St. Louis Community College

Forest Park
Florissant Valley
Meramec

Instructional Resources
St. Louis, Missouri

GAYLORD

The Watchful Eye

AMERICAN JUSTICE IN THE AGE OF THE TELEVISION TRIAL

Paul Thaler

PRAEGER

Westport, Connecticut
London

Library of Congress Cataloging-in-Publication Data

Thaler, Paul.
    The watchful eye : American justice in the age of the television
trial / Paul Thaler.
       p. cm.
    Includes bibliographical references and index.
    ISBN 0–275–94215–5 (alk. paper)—ISBN 0–275–95133–2 (pbk.)
    1. Video tapes in courtroom proceedings—United States.
2. Conduct of court proceedings—United States. 3. Free press and
fair trial—United States. I. Title.
KF8725.T47   1994
347.73'5—dc20
[347.3075]   93–4257

British Library Cataloguing in Publication Data is available.

Library of Congress Catalog Card Number: 93–4257
ISBN: 0–275–94215–5
      0–275–95133–2 (pbk.)

First published in 1994
Paperback edition 1994

Praeger Publishers, 88 Post Road West, Westport, CT 06881
An imprint of Greenwood Publishing Group, Inc.

Printed in the United States of America

∞™

The paper used in this book complies with the
Permanent Paper Standard issued by the National
Information Standards Organization (Z39.48–1984).

10 9 8 7 6 5 4 3 2 1

Copyright Acknowledgments

The author and publisher are grateful to the following for allowing the use of material:

Katherine Anderson, interview with author, January 1989.

David Bookstaver, interview with author, January 1989.

Steven Brill, president and editor in chief, Courtroom Television Network, interview with author, February 1992.

Merrill Brown, interviews with author, February 1992 and July 1993.

Susan Brownmiller, interview with author, January 1989.

Michael Callaghan, interview with author, January 1989.

Peter Casolaro, interview with author, January 1989.

Dr. Aglae Charlot, interview with author, January 1989.

Timothy Clifford, interview with author, January 1989.

Jeremiah Cole, interview with author, January 1989.

Courtroom Television Network, still photos taken from Court TV air.

Adrian DiLuzio, interview with author, January 1989.

T. S. Eliot. Excerpt from "The Hollow Men" in *Collected Poems 1909–1962* by T. S. Eliot, copyright 1936 by Harcourt Brace Jovanovich, Inc., copyright © 1964, 1963 by T. S. Eliot, reprinted by permission of the publisher. World rights (excluding U.S.) by permission of Faber and Faber Ltd.

Roberta Entner, "Encoding the Image of the American Judiciary Institution: A Semiotic Analysis of Broadcast Trials to Ascertain Its Definition of the Court System," Ph.D. diss., New York University, 1993.

Dr. Azariah Eshkenazi, interview with author, January 1989.

Pamela Ferrero, interview with author, January 1991.

Ellen Fleysher, interview with author, January 1989.

Walter Goodman, interview with author, July 1992.

Tony Guida, interview with author, January 1989.

Pete Hamill, interview with author, January 1989.

Allen Jared, interview with author, January 1989.

Dr. Patrick Kilhenny, interview with author, January 1989.

Dr. Mary Elizabeth Lell, interview with author, January 1989.

Jack Litman, interview with author, January 1989.

Ira London, interview with author, January 1989.

John McCusker, interview with author, January 1989.

Dr. Douglas Miller, interview with author, January 1989.

New York Newsday, jacket photo of Judge Harold Rothwax by Bruce Gilbert; jacket photo of Joel Steinberg by Susan Farley.

Steve Paulus, interview with author, January 1989.

Mike Pearl, interview with author, January 1989.

Steve Reece, photograph of Harry Washburn murder trial, *Waco-Tribune*, December 1955. Reprinted in "Televised Trial, World's Attention Attracted to 1955," *Waco Tribune Herald*, July 23, 1978, p. C1.

Perry Reich, interview with author, June 1989.

Marty Rosenbaum, New York State Defenders Association, interview with author, September 1992.

Judge Harold Rothwax, interview with author, January 1989.

Judge Steve Russell, letter from Judge Russell to Court TV, June 18, 1992; interview with author, December 1992.

Barry Scheck, interviews with author, January 1989 and December 1992.

Paul Smirnoff, interview with author, January 1989.

Joel Steinberg, interviews with author, June 1989 and October 1992–August 1993.

Shirley Unger, interview with author, January 1989.

Marilyn Walton, interview with author, January 1989.

Every reasonable effort has been made to trace the owners of copyright materials in this book, but in some instances this has proven impossible. The author and publisher will be glad to receive information leading to more complete acknowledgments in subsequent printings of the book and in the meantime extend their apologies for any omissions.

To my mother and father

Between the idea
and the reality
Between the motion
and the act
Falls the shadow.

T. S. Eliot

Contents

Photographs follow page 92.

Preface

The idea for this book originated long before I was ever conscious that it existed. Writing can be a painfully slow process that often begins with a whimper of a thought that is at first barely noticeable to the mind's eye. The process somehow began for me in a New York University classroom where scholars by the names of Neil Postman, Christine Nystrom, and Terrance Moran rekindled old fires of intellectual curiosity.

This book is about one idea that caught on six years ago and has not let go since. Writing *The Watchful Eye* has been an extraordinary journey that began in 1988 when Neil Postman was asked to serve as a member of a state advisory committee, a group of prominent journalists, academicians, and attorneys who were assigned to study the recently enacted camera-in-the-courtroom law in New York. Characteristically, Neil opened the intellectual gates to his students, proposing that a small group of "media ecologists" help to investigate the ramifications of an experiment that had been embraced by the vast majority of states across the country. Our studies soon shifted from the theoretical to the pragmatic as we explored this newly mediated environment.

Two of my colleagues took different paths of study. Roberta Entner conducted a meticulous semiotic study of trial telecasts, making sense of television's "language" and manipulative power in shaping and defining courtroom images. William Petkanas laid to rest longstanding claims that the in-court camera was an educational tool that could elevate civic understanding of the justice system, a key rationale used by camera proponents. Both studies are referred to in this book, and I am grateful for my colleagues' scholastic wisdom and even more so for their genuine friendship during these past years.

My own research took me from a criminal courthouse in lower Manhattan to a maximum security prison in upstate New York. Through the perceptions of participants at a celebrated trial in 1988, I sought to narrow the camera debate to a fundamental and critical question that has persisted for nearly 40 years: Could television be responsible for altering the attitudes, judgments, and behaviors of trial participants, creating a radically new relationship between media and the courts?

Since 1977, dozens of state-sponsored questionnaires had attempted to quantify the human experience in a televised courtroom through closed-ended surveys. At best, they have proven to be short-sighted, bringing a researcher no closer to understanding the often subtle, yet important, shifts evident in an electronic courtroom. Even anecdotal accounts from trial members—judges, lawyers, jurors, and witnesses—have been cursory and decontextual. Ignored altogether are the observations of defendants, those individuals, needless to say, who have the most to lose in a televised trial.

The central idea for this book crashed headlong into a highly publicized trial that riveted New York City in October 1988. Joel Steinberg, a 46-year-old criminal attorney, had been accused of killing his 6-year-old daughter, Lisa. Even beyond the accusations of debased criminality, the case resonated on many levels. Hedda Nussbaum, Steinberg's live-in companion, was a severely battered woman, and their life style appeared to be one of drug abuse and degradation. The case seemed to touch a public nerve, and in the workplace and on city streets the Steinberg trial became a volatile topic of intense interest. Feeding into this emotional public discourse was television. The electronic press had been given access to the trial, and the pictures broadcast to the nation and even around the world were intimate and ultimately horrifying.

The Steinberg trial represented a historic opportunity to study New York State's camera experiment, although from a personal viewpoint it posed what could be described as an intellectual dilemma. As a former reporter who has traded in his daily news beat for an academic robe, I have long shared the media's sensitivity toward a free and vigorous press, a point of view invariably asserted by camera advocates. Had the book simply enunciated the "free press" perspective, it need not have been longer than any one of a handful of ringing *New York Times* editorials that chimed the virtues of the electronic press. But my research opened a broader realm of understanding, one that was particularly attuned to the evolution of an emerging technological society and the radical clash between traditional American culture and a new generation of once-unimaginable machines. In other arenas of sociopolitical life, critics such as Susan Sontag, Roland Barthes, Marshall McLuhan, George Gerbner, and Neil Postman have written eloquently about our emerging technological society, and their thoughts are the grounding for this book.

The study moves from a theoretical perspective of television to an investigation that carefully probes beneath the surface of the "electronic courtroom." Its aim is to examine how television works within a courtroom setting by asking several critical questions: In a television trial, who benefits and who loses? What new ways of thinking are encouraged, and which ideas are made obsolete? Which behaviors and judgments are reinforced, and which others are not? Unlike the conclusions drawn in survey reports, which exude a type of statistical certainty, this book offers no definitive answer; instead, it offers a viewpoint that takes into account the ambiguity that is integral to the human experience.

Research evidence for the Steinberg case study was collected from December 1988 through July 1989. Interviews were conducted with 40 individuals connected to the trial in either a judicial or a journalistic capacity. Most interviews were completed immediately after the trial's conclusion to ensure that observations and recollections were still clear. For the most part, participants were willing, and even eager, to share their experiences and observations about the trial. In total, the presiding judge, 6 attorneys, 9 witnesses, 10 jurors, the defendant, and 13 journalists joined in the research. The research was not complete until Steinberg himself was given the chance to offer his own perspective during extensive interviews, first at the Clinton Correctional Facility following his sentencing, and then, after his transfer, at the Southport Correctional Facility. These key trial participants are very much a part of the writing of this book, and my deep appreciation is extended to them. Their names are listed in the appendix. More than 500 pages of transcripts were generated from the interviews, making the case study the most comprehensive of its kind. To supplement my understanding of the case, I also scrutinized a wealth of public and private documents connected to the specifics of the case.

To aid in further assessing the impact of television in the courts, I attended various sessions of the trial itself, including the testimony of key witnesses, the defense attorneys' summation, and the judge's two-and-a-half hour charge to the jury. I also followed the extended live television coverage of Hedda Nussbaum's testimony and Judge Rothwax's sentencing of Joel Steinberg. Visits to the courtroom enabled me to observe firsthand the interactions among participants, which would later prove helpful in designing interview questions. Outside the courtroom, reporters were particularly forthcoming in interviews conducted in the first-floor press office at the Criminal Courts Building and later in follow-up discussions conducted by telephone.

The lengthy jury deliberations allowed court participants extended time to discuss their role and the role of others in the televised trial. Many awaited the jury's verdict by remaining in the courtroom or the hallway corridor. In a rigorous interview with Judge Rothwax in his chambers, it became evident that he had given considerable thought to the camera issue. A follow-up interview by telephone was conducted several months later to allow the judge the chance to respond to the observations and comments made by other participants about his actions and behavior within the courtroom.

Interviews with defense counsels Ira London and Adrian DiLuzzio also were conducted while jury members deliberated the case. Prosecutors agreed to discuss their observations following the verdict, and I later met with Peter Casolaro and John McCusker at their offices across from the Criminal Courts Building. Perry Reich, who replaced Ira London as Steinberg's legal counsel, was interviewed after sentencing. I also met with Barry Scheck, who represented Hedda Nussbaum, for an extensive interview at the Cardozo Law School. He provided thoughtful commentary and opinions about the use of the in-court camera and its influence on the courtroom environment. From his office, he telephoned Nussbaum, then a patient at Four Winds psychiatric hospital in Katonah, New York. With Scheck mediating the call, Nussbaum answered questions. He declined to allow her to be interviewed directly, citing pending litigation against her.

Within a week of the verdict, telephone interviews were conducted with 10 of the 12 jurors. I believed it important to reach them quickly before their recollections faded. Similarly, witnesses were also sought out immediately after the trial had concluded. The most challenging interview for the study was conducted with Steinberg. Our far-ranging discussions, spanning more than 50 hours, probed various aspects of the trial and the media's influence in shaping public perceptions of his case. Virtually no study has gone so far as to broadly frame the camera debate from a defendant's vantage point. This study devotes a chapter to Steinberg's insights about the media, and they are reported straightforwardly.

Since the Steinberg trial, the camera question remains far from resolution, even as the number of states allowing televised trials continues to grow. Part One places the current debate inside a far-reaching historical and theoretical framework. To that end, I am grateful to Susanna Barber's impressive documentation of events leading up to the present-day debate. Also singled out as part of this analysis is the dramatic debut of the Courtroom Television Network. As of this writing, it may be too early to fully evaluate the significance of the fledgling cable channel; clearly, however, the Courtroom Television Network (Court TV) has inspired a radical change in the way in which the courts are covered. Steven Brill, the founder and president of Court TV, and Merrill Brown, senior vice president, were both forthcoming in granting interviews, opening studio doors, and allowing me to observe firsthand their editorial meetings. Susan Abbey, the director of marketing, and also Alex Gomez, were generous in permitting trial photographs to appear in this book.

Other sources have also contributed to this book. I gratefully acknowledge the research expertise of Srivalli Rao and the Mercy College library staff; the legal acumen and documentation provided by Marty Rosenbaum of the New York State Defenders Association; Mary de Bourbon of the New York Office of Court Administration; and Erick Low and Kriss Winchester at the National Center for State Courts in Williamsburg, Virginia.

The Watchful Eye began with an idea that never would have been nourished had it not been for the personal and intellectual support of colleagues, friends, and family. The solitary act of writing is an exhausting, but exhilarating, experience, akin to stepping out into open space. Jay Rosen and Marcia Rock of New York University inspired me to enjoy the intellectual freefall, and I am grateful for their perceptive comments in shaping these ideas. Special thanks are due to my friend and long-time colleague Fay Greenwald of Mercy College. During the past decade we have shared a ramshackle building that is home to our English and Journalism Department. Invigorated by intellectual energy and also a humane, civilized spirit, it is a place in which a project like this can grow. My appreciation goes also to Jay Sexter, Mercy's president, and to those faculty members and students whose talented efforts contributed to my original research and writing.

The book has been six years in the making. From the early stages, Praeger Publishers has been one of its most enthusiastic supporters. Mary Glenn, my first editor, genuinely shared my belief that the book could significantly contribute to our understanding of television and the American justice system. Andrea Morgan, my production editor, has diligently followed through to keep both the book and myself under control during critical deadline schedules.

Finally, my deepest gratitude goes to my family and friends who lived this project with unswerving support. My wife, Amy Wolfson, with a perceptive eye and a strong measure of common sense, has immeasurably helped me past the critical junctures of this work. As such, her imprint is as much a part of this book as my own. Enid Wolfson and Marjorie Wolfson have opened their hearts and minds to my work from its origins. I am particularly indebted to Mel Wolfson who scrupulously pored over a weighty manuscript. His sensitive red pen has held me to my own aspirations of clarity and honesty. Fred Thaler and Linda Kaplan Thaler, two wonderfully creative people, have enriched our family's life with music and words (and a son, Michael). Through example they have challenged me to discover my own voice in the world, and I hope this book measures up to that ideal.

Foremost, I dedicate this book to my parents: in honor of my mother, Rose Thaler, whose unqualified love and beautiful spirit I cherish; and in memory of my father, Max A. Thaler, whose soft-spoken wisdom was matched only by the love he gave to his family. Dad was my greatest teacher, who gently and lovingly showed me the way.

Introduction: The Faustian Bargain

On a winter's day in December 1955, the District Court in Waco, Texas, was the site of two very distinct trials. In one, Harry L. Washburn was accused of murdering his mother-in-law by planting a bomb in her car. In the other, the defendant was television itself. For the first time, an in-court camera would bring a "live" criminal trial into the living rooms of an intrigued Waco community. History would forever tie the Washburn case with television, marking the birth of a new type of American trial. Observers reported at the time that the medium acquitted itself quite well, but, still, there were lingering doubts held by some reporters who called for restraints on this new courtroom technology. One key participant dismissed such concerns. Asked if he minded live television coverage of his trial, a dispassionate Harry L. Washburn remarked before being found guilty of murder: "Naw, let it go all over the world."[1] Court members may not have viewed Washburn's comment as a harbinger of an emerging technological era, but Waco was only the beginning of a national experiment that has, for the most part, now ended. From New York to California, courts are replicating each day the experiment in justice that began in Texas nearly 40 years ago. While a murmur of discontent is still heard occasionally, the American judiciary has adjusted nicely to an age it can hardly understand or even name. I call it the age of the Television Trial.

To an extent this book is about the ideology of technology, a deep-rooted belief that is exalted within the American congregation, but that is also worrisome to nonbelievers. In his dark vision of a nation increasingly obedient to its machines, media theorist Neil Postman warns: "In America, we have been so dazzled by the alluring promises of technology that we have placed our culture entirely at its service. Whatever technology has created we have rejoiced in. Whatever it has destroyed we have endured without complaint. To technology's demands we have replied with a Biblical simplicity: Wherever thou goest, we shall go."[2]

Postman's prophecy rings an eerie truth as Americans, hovering on the brink of the imminent technological shifts of the twenty-first century, are locked in a perilous dance between old and new. For the most part, we have come to think of this technological torrent as progress, a step toward a more sophisticated and enlightened society. It is this very belief that is at the center of a sweeping social experiment that has invaded the nation's judicial system, an experiment that has come to be identified by its sobriquet, "cameras in the court."

Across the country, throughout 47 states, a person can turn to television to watch events unfolding at an ongoing trial.[3] Even federal courts, once shielded from the camera, are now televising civil trials. And, in all likelihood, virtually all state and national courts, including the U.S. Supreme Court, could be wired for television in the not-too-distant future, airing trials across the country via an emerging cable television network. We have entered a new technological era, and the courts, once an inaccessible and shadowy institution to most Americans, are no longer off-limits to the camera lens or the public eye. Television is providing an intimate view of the judicial process, the camera visually escorting us behind closed doors to witness some of the most dramatic proceedings in the annals of American law.

These trials have tapped an emotional core, one heightened by the medium's use of powerful images. They are pictures that remain indelibly etched in the public mind: a New York lawyer convicted in the death of his six-year-old daughter, his common-law wife shockingly disfigured by years of abuse and beatings; a notorious mobster, neatly coiffed and elegantly dressed, smirking into the camera lens after being acquitted on a string of racketeering charges; the son of a famous American actor, disheveled and wild-eyed, facing charges that he murdered his sister's lover; a confessed serial killer, staring nonplussed during an insanity hearing in which the sordid details of his multiple killings are explicitly recounted amid the anguish of victims' family members; a member of a renowned American family standing accused of rape, listening intently to the testimony of his accuser as she graphically describes the night of her attack; a 17-year-old woman, branded by the press as a "Long Island Lolita" for shooting the wife of her alleged lover, facing her victim's condemnation in court before being given a lengthy prison sentence. Some, like Joel Steinberg, John Gotti, Christian Brando, Jeffrey Dahmer, William Kennedy Smith, and Amy Fisher, have achieved a momentary fame, largely because of television and the blue smoke of celebrity it spews. Others are immediately more familiar: Paul Newman, William Hurt, and Zsa Zsa Gabor, glittering stars who play out their roles on the silver screen or the public stage, have also become the focus of the courtroom camera. All have faced criminal or civil actions.[4]

For the most part, we have grown accustomed to these images and others like them. In its eager embrace of this relatively recent television genre, the public has come to expect that the televised courtroom will yield "visual truth" not only about the proceedings themselves, but also about the social issues attached to them. Indeed, in most state courts, the question of whether or not to allow television cameras is moot. "We don't talk about courtroom cameras anymore— people just accept them as a matter of course," acknowledges Pamela Ferrero, an assistant district attorney in the 1990 McMartin Pre-School child-abuse case in California. As the lead prosecutor, Ferrero had some familiarity with the workings of a televised courtroom. The trial was showcased throughout the national media, and she noted with some resignation that "everyone accepted we were going to have cameras [during the trial] without flinching."[5] Staging her own personal protest during her closing remarks to the jury, Ferrero strategically placed a large board between herself and the camera and later explained that it was her objective to direct her arguments to the jury and not to a television audience. The effort was thwarted, however, when the position of the camera was merely shifted and Ferrero's remarks were captured on videotape. But the attempt may be symbolic of a growing frustration felt by the opponents of this national experiment and exemplifies the futility intrinsic in their efforts.

One point remains clear: Once television has infiltrated a critical arena of American sociopolitical life, it seems to find a permanent home. It is certainly the case in the camera experiment. Only one state, New York, after a three-year experiment beginning in 1987, has ever reversed a law permitting television access to the courts.[6] But even then, New York's move to ban the camera was merely an aberration, a glitch that would be rectified in 1992 when the state legislature, under intense pressure from media and legal lobbyists, would reinstate courtroom television.

Curiously, it is this nearly untarnished record that is often cited by advocates as proof that the medium is an ally of the judicial system. Reasons for the widespread acceptance vary. But, primarily, the courts are not unlike other forums that have come to trust the electronic press as an impartial and quiet observer, a helpmate as well as a friend. From congressional hearings to community board meetings, the television camera has found a comfortable niche and has become a welcomed guest. As a medium that is regarded as "mythic" in our culture, we have readily accepted its presence as part of our natural universe, bestowing upon it a crown of legitimacy as an electronic press.

For the most part, our faith has been unblemished. It is easy to understand why. The mythology of television has been translated into an amalgam of social agendas that we consider sacrosanct. For members of the legal community, television coverage promises to enhance public understanding. For the public at large, it is a powerful communications link that bridges the gap between judicial proceedings and public inquiry. For the press itself, the camera is a useful, even necessary, journalistic tool that helps the electronic media tell their story, not unlike the pads and pens of their print counterparts. In essence, advocates conclude, the camera helps the nation construct a clearer "reality" of the American courts, which can only enhance and legitimize the processes of law and renew faith in the justice system.

The applause in some quarters has been deafening. For proponents of the courtroom camera, such as Anna Quindlen of the *New York Times*, television has proven to be a valuable, even crucial, tool for social democracy. So enamored was Quindlen with the medium that she has referred to the year 1991 as a watershed for teledemocracy. Metaphorically, she calls it the year of the "glass eye."[7] For Quindlen, it is an inviting metaphor. From the Persian Gulf war, to the Supreme Court confirmation hearings of Clarence Thomas and the accusations of sexual harassment by Professor Anita Hill, to the William Kennedy Smith rape trial, television was translucent, allowing light to shine upon a democracy bent on the free flow of information. The "bogeyman" evoked in George Orwell's *1984*, Quindlen assured us, was confirmed dead. Big Brother was no longer watching; instead, television was.

In 1991 in America, she explained, the glass eye of television fostered a truer sense of the democratic dream. As television funneled critical national forums to an awaiting and eager public, Americans could see for themselves the processes of war and of law. "We came, we saw, we decided," she concluded. "The raw material from which we reporters build stories on—most of it was there on screen. It was the first time I can remember that I could cover a story just as well from my living room as I could at the scene."[8]

But Quindlen's "glass eye" metaphor has proven to be an incongruous meditation. Metaphors are important symbolic markings that carry significant psychological weight: They paint a picture of what the world is supposed to be like. Quindlen's "glass eye" implies a transparent medium free of those filters, biases, and distortions that misshape the message. Viewers are left with the notion that they are the ultimate arbiters of what is genuine and real. Paradoxically, as metaphor, a glass eye also brings to mind an opaque technology *incapable* of processing light—indeed, a blind instrument that gives the appearance of seeing, but cannot.

But the in-court camera is neither translucent nor blind. The powerful courtroom images that emanate from the screen, and our attention to them, defeat both metaphors. Taking another metaphorical vantage point, the camera issue makes more sense. Television is hardly a glass eye, a benign and remote technology; rather, it is a powerful and active observer—a watchful eye—that narrowly frames the world. In its frames, pictures are enlarged, reduced, or eliminated altogether to dictate "meaning" that fits into the specific constraints and structural makeup of this image-driven medium. As audience members, we are affected and influenced by what we see, but so, too, is the event itself.

That the court camera has gained widespread acceptance does not negate the disturbing questions that continue to haunt an experiment that remains widely misunderstood. They relate to our understanding of how television works, what it can "create" within a particular environment, and, ultimately, how the medium affects and changes that which it focuses on. Perilously, it seems, we have failed to heed the red signals that point to the possible dangers inherent in this new judicial technology. In our rush to judgment, we may have been too quick to ignore an important warning that has been underscored by social and media observers: With each new technology comes a corresponding "trade-off," a disadvantage for which we have to pay a definitive price.

By embracing the courtroom camera, we may have entered into a Faustian bargain, where part of the soul of our judicial legacy is traded for what we believe is a measure of progress. We have assumed that there is a substantial gain to be had by opening the gates of justice to television—and perhaps there is some. But concealed in the umbilical relationship are questions that are crucial to our understanding of this newly mediated environment: What do we forfeit when we readily allow television into the court system? In the arena of American justice, just what will this powerful communications medium do? Or, even more pertinently, to borrow a question asked by a colleague: "What will this medium undo?"

The purpose of this book is to closely "watch" television to determine its effect on the American system of justice. If there is a prefatory conclusion to be drawn here, it is that in our fervor to believe in the benevolence of technology, we may very well have followed the camera into the courtroom with our eyes half shut, groping in the darkness, without fully recognizing the powerful, active nature of this image-based medium. Immersing the courtroom into the cauldron of public scrutiny via the camera lens may have consequences yet to be unearthed. Far from being a measure of progress, the social experiment we call "cameras in the courtroom" may bring about a dramatic and irreversible shift in the way we think about and act upon justice in America.

Part One

The Age of the Television Trial

The Theater of the Television Trial

We exist in an electronic culture, and there is perhaps no single American institution that has not felt the unique and penetrating inoculation of television. The medium that transformed the political scene has also changed—and trivialized—the way in which we perceive and conduct American family life, business, sports, and religion.[1]

Historically, the American courtroom has been the most recalcitrant public institution to extend a welcoming hand to television, but that stance has severely eroded during the past 15 years. Writing in 1980, George Gerbner, the noted communications scholar, warned that the camera-in-the-court debate may be "at the point of no return," our last opportunity to evaluate television's influence on public perception of law and the courts.[2]

Television presents a coherent world of images and messages serving its own institutional interests. The question is whether the judiciary should be enlisted to add further credibility to media mythology. Plugging courtrooms into the television system can make them appendages of that system. Once televised trials attract a large national following, the process will be irresistible, cumulative, and probably irreversible.[3]

Even at the time of his writing, Gerbner may have realized he was tilting against a technological windmill. In the past two decades, "the court story," both fictional and real, has become an integral part of television programming—and the national consciousness. If television has tried to distinguish the real from the make-believe, it has failed, and for good reason. As we have come to learn, television remains trapped in its predominant identity, incapable of overriding its primary function as a picture-producing technology. At its root, it is inextricably tied to its visuals—fleeting, but alluring, images meant to arouse and entertain, grinding trial proceedings into palatable 15- to 30-second sound bites, as easily digested as advertisements for breakfast foods.

Video clips from trial proceedings are not unlike the television commercial itself, or other types of entertainment programming. The visuals are chosen to excite the senses and ultimately persuade us that they are real and should be believed. But such images are only impressions, shallow imprints that lack contextual truth. "Surface appearances are more likely to conceal than reveal how the judicial system operates," warns Gerbner. "Television will create popular spectacles of great appeal but deceptive authenticity as it selects and interprets trials to fit the existing patterns of law in the world of television."[4] The NBC-TV series "L.A. Law" thus becomes a working model, and not a fictional counterpart, for a news producer making decisions about trial footage to be used for the evening report.

As a medium that is locked into a commercial structure reliant on the presentation of fast-moving images, television is at its weakest when dealing with complex matters that are abstract and conceptually based, the very symbolic stuff of print media. Its technological bias is sensory rather than temporal, which is why we turn to television for its speed, not for its exposition; for its pictures, not for its words. Simply stated, we watch television because it is entertaining.

Even attempts to expand and elevate television coverage of trials to a higher standard eventually reduce the complexities of a trial to entertainment fare. A case in point is the $40-million venture by Time Warner Inc., a national 24-hour cable network called the Courtroom Television Network (Court TV), which made its debut in July 1991. Production crews are deployed to selected trials around the country, feeding live and taped proceedings to an anchor desk in New York. An experienced editorial staff, featuring Fred Graham, a former CBS legal affairs correspondent now turned network anchor, then chooses among them, telecasting what has been described as a "Wide World of Courts." Steven Brill, Court TV's president and editor in chief, explains that the anchor desk "peppers the proceedings with voiceovers and intermission commentary from highly skilled newsmen and a star cast of prominent lawyers."[5]

Special programs include "Prime Time Trial Story," a network "feature presentation," that reduces selected trials to a single or multipart movie format and airs at least six times weekly. Programs have included "Pam Smart's Calculated Crime of Passion," about a New Hampshire schoolteacher tried and convicted in the murder of her husband; and "The Christian Brando Story," with a cameo from Marlon Brando, who makes an impassioned plea to the court on behalf of his son, who was accused of killing his half-sister's boyfriend.

Brill concedes that success will be measured in terms of the show's ability to garner a mass audience. His proposal boasts a "unique marriage of upscale 'serious' programming with the appeal of 'tabloid' television." "Will we televise murder trials and other tabloid fare?" he asks. "Of course we will, because it will engage our viewers." But he also promises that other types of less sensational cases—tort suits, civil rights suits, employment discrimination trials—will be televised "to get people to watch and learn from the real thing."[6]

Whether or not viewers will actually learn anything from such programming is questionable and perhaps irrelevant. More to the point is whether the cable network will be able to deliver an audience large enough to sustain itself. It may be successful if Brill can effectively convert judicial proceedings into a sort of television theater imbued with typical entertainment values. When real trials fail to meet such standards, Court TV may find other, more fictional venues to reach their audience. Such was perhaps the motivation in a peculiar national broadcast aired August 10, 1992, with the lofty title "The Trial of the Century: USA v. Lee Harvey Oswald." The mock trial of President John F. Kennedy's assassin was enacted by the American Bar Association at their annual convention in San Francisco. Feeding off a recent frenzy of interest surrounding the Kennedy assassination, spurred by a popular film directed by Oliver Stone, both the association and Court TV perceived that television could commercially exploit the issue, while promoting the legal industry and the network itself. To that extent they were correct in their judgment, since the program—in essence, a media event—attracted extensive media coverage and good ratings.

Mainstream television is also targeting trial coverage as a potential source of entertainment programming. With the availability of actual footage, trials now can be tailored to suit the specific needs dictated by a mass audience. Using popular thematic devices that depict high courtroom drama, sex, scandal, and greed, real-life trials are easily molded to fit the narrative line of their fictional counterparts. The "tabloid-styled" "Inside Edition" and "A Current Affair" and the "magazine-formatted" "48 Hours" and "Prime Time Live" are national programs that have generously used trial footage in their reports. Indeed, courtroom videotape is a primary source of visual "information," if not the sole reason for the selection of a particular case in the first place. In the surrealistic theater of television, "relevancy" is linked less to journalistic convention and more to the medium's ability to produce forceful images.

One lengthy segment of ABC-TV's "Prime Time Live," for example, was notably bizarre, yet perfectly ordinary in the world of televised justice.[7] The Menendez murders in California received widespread media attention in 1990 after Jose Menendez, a high-powered Hollywood entertainment executive, and his wife, Kitty Louise, were found brutally murdered in their Beverly Hills mansion. Their sons, Lyle and Erick, stood accused of the crime. The "evidence," as depicted in the show, skillfully blended the "testimony" of a single witness and dated police reports with quick snippets from the brothers' bail hearing. Voiceovers describing the tormented and twisted minds of the young men were juxtaposed against visuals obviously selected for their imagistic intensity. Underscoring the picture of guilt, a year-old videotape of a pretrial hearing was added, showing the defendants, dressed in jailhouse fatigues, entering a courtroom. Close-ups and still shots were selectively pieced together to drive home the point that the brothers were unremorseful and, we may deduce, pathological.

Although the case had yet to come to trial, ABC teased its audience with a sneak preview. Framed in the guise of a legitimate news show and professionally anchored by prominent journalists Diane Sawyer and Sam Donaldson, the story was clearly emotionally engaging—and manipulative—as powerful images revealed visual connotations that went beyond a prepared script. After taking on the roles of judge and prosecutor, Sawyer promised that additional witnesses would be testifying on the program in subsequent weeks so that the audience "can decide for itself" the guilt or innocence of the Menendez brothers. There was, of course, the outside chance that since this media-wise public jury was already empaneled, program executives might feel inclined to poll them and announce their "verdict" on the air (certainly not a far-fetched idea at a time when many news shows are promoting such audience response polls).

CONSTRUCTING THE "REAL WORLD"

Sawyer and other journalists would be most likely to justify such reports as helping the public understand the specifics of a particular case and the workings of the judicial system at large. Through television, the public could witness "justice" at work. We have come to discover, however, that the medium is not merely a innocuous "info-tainment" tool, but rather a distinct and separate entity that imposes its own set of rules upon the world. By constructing the "real world" through brief, opaque images, television refracts reality, rather than mirrors it. Visual transcriptions of an event must be shaped to fit the constraints of a medium where simple ideas accompany quick-moving pictures. In this way, television does not just accommodate the message, but changes it.

Television's power lies in its inherent capability of making images appear as exact visual transcriptions of the real world. For many Americans, there is little to distinguish the Television Trial from the real thing: In the universe of television, seeing is believing. Our sensorium confirms that what passes through television's screen is grounded in a certain reality. In short, states Roberta Entner, a communications scholar from New York University, "images have a way of passing themselves off as natural."[8] Or, as critic Barry Brummett notes, "It is the business of media to create an illusion that their world is no different from that of unmediated reality. The public comes to think of media as not only continuous with other types of experiences, but as essentially the same as this world."[9] Television achieves this end by presenting a continuous bombardment of images that are intensely familiar in terms of their structure and form. The codes of the medium are so instantly recognizable as to appear indistinguishable from the natural way of seeing the world.

In the theater of the Television Trial, images appear to correspond to the court scene, but as Entner explains, the camera creates a visual scenario that "does not merely convey the court system but constructs [it]." She elaborates: "As the viewers see moving pictures of trials on their nightly news, their understanding of the courts is not simply a correspondence to what actually took place. Instead what is communicated depends upon a unique combination of what is shot and what the viewer expects to see."[10]

Essentially, both the courtroom and television work with a similar set of facts, people, and social and legal agendas. They are both storytelling institutions, but the compelling narratives that they weave are far different and often at odds with one another. In the courtroom, each attorney seeks to present a story about his case that is convincing and consistent. Their purpose is evident: to persuade a judge and jury that their chosen story line is the one most credible. The information, witness testimony, and physical evidence they select and emphasize are meant to complement the narrative. Those pieces of the judicial puzzle that do not correspond with a particular story are simply left out. As part of the adversarial process, the defense and the prosecuting attorneys may try to discredit one another, but their stories are built carefully, piece by piece, and presented slowly over the entire trial, which may last as long as several months. Each point of the narrative is relevant only as it pertains to the context of the entire story.[11]

According to media critics like David Altheide, the television court story carries a different agenda. First, stories "are likely to originate from the reporter's or producer's predefined angles based on what is most interesting to the audience, rather than what is central to the trial." Second, most television reporters are not schooled in court procedure or highly knowledgeable about rules of evidence, or the legal weight attached to testimony. It is important to note, states Altheide, that these reporters often are unaware of the significance of the story line in court cases. Third, the very format of the newscast requires very little of the television reporter. Since the court report will last anywhere from 15 seconds to two minutes, "there is really no need to become knowledgeable of the complex issues and approaches used by the attorneys within the courtroom setting."[12] Fourth, the medium dictates that the reporter match images with his report or, more exactly, that he fit his report with the most effective trial footage. In the theater of the Television Trial, pictures rule and are often selected to emphasize the dramatic (a lawyer raging, a witness in tears) and not necessarily those legal issues central to the case. Finally, the constraints placed by the medium—its "image bias" and sound bite vocabulary—reduce and simplify legal issues for the viewing audience. In essence, concludes Altheide, television trial coverage is inherently at odds with courtroom accounts of the case.

TV news reports of court cases will be much different than the [trial] accounts and issues because the purpose of TV is different: Television's main function is to keep viewers interested in the case. However, if court cases are transmitted to the public via TV news stories, the public essentially may be uninformed about the general legal process as well as particular cases and issues.[13]

It is often argued that television is but one medium used to inform the public about the courts and the law. However, television must be considered the most pervasive and potent source of information and news—and also the most manipulative. Television's message is a complex process in which two components—the verbal and visual—are deliberately melded to create a story. The verbal consists of "stand-ups" (where a reporter speaks directly to the camera), voiceovers (where the spoken report is placed over the visual), or direct commentary from a subject. Typically, the verbal message is overwhelmed by visuals being flashed on the screen. The image is itself a subtle, but powerful, "language," with meanings that lie beneath the surface of the conscious mind of the television viewer.

Media analysts have pointed out that television's "reality" is often created through the juxtaposition or linking of images. Combining one shot with another infers a causal relationship—when, in actuality, there may be none. "Unfortunately, television's reliance on such an associative grammar has dulled the viewing public's analytic abilities," maintains Entner. Unaccustomed to questioning the causality between two consecutive visuals, the television audience has learned to "read" such a visual connection as a factual relationship.[14]

In her illuminating semiotic analysis of courtroom television, Entner makes the case that "the ease by which we interpret images on television might make one overlook the importance" of how television functions. Yet, through the use of space, camera angles, lighting, juxtaposition, editing, and other elements of the medium, which form the basis of how images are perceived, "our perception and thus the meaning of these images are manipulated—with little recognition of manipulation."

Visuals operate as if this really happened, just see for yourself. But the choice of one moment of an event rather than another, the selection of this person instead of that and the decision of this camera angle rather than that makes these visuals a highly selective and interpretative procedure. Although photographic images have a way of passing themselves off as natural, the naturalness of that relationship is contrived.[15]

The very choice of images must conform to the parameters of the trial "genre." Easily identifiable images are chosen to readily summarize an event or help promote the mythical nature of the court and legal process. Since ratings are a primary factor, visual action coverage is encouraged. These images often are used to represent a larger frame of criminal activity. An image no longer is a "fact," but a visual "symbol," a powerful representation that stands for something outside the specific boundaries of a particular trial. Courtroom images can become symbolic of "child abuse" or "organized crime" or "lovers' triangle" or other social taboos. To enhance the story line, visuals of trial participants are framed to fit the neat stereotypes of the judicial process. The judge is representative of an authority figure, lawyers symbolize an adversarial process, and so on.

Once participants are labeled, they are then placed within a courtroom setting. Entner explains that "the television frame is a kind of territory." The positioning of the subject in his territory "suggests the amount of intimacy the audience feels with him." The close-up is the most intimate shot and is often used to frame sympathetic witnesses; the three-quarter is more emotionally detached and is used to show lawyers; the profile conveys a sense of remoteness and typically is used to portray the defendant.[16]

Television uses other crucial techniques to create a story, including camera angles, camera movement, and editing. Of these three, editing techniques may be most critical. The process of selecting and ordering pictures can significantly alter meaning. Media scholar Edward J. Epstein points out that television news employs codes of editing to enhance the dramatic appeal of a trial story.[17] Editing attempts to eliminate segments containing little visual interest. The methodical unfolding of testimony is then replaced with the punchy sound bite or courtroom histrionics. The courtroom "action" is enhanced as editing condenses time, giving the appearance that the trial is a continuous flow of activity. The juxtaposition of images is also used to promote courtroom theater: For instance, a camera shot of the victim placed after a picture of the defendant has intentional dramatic play.

During her extensive research, Entner conducted a frame-by-frame analysis of footage of selected criminal trials televised in New York. Her examples point to the medium's power in creating meaning through camera techniques. For instance, the constant and repetitious visuals of the courtroom setting—the American flag, the judge's bench, the court stenographer, the uniformed court officials, the workings of the attorneys and presiding judge—set up the mythical context of the American courtroom.

Thus, the trial is a process involving an omnipotent judge, objective attorneys and a blameworthy defendant. The trial takes place in a professional setting of uniformed court officials which is dutifully recorded by a stenographer. The procedure involves a question and answer duel to uncover information against a culpable defendant. The criminal is entitled to counsel, who has the freedom to explore a possible defense. Such fairness under the American Flag is inherent in the judicial system. However, in the presence of God, the evidence disclosed and associated with the defendant will find him guilty.[18]

Of all participants, the defendant appears to be most vulnerable to the camera lens. In the tapes reviewed by Entner, the defendant is typically cast as an unsympathetic and culpable figure. The presumption of innocence, an integral concept of American jurisprudence, is not the concern of the camera, as illustrated by WKBW-TV coverage of the Charles Mixon case in Buffalo. The trial involved a man accused in the arson murder of his stepchildren and wife.

Camera distance, proxemics [space] and juxtaposition created a very unsympathetic pose for the defendant. The case begins with a medium close-up of the defendant who is photographed in profile. The profile is a remote position, causing an unfeeling reaction by the viewer. This lack of feeling for the defendant develops further in the next frame where he is shown again in profile, but in extreme close-up. Such a shot focuses on his prominent nose and mustache, often the symbol for the villain. Negative feelings for the defendant grow as he is linked to the eyewitness through the juxtaposition of shots. Thus, after the eyewitness speaks, the next shot is of an extreme close-up, profiled defendant, connoting his guilt. The association, however, is due to a TV producer's choice of shots rather than any revelation by the eyewitness, since this neighbor could not identify the defendant.[19]

TELEVISION'S TRUTH AND CONSEQUENCE

The courts are only the most recent institution to feel the shaping power of television. We are only now coming to grips with the havoc that the medium has wrought in other arenas of sociopolitical life. The American political scene, as one example, has undergone a dramatic metamorphosis since its submersion into the television age. The demise of traditional election campaigns has long been noted by media observers who now routinely expound on "image candidates" and their media platforms, their message the electronically enhanced product of a new political universe.

Television's imprimatur is apparent. In reshaping the political scene, the medium has sharply reduced the need for language, creating the "sound bite"—a bumper-sticker vernacular devoid of context or explanation. The trend moved researchers at Harvard University to quantify the length of coverage given to candidates' political pronouncements in the electronic press. The results were hardly startling: The compression of sound bites has gotten steadily shorter, from 42.3 seconds in the 1968 presidential campaign to an average of 9.8 seconds in 1988.[20]

So linked is the medium and the truncated message that even attempts to reshape television fall flat. During the 1992 presidential campaign, "CBS Evening News" responded to complaints about sound bite journalism by requiring that snippets of sounds from a candidate's mouth last at least 30 seconds. The experiment proved to be a lesson in absurdity as viewers heard less, not more, from the candidates. Apparently, network officials were forced to discard some bites altogether after they either fell short of the 30-second requirements or were considered too unwieldy to fit into the report. Reporters were left to paraphrasing quotations and presenting the information as part of the account. "Clearly, they're struggling to find out how to fit 1968 sound bites into the 1992 MTV election stories," said S. Robert Lichter, co-director of the Center for Media and Public Affairs, which analyzes news coverage.[21]

Lichter's point is well taken. As Neil Postman eloquently concludes: "In the world of television, 'political knowledge' means having pictures in your head more than words."[22] Significantly, the sculpted media "image" has *become* the "content"—the telegenic billboard of the modern political campaign. It is with no surprise that we have come to view the 15- to 30-second political advertising "spot" as a candidate's major weapon in his televised political arsenal. This television platform has become a modern-day soapbox, and candidates are judged by how well they speak the TV shorthand. More important, the commercials, equating images with a sort of visual truth, are often the definitive factor for many in deciding where to place their vote.[23]

In point of fact, television has radically transformed the modern political campaign. According to Harvard University's Kiku Adatto, "Television [has] displaced politics as the focus of coverage. Like a gestalt shift, the images that once formed the background to political events—the setting and the stage-craft—now [occupy] the foreground." In her study of the three major networks during the 1968 and 1988 presidential elections, Adatto found that as networks devoted less time to the candidates' words over the past 20 years, they increased the time given to visuals of the candidates, unaccompanied by words, by over 300 percent.[24]

It is the medium's growing imagistic power that raises serious questions about the future of political discourse and "the democratic prospect." Asks Adatto: "What becomes of democracy when political discourse is reduced to sound bites, one-liners, and potent visuals? And to what extent is television responsible for this development?"[25]

As television enters the judicial system, there are unsettling parallels to be drawn. Traditionally, the courtroom has been a sanctuary for the spoken and written word. Through the careful analysis of testimony and the weight of written laws and legal precedents, judgments are reached. A trial is often a long, methodical process that can at times seem belabored and, for most observers and even some participants, rather tedious. But it is this cautious unraveling that gives credence to an equitable jurisprudence that allows the system to function.

Television has changed that equation. The judicial process is one inherently adverse to the demands of the medium, and the camera's presence imposes a reordered environment that shifts existing power relationships. Some individuals and groups are empowered by this shift; others are disenfranchised. The Television Trial is a very different one. Whereas the courts traditionally have

attempted to balance a defendant's rights with the public demands for per-
secutorial justice, the courtroom camera has realigned the scales of justice.

It is not the first time in the history of modern Western law that a new
medium has infiltrated and reshaped the judicial environment. The idea of
law as being tied to the written word was introduced into the English courts
in the seventeenth century when written pleadings and decisions began to
supplant those traditional practices that were orally based. The effect of
writing was twofold: It curtailed the court members' practice of shifting
tentative legal positions, and written pleadings tended to be more focused,
reducing controversy to a narrowly singular point (often earmarked in written
decisions that later became precedent for subsequent cases).

If writing organized the early courts in one way, the televised trial does so in
another. Unlike the written word, however, television has added an entirely new
dimension to the process: a vast, mediated public, emotionally involved with
the issues and controversy attached to a particular case. At first glance, it is an
involvement that seems to have positive consequences. In the Dr. Veronica
Prego civil trial in 1989, for example, television helped to heighten awareness
about unsafe hospital practices associated with AIDS treatment. The televised
McMartin trial piqued public interest and sensitivities to the issues of child
abuse. Following the Big Dan Tavern gang rape case in New Bedford, Massachusetts, Susan Brownmiller, the noted feminist and author, commented:
"The case became a public morality play which served to enlighten a nation as
to what actually happens in a courtroom."[26]

But even camera advocates can never rely on television to educate and shape
the public agenda. The William Kennedy Smith trial is a case in point. When
Smith was brought before a Palm Beach, Florida, criminal court in December
1991, accused of raping a 30-year-old woman at the Kennedy family estate, the
case was critiqued as part of a larger commentary on "date rape." After Smith
was acquitted, many of the same commentators scrambled to salve the fears of
the very people they had originally sought to reach. Of particular concern were
women who had been victims of sexual assault and now were fearful of
becoming involved with the criminal justice system because of the possible
television publicity.[27] "The perception is that what people see on TV in high
profile cases is typical," said Ruth Jones, a staff lawyer with the NOW Legal
Defense and Education Fund in Washington, "[but] it's a false perception that
this is what happens in a rape case."[28]

Irrespective of television's forays into elevating public discourse, significant
aftershocks rumble when the camera melds with the courtroom. In point of fact,
the trade-off required when a trial is televised may not only deviate from, but
also imperil, traditional norms of justice. At risk are fundamental liberties that
are embedded in the American system of laws. Although these principles have
always been subject to varying interpretations, the Television Trial potentially
makes them obsolete.

On tenuous ground, for instance, is the fundamental concept of "equal justice," that is, the presumption that each individual is entitled to fair and equal treatment under the law.[29] The courtroom camera pulls against this principle that is woven into a defendant's right of due process. The very selection of a trial to be televised can stamp in the minds of the court members, the media, and the public that this particular case is a more important one. Of course, it may not be—a trial may simply be showcased because of the singularly lurid and sensational aspects attached to the case. Nevertheless, its participants are held up to a more radiant light overshadowing the accused, placing him in a more defensive posture. Charged with a specific crime, he may now personify the broader social issues attached to the case. Widespread child and spousal abuse, random violence, and rape now have readily identifiable faces that can forever mark a defendant as a pariah in the eyes of the community, regardless of the ultimate verdict reached. Television virtually eradicates the possibility that a defendant may ever reenter society, since he may be unable to overcome the labeling that has become part of his public identity. Although only one source of public information, television is by far the most pervasive and dynamic.

Connected to this principle of equal justice is a second judicial doctrine imperiled by the camera. The doctrine of "presumed innocence" is often weakened in a high-profile trial, but in a televised courtroom it can be obliterated altogether.[30] Although constitutional law mandates that all defendants be considered innocent until proven guilty, highly charged courtroom visuals instigate a "presumption of guilt" by presenting a defendant in a vulnerable and subjective light even before a trial is under way. Even in a nontelevised, high-profile trial a defendant would probably be subjected to pretrial publicity that could undermine his due process rights. But the hazards imposed by television images lie in their ability to be powerfully suggestive and are therefore far more destructive, especially when driven into the public consciousness night after night. These visuals connote "meanings" that are almost impossible to dispel, the primary one being that if the accused looks guilty, he must be. Such perceptions are clearly illustrated in a videotape presentation made by the New York State Defenders Association. In one televised pretrial hearing, a defendant was shown being led before the bench in shackles and prison garb.[31] During a nationally televised bail hearing, a judge openly declared that the defendant "will probably be found guilty" of second-degree murder as part of his overall evaluation of the case.[32]

The "presumption of guilt" is magnified by the way in which videotape is selected and edited. Rather than enlightening its audience about the judicial process, television often feeds viewers a misshapen version of a trial in half-minute film clips seen on the nightly news. By selecting clips of high visual intensity above those of actual legal significance, a trial can be transformed into a *cause célèbre* that has the potential to inflame and sway public opinion.

Joel Steinberg, convicted in the beating death of his six-year-old daughter, argued that during his trial he was as much a prisoner of the camera as he was of the legal system. He charged that by choosing images that were one-sided, the medium created an avalanche of public opinion calling for his conviction. An avid media observer, Steinberg opined that his televised trial was not unlike others in which television creates stereotypical themes in order to form a strong narrative line. Images and information that fail to conform are simply disregarded or de-emphasized. The outcome is a highly biased and unfair portrayal of the case put forth to the public.[33]

Regardless of television's intent, legal analysts agree that fleeting and powerful visuals lacking a broader context are more likely to confirm the worst of public opinion. Because of the medium's inclination to promote "a climate of guilt," some defense attorneys are fighting more forcefully to keep the camera out of the courtroom. Jack Litman, a nationally prominent criminal defense lawyer who represented accused murderer Robert Chambers, openly criticized media coverage and speculated about the danger to his client had television been allowed access to the proceedings. The press, Litman charged, had already made up its mind that Chambers was guilty of killing 19-year-old Jennifer Levin during a sexual tryst in Central Park: Television would merely select the appropriate trial visuals to paint this negative "portrait" in the public mind.[34] "My view was that television would air the most salacious 30-second sound bite or what they believed was the most damning piece of evidence against Chambers, and of course leave out all the mitigating circumstances and all the favorable evidence for Chambers," he said. "And I didn't want that portrait on every night in a way that could impact negatively on the jurors." "The public pressure," he stated, is usually "a pressure to convict."[35] Litman noted that television was excluded from the trial and the jury hung 7–5 in favor of acquittal for Chambers, resulting in a plea to a much reduced charge.

THE ECOLOGY OF THE TELEVISION TRIAL

Beyond televison's propensity to trivialize legal proceedings and upset fundamental principles of law are issues related to the medium's expansive power within the judicial system itself. They revolve around fundamental questions: To what extent does the courtroom camera affect the behavior and judgments of trial participants, and do such shifts threaten the fair administration of justice? Do court participants, under the scrutiny of the television eye, change their courtroom stance to fit the demands of the medium itself? These questions are crucial in evaluating the national camera experiment and will be fully explored in a broad-based case study in Part Two.

It is sufficient here to conclude that most state investigations have failed to answer this central query, suffering from a statistical myopia. Attempting to quantify their results through close-ended, narrowly focused surveys of judges, lawyers, jurors, and witnesses involved in televised trials, the states have elicited no more than a popular vote on the camera-in-the-court question. Even in cases where trial participants have expressed strong reservations about courtroom television, their responses are seen as anomalous, mere statistical aberrations in an experiment prematurely deemed a success. The best and worst of these studies are the 1980 California survey, which presented a comprehensive, if not misleading, statistical analysis of courtroom impressions of in-court cameras; and the 1988 New York study, considered to be an unreliable and shoddy investigation.[36] They share a common conclusion summed up in a 113-page New York report stating that "audio-visual coverage does not adversely affect judicial proceedings."[37]

By and large, however, these studies are virtually deficient of any dialogue or observation that explains the subtle interactions and psychological changes that, in fact, exist between the court participant and the camera. Such changes are typically dismissed as being irregular or deviant from "normal" responses. These state reports glaringly miss the very essence of the camera question, reflecting a basic confusion about the medium's powerful activism within the courtroom and, indeed, within the culture at large. The confusion that prevails over the camera experiment stems from the perception that television is a mere *additive* to the courtroom. Place a television at a trial, contend proponents, and we have both camera and courtroom, distinct entities that work in tandem. This viewpoint argues that the camera is simply a reportorial tool that facilitates media coverage not unlike the reporter's prose description or the artist's sketchboard rendition. Soon after the camera is in place, the argument continues, it becomes a "part of the courtroom furniture," virtually fading into the background, invisible and unthreatening to proceedings.

In a certain sense, those who hold this viewpoint have a valid point. The days of noisy motor drives, harsh lights, and cumbersome equipment are long gone, replaced by a more streamlined technology capable of operating quietly and inconspicuously. The very development of the light-sensitive, noiseless camera has allowed the judicial system to work with and ultimately to trust in television's stealthy efficiency. Critics can no longer claim that the medium calls attention to itself, undermining the concentration of court members and preventing "a sober search for the truth."

But it is a conclusion that fails to satisfy a deeper analysis. Even advocates who argue that the camera is a passive technology that simply mirrors the events taking place before it are forced to concede that underlying and inexplicable shifts occur when a trial is televised. Television's expansiveness is one that undulates, much like a stone tossed into water. The rippling effect created extends far beyond the boundaries constructed by the legal system. How participants weigh and interpret their role before the camera eye often has a direct bearing on their judgment and behavior in the courtroom. In effect, the camera suddenly becomes a viable entity, a force to be dealt with and confronted.

Inevitably, the camera compels each court member to confront his courtroom "image" as it is electronically bounced off a television audience. Participants can suddenly find themselves as part of the audience, since televised proceedings allow them to interact with their own performances. They can scrutinize their remarks, body language, and nuances of their performance as broadcast on television. As the distinction between actor and audience is blurred, so, too, is the fine line between impartiality and self-conscious performance.

The danger is made clearer by anecdote. In the Joseph Hazelwood hearing, in April 1989, on Long Island, New York, the presiding judge was roundly criticized by the legal community for apparently buckling under the weight of public pressure. Hazelwood had been the captain of the oil tanker Exxon *Valdez*, which ran aground in Prince William Sound, spilling millions of gallons of oil and devastating the Alaskan shoreline and the area's wildlife. Wanted in Alaska on three misdemeanor charges, he voluntarily surrendered to authorities.[38]

During the televised bail hearing, prosecutor Philip Castellano accused Hazelwood of being "an architect of an American tragedy" and requested that bail be set at $50,000. Hazelwood's lawyers argued for a lesser sum of $5,000, describing the 35-year-old Suffolk County resident as "a family man," charged with relatively minor crimes. But Hazelwood's freedom would ultimately lay in the hands of Judge Kenneth Rohl, and in a decision that visibly stunned the courtroom, the judge set bail at $1 million, 20 times the prosecutor's request. In a voice laced with anger and outrage he addressed the court, calling Hazelwood's actions "misdemeanors of such magnitude unequaled in this country. This is a level of destruction we've not seen since Hiroshima."[39] Hazelwood stood impassively throughout most of the bail hearing, but was noticeably shaken by the judge's decision as he was led away in handcuffs to a county jail in Riverhead.

To many observers, Judge Rohl's performance and judgment were suspect. Addressing a public audience, his remarks clearly indicated an awareness of the broader implications attached to the case. His recognition of the international impact of his decision was evident when he concluded, "This will send a ripple around the world."[40] Even if Rohl's decision was untainted by public pressure, there still remained the very perception that television had unfairly influenced the process.

Indeed, Judge Rohl's ruling was subsequently overturned by a review board that cited the $1 million bail bond as "constitutionally excessive." Hazelwood's bail was reduced, and he was released, but not before sparking a wave of criticism. The judge was openly accused of "grandstanding" in a televised case that touched public sensitivities worldwide. According to attorney Jack Litman:

"Although the case had large environmental impact, the charges against the accused were very minor, and the judge, in the minds of many, used that forum to grandstand, portraying himself as a committed environmentalist and outrageously setting bail at $1 million. He did so only because the cameras were there."[41]

The Television Trial is a new entity altogether, one that encompasses a broad social and legal spectrum. Clearly, these changes instigated by television are not merely additive—singular and momentary shifts—but *ecological*: In the world of the televised courtroom *every* aspect of the judicial process changes. As conventional rules that once defined the connection between the courts and the public begin to dissipate, they are replaced by a new mediated compact. For trial participants, there are distinct risks embedded in an environment in which they are, in effect, prompted to judge how they are being judged.

This perilous transformation within the American courtroom is at the core of our investigation.

The Early Years

THE REELING TWENTIES

Even before the advent of television, the medium's technological predecessors—still and newsreel cameras—had made inroads into the courtroom. From the beginning, though, the camera butted up against a judicial system fearful that an obtrusive medium might hamper trial proceedings and damage the reputation of the courts and "the sanctity of the judiciary."[1]

It was a point of view subscribed to by the Illinois State Supreme Court, which, in a 1917 decision, became the first legal authority to officially advise state courts to bar cameras during their trials. In calling for a ban on still and newsreel cameras, the court ruled that such coverage was "not in keeping with the dignity a court should maintain, or with the proper and orderly conduct of its business."[2] Until the Illinois high court decision, photojournalists had broad access to the state's courts, although permission to photograph proceedings was left to the discretion of each judge.[3] The move by the Illinois high court reflected the growing sensitivity to camera coverage in relation to the rise of tabloid newspapers after World War I. Most notable among the tabloid press was the *New York Daily News*, which aggressively pursued courtroom photography for its regular editorial features.[4]

Some media historians have made the case that even certain members of the press actively gave their approval to state recommendations that banned cameras from the courts. An agreement between journalists and the Chicago Bar Association in the early 1920s called for the exclusion of cameras from the courtroom. In 1925, at the urging of the bar association's Committee on

Relations with the Press to Judicial Proceedings, 45 Chicago judges voted unanimously to prohibit the photo-press in courtrooms around the state. Andrew R. Sherriff, chairman of the committee, claimed that the recommendation to ban cameras had the approval of attending editors and lawyers alike.[5]

Inevitably, the Chicago rules outlawing court photography fell under the weight of competition and a growing interest in this emerging technology. More newspapers were investing in photojournalism, and even those that had agreed in principle with the camera prohibition found it virtually impossible to abide by the decree of the city's legal community in order to stay competitive with other newspapers that featured trial pictures. The *Chicago Daily News* conceded that it assigned photographers to the courts because other newspapers had done so, "but, in the interest of orderly and dignified procedure, it has long advocated the banishment of cameras during trials."[6]

Still, the decree by Chicago's judges and the bar association was not met with enthusiasm by the national media and segments of the legal establishment. The American Bar Association (ABA), for instance, refused to endorse a national standard to regulate cameras in the court, while judges in several high-profile trials were not dissuaded from granting permission to news photographers. The most notable dissenter was Judge John T. Raulston, who presided at the John T. Scopes "Monkey" trial later that year. On July 10, 1925, in Dayton, Tennessee, Raulston opened the courtroom to camera as well as radio coverage. Scopes, a Kentucky schoolteacher, had challenged Tennessee's Butler Act, which prohibited the teaching of evolutionary theories that denied the Biblical version of Divine Creation. The penalty for the offense was $100 to $500, but Scopes, encouraged by local businessmen and civic leaders interested in attracting business for the Dayton community, agreed to the test case.[7]

The trial ignited public attention when two of the nation's preeminent trial attorneys announced that they would voluntarily serve the court: William Jennings Bryan, a three-time Democratic nominee for the presidency, and Clarence Darrow, a nationally recognized criminal attorney from Chicago, would act, respectively, as state prosecutor and defense counsel. News photographers were permitted to take photographs during critical junctures in the trial, including one of Darrow addressing the court and another of Scopes during sentencing. But it was radio that was thought to be most responsible for bringing the Scopes trial to the public.[8] Quin Ryan, the sole broadcast announcer at the trial, recalled that both Darrow and Ryan were led to believe that the trial broadcast had a limited range outside the courthouse, and neither lawyer competed for the radio microphone. Despite a devastating cross-examination by Darrow of Bryan (which revealed Bryan's pointed shortcomings as an expert witness on the Bible and as a student of biological science), Scopes was convicted and fined $100. A Tennessee appeals court later reversed the conviction. It based this action not on the unconstitutionality of the statute, but on the grounds that the jury could not impose a fine in excess of $50.[9]

Judicial opinion about the use of cameras still remained divided in the aftermath of the Scopes trial. In a Maryland murder case two years later, a presiding judge cited two photographers and three editors from William Randolph Hearst's *Baltimore News* and the *American* for contempt after discovering that photographs had been surreptitiously taken during the trial and later published.[10]

Prior to the trial, Judge Eugene O'Dunne caught William Klemm, a *News* photographer, taking pictures of the defendant as he was being locked in the courthouse jail. After confiscating the film plate, the judge discovered that Klemm had switched a blank plate for the real one. The following day O'Dunne announced that all press photography would be banned from the trial.[11]

The judge's ruling still did not stop the newspaper's city editor from assigning another photographer, William Strum, who secretly took seven photographs during the opening day of the trial. Two of the photographs were published the following day, a move that infuriated the judge who cited the five members of the news staff for contempt. The newspaper argued that while the judge had discretionary power, he could not ban cameras completely. But the Maryland Court of Appeals concluded that a judge could act to limit and even prohibit cameras in order to protect a defendant's rights and to maintain judicial decorum. The newspapers were forced to pay a $5,000 fine, and the five editors and photographers were sentenced to one day in jail.[12] As noted by Susanna Barber, the judge's contempt citation was prompted more out of resentment that his authority had been willfully disobeyed than any problem with photographic coverage. Apparently the *News* photographer was so noiseless that Judge O'Dunne only learned that pictures were taken when he saw the published photographs the following day.[13]

The Maryland high court decision still had not cemented a national judicial stance, and the decision to allow courtroom cameras was left up to the predilections of individual judges. While some judges banned photography entirely, others allowed and even endorsed the use of cameras as a judicial and journalistic tool. In a 1931 murder trial, the presiding judge dismissed a juror's complaint that photography was distracting and declared that publicity helped to protect the integrity of the criminal justice system by making the public more aware of court proceedings. And in 1933, a judge in an Oklahoma City kidnapping trial, in stating that the public is "living in an age of pictures when people get their information from seeing as much as reading," declared that Americans are within their constitutional rights to see trials in a photograph as well as in print.[14] It is this very belief that would echo two decades later when television would enter the scene.

THE TRIAL OF BRUNO HAUPTMANN

This division among jurists would soon be overwhelmed by the explosive events surrounding a landmark six-week trial in Flemington, New Jersey, in January 1935. The trial of Bruno Richard Hauptmann, a German immigrant accused of kidnapping and murdering the baby of Charles Lindbergh, the world-famous aviator and national hero, would quickly galvanize opinion within the legal community against the use of the courtroom camera.

Judge Thomas W. Trenchard, of the state supreme court, had considered banning the photo-press before deciding to allow restricted use of newsreel and still photography. Four photographers were given permission to take pictures before court proceedings began, during recess, and after the court adjourned for the day. Newsreel cameramen also faced court restrictions: A silent camera was permitted on the courtroom floor and sound cameras in the balcony. While no filming was allowed when the judge was seated on the bench, witnesses could repeat highlights of their testimony to photojournalists following the day's proceedings.[15]

In the trial's aftermath, scholars, journalists, and legal authorities argued about the exact circumstances that led to what was widely perceived as a media circus both inside and outside the Hauptmann courthouse. Describing the courtroom scene, one newsman called it a "Roman holiday" where "photographers clambered on the counsel's table and shoved their flashbulbs into the faces of witnesses."[16] Blame for the pandemonium was also leveled against a highly charged print press for disturbing court proceedings and for publishing slanted stories convicting Hauptmann before a verdict was reached. Editors, too, were accused of hiring detective story writers, fashion writers, and gossip columnists to report the trial. News photographers were similarly criticized for their bad taste in taking pictures and for harassing witnesses outside the courtroom.

Still, some media analysts dispute the notion that the photo-press was out of control. They believe that despite keen competition among the 700 writers and broadcasters, and 132 still and newsreel cameramen, there were few breaches of courtroom protocol and no single transgression disrupted the trial.[17] It was not the tumult caused by an unruly press or overzealous photographers that led the judge to withdraw permission for all photographic coverage in the courtroom. Instead, argue some critics, it was a hidden newsreel camera that had been so well soundproofed that its existence was discovered only after footage was released to the public. This incident marked one of the first instances when sound cameras taped court actions for public consumption. The film from the Hauptmann trial played in 10,000 of the nation's 14,000 movie theaters.[18]

The media frenzy surrounding the Hauptmann trial was not limited to the excesses of the photo-press. Lending to the media circus were newspaper reports with damning headlines that all but convicted Hauptmann. The *New*

York Post described the defendant, during his testimony, as "a thing lacking in human characteristics."[19] Trial attorneys played to the media's appetite for sensational reports, granting regular press conferences at which they commented on the day's proceedings and on testimony yet to be presented in court. Key witnesses also gave highly prejudicial out-of-court interviews, and even Hauptmann, beleaguered and confused, made statements to the media. Judge Trenchard chastised photographers who disobeyed his instructions, but he failed to stop sensational and inflammatory newspaper reports that undermined the defendant's case and to prevent trial participants from making damaging statements.

Chaos reigned outside the courtroom as the media and the public jockeyed for position. An estimated 20,000 people converged on the small courthouse; throngs of spectators crammed into hallways and even broke the glass entrance doors. Oscar Hallam, a former Minnesota court justice, describes people perching on windowsills, craning over balcony rails, and standing on tables to get a glimpse of the proceedings. Inside the Flemington courtroom, a maximum of 260 people were allowed to be seated, a restriction that did not deter some 275 spectators and witnesses; 135 reporters, trial participants, and court personnel; and for a part of the proceedings a panel of 150 prospective jury members from cramming into the space. Despite warnings from the judge, the noise inside the courtroom was so penetrating that Judge Trenchard had difficulty hearing the questions asked by trial counsel. The trial soon became a public spectacle as rowdy spectators persisted in laughing and commenting throughout the entire proceedings. During the verdict, the court clerk told the judge that he could not poll jury members, since he could not hear them over the din.[20]

A month after the trial, *The New Republic* with evident disdain concluded that the Hauptmann trial was a case in which "both the defendant and society were found guilty. The best thing one can say is that it is over. It was a microcosm showing us many of the faults of our system of justice—and indeed, of our society as a whole—in one vivid and humiliating example."[21] Even a year after the verdict, media critics were scathing in their recollections of the trial. Richard Knight in *The Forum* described the trial as taking place "in the midst of a mob of peanut eaters in an atmosphere suggestive of a cockfight rather than a court."[22]

Susanna Barber argues that the blame for the spectacle, what one headline called "The Flemington Circus—This Way to the Big Tent," cannot be placed at the doorstep of newsreel and still photographers. She cites only several instances when cameramen violated Judge Trenchard's order, and "there is little evidence to substantiate the myth of a media circus [among camera personnel] while the trial was in progress. The so-called 'Roman holiday' that existed during the trial was perpetrated instead by the prejudicial and notorious nature of the publicity accompanying the trial."[23]

Clearly, it was not an opinion later shared by a special committee appointed by the American Bar Association. The committee pointed a condemning finger at the news photography as the spark that lit the judicial conflagration at Flemington.

CANON FIRE

While the print press was severely criticized for its sensational treatment of the Hauptmann case, the photo-press was officially singled out for condemnation by the ABA. Shortly after the trial, the organization empaneled a Special Committee on Publicity in Criminal Trials, headed by Oscar Hallam, who later commented that "there was never a case that lent itself to greater temptation to lurid or excessive publicity, never a case more provocative of trial out of court, never a case beset with greater menace of disorderly procedure."[24]

The committee delved deeply into the events surrounding the Hauptmann trial, and it finally issued a lengthy report offering 16 recommendations that would regulate the behavior of the press and legal personnel. One advised that U.S. courtrooms bar all news cameras. Eventually, this recommendation to prohibit camera coverage in the courts would be accepted and codified by the ABA in what was to become Canon 35.

The committee report also encouraged the ABA to work with journalism organizations to formulate a set of guidelines governing press coverage in criminal trials. In response, a joint bar-press committee headed by Newton D. Baker was established in 1937. Baker had previously characterized the Hauptmann trial as "perhaps the most spectacular and depressing example of improper publicity and professional misconduct ever presented to the people of the United States in a criminal trial."[25] Baker, however, held a view of cameras different from that of his predecessor. While the Hallam report had advised against the use of courtroom photography, the joint bar-press committee was closing in on an opinion endorsing the use of trial cameras with specific limitations.

But before a final recommendation could be made, the committee's work was quashed when the ABA's Committee on Professional and Judicial Ethics and Grievances issued an updated version of Canon 35. Circumventing the work of the Baker committee, it called for a total ban on news cameras and radio broadcasting. Entitled "Improper Publicizing of Court Proceedings," Canon 35 stated that courtroom photography was "calculated to detract from the essential dignity of the proceedings, degrade the court and create misconceptions [about the judicial process] . . . in the mind of the public and should not be permitted." Although ABA canons do not have the force of law, Canon 35 had a significant impact on the relationship between the courts and the media.[26] While there remained scattered instances where cameras were allowed by a presiding judge (or were operated surreptitiously), Canon 35 became the guiding principle behind banning still and newsreel cameras, and, later, television cameras, from most state courtrooms. Nine years after Canon 35 was updated, Congress enacted legislation—Rule 53 of the Federal Rules of Criminal Procedure—forbidding radio and photographic in-court coverage of criminal cases in federal courts.

Media analysts maintain that the photo-press was singled out for misconduct because of the ABA's desire to "insulate the profession's status in society." According to critic Richard Kielbowicz, there is a tendency for established professions to resist public scrutiny of their work because it "demystifies their realm of expertise" and "reduces public respect for their profession." He further contends that "cameras threatened to open the judicial process to public scrutiny" and that "Canon 35, however, helped keep the public largely ignorant of the judicial process." Canon 35, Kielbowicz concludes, "appears now to have been an exaggerated response to an exceptional situation. On balance, the photojournalists probably acquitted themselves well in the Flemington courtroom."[27] But after the Hauptmann trial there was no unanimity of opinion. Many journalists criticized the legal profession itself, in particular attorneys who vied for public attention by giving self-serving out-of-court statements.

TELEVISION COMES TO COURT

The split between the national bar and the photo-press intensified when television entered American living rooms. The emergence of this new medium prompted the ABA to revise Canon 35, and in 1952, the canon was amended to specifically prohibit television cameras. During the next two decades, several advisory committees within the ABA examined Canon 35, but each committee upon review would recommend to retain it, agreeing that photography and the broadcast of trial proceedings were unfriendly to the courts. The ABA actions still did not stop some lower-court judges who permitted the photo-press to work unhampered. In several states, judges took bolder moves by opening courtroom doors to television cameras and radio microphones.

A year after the amended Canon 35, an Oklahoma City court became the first to allow televised trial coverage. From a booth in the rear of the courtroom, television personnel recorded the trial of Billy Eugene Manley. A hidden microphone was placed in front, while additional lighting was attached to the courtroom chandelier. The trial judge had the discretion to halt the operation of the television camera by pushing a button attached to his bench. Most Oklahoma City residents saw the trial through the edited footage on WKY-TV news, depicting the jury selection, witness testimony, and sentencing.[28]

Although cameras were subsequently barred in Oklahoma courts in the late 1950s, the Oklahoma Supreme Court made an exception during the pretrial hearing of Gene Leroy Hart. The defendant had been accused of murdering three young Girl Scouts, and the court's decision to allow television cameras centered, in part, on the intense public interest in the case and the inability of the courtroom to accommodate a large number of spectators. The trial judge permitted television cameras to broadcast on closed circuit from the courtroom to a nearby auditorium; no rebroadcast of the proceedings was allowed.[29]

The nation's first live television broadcast of a trial took place in Waco, Texas, on December 6, 1955, with the approval of the judge, the jury, and even the defendant, Harry Washburn. KWTX-TV placed its camera on the rear balcony of the courtroom and carried only brief running commentary. All other sounds heard by viewers came from the courtroom. Jury members were not told that the trial would be televised, but soon suspected that something was different about this case. "By the time it was over, some of us had a suspicion there was something special about this trial," said jury foreman Jack Woods. "It was so intense. We became intense."[30]

Following the trial, a documentary report prepared by Abner V. McCall, dean of Baylor University Law School, found that the television station had received near-unanimous support from viewers for airing the Washburn trial.[31] The Waco–McLennon County Bar Association also polled its members who had watched at least part of the trial on television. According to the survey results, 59 out of 61 members considered television to be the least intrusive medium covering the trial. The bar association's report concluded that television coverage appeared to "dignify the proceedings" and "was no more distracting then a court reporter taking notes, or an electric light burning in the courtroom."[32]

In spite of public opinion favoring television cameras, the influence of the ABA's Canon 35 loomed over state legislatures. Under harsh attacks by the media, the ABA in 1963 affirmed its position with a resolution that "Judicial Canon 35 remains valid and with minor deletions should be retained as an essential safeguard of the individual's inviolate and personal right of fair trial." The association pushed further by recommending that the canon be incorporated in the rules of court of every state. By 1965, virtually all states had codified the canon into law, banning cameras from their courtrooms. Colorado and Texas were the lone states to reject Canon 35, and both would eventually become embroiled in televised trials that would serve as the warring grounds on which a contentious national debate would take place.[33]

Television cameras finally found a permanent home in Colorado courthouses in 1956. The new law was formulated as a result of a unique compromise between the media and the courts in the case of John Gilbert Graham, on trial for planting a time bomb on an airline flight to Portland that exploded in mid-air killing 44 people, including his mother. Graham had placed the bomb in his mother's luggage after taking out insurance policies on her life.[34]

His arraignment was covered by television cameras, but they were barred from subsequent hearings. Media representatives protested the ruling and petitioned the court. During a week-long hearing, they argued that Canon 35 violated press rights and that photographic and broadcast coverage could be conducted quietly without disrupting court proceedings. To further enhance their case, the media established a set of recommendations regulating the number of cameras during court sessions. They agreed to limit television equipment, pool resources, and also install a cutoff switch that would enable judges to stop camera coverage at any time during the trial. Significantly, this compromise between the television press and the courts would serve as a model for future state laws allowing cameras under the authority of the trial judge.

In the Graham case, Judge Otto Moore subsequently ruled in favor of the camera and then took another judicial step by recommending to the Colorado Supreme Court that Canon 35 be replaced by a new code of judicial conduct.[35] Furthermore, Moore criticized supporters of Canon 35 who "have failed to, neglected or refused to expose themselves to information, evidence, and demonstrations of progress which are available in this field." As a result, Colorado Rule 35 was adopted, and Colorado became the first state to permit in-court cameras to operate with the permission of the presiding judge.[36]

During the 1950s and 1960s, the debate over photo access to court proceedings came to include far-ranging constitutional issues. Originally, Canon 35 was a response to the physical intrusion of cameras and their effect on the court's dignity and decorum. These arguments weakened as media technologies improved and television became less physically intrusive. But other arguments began to surface and were articulated by members of the legal profession who continued to call for a camera ban. Legal scholars now perceived that television was not merely a neutral observer of a courtroom scene, but could instigate psychological repercussions among court participants and potentially undermine proceedings. It was a point of view sharply defined in the Supreme Court's 1965 decision called *Estes*.

THE BILLY SOL ESTES DECISION

As the 1960s unfolded, the camera-in-the-court question shifted into a constitutional arena, pitting a defendant's right of fair trial against the press's rights to freely cover judicial proceedings. The media did not have a friend in the ABA, which contended that the "fair trial" component of due process was paramount and that greater media access to courtroom proceedings should be granted only if it does not interfere with the defendant's right to a fair trial. Against this backdrop, the case of *Estes* v. *Texas* came before the Supreme Court in 1965.[37]

Billy Sol Estes, a prominent political figure, had been tried in a Texas courtroom in 1962 and convicted of fraudulent financial dealings. He was alleged to have swindled lending institutions and farmers out of an estimated $32 million through a phony liquid fertilizer tank scheme. Estes's reputation was that of an avowed liberal, a lay preacher, and a friend and political ally of President John Kennedy and Vice President Lyndon Johnson.[38] The intense public interest in the case prompted the trial judge to allow photographers and television cameras during pretrial hearings. The behavior of the photo-press during these proceedings was later compared to that of the Hauptmann trial and became the focus of the 1965 Supreme Court ruling which reversed Estes's conviction on the grounds that the televising of a "notorious" criminal trial was a denial of the defendant's right to due process as guaranteed by the Fourteenth Amendment.[39]

The Supreme Court's dilemma in its decision to overturn the Estes conviction centered on the physical disruption created by the plethora of cameras, wires, and lights, as well as the psychological impact of television. During the trial, camera operators and photographers roamed the courtroom at will, while photographers snapped pictures from behind the judge's bench. The "carnival atmosphere" surrounding the pretrial proceedings was illustrated in a concurring opinion by Chief Justice Earl Warren:

A television motor van, big as an intercontinental bus, was parked outside the court-house and the second-floor courtroom was a forest of equipment. Two television cameras had been set up inside the bar and four more marked cameras were aligned from outside the gates. A microphone stuck its 12-inch snout inside the jury box, now occupied by an overflow of reporters from the press table, and three microphones confronted Judge Dunagan on his bench. Cables and wires snaked over the floor.[40]

But the 5–4 Court ruling moved beyond earlier arguments that television cameras were essentially obtrusive and interfered with court decorum. In a broad condemnation of television, the Court found that the use of the cameras was itself unfriendly to the judicial process. Conceivably, it could corrupt a juror's impartiality, impair the testimony of witnesses, affect a judge's decision making, and subject the defendant to "a form of mental if not physical harassment, resembling a police line-up or the third-degree."[41] In effect, said the Court, television coverage usurped a defendant's right to a fair trial by influencing trial participants.

Justice Tom Clark also noted that courtroom cameras could have a deleterious effect on a juror's judgment and thus affect the outcome of a trial. Jury members could become self-conscious, view the case as part of a larger agenda, or be pressured to conform to a perceived community viewpoint. "We are all self-conscious and uneasy when being televised," Clark acknowledged. "Human nature being what it is, not only will the juror's eyes be focused on the cameras, but his mind will also be preoccupied with the television rather than the testimony."[42]

The presence of a television camera during a trial, the Supreme Court concluded, could influence the performance of attorneys, judges, witnesses, and jurors and perhaps subvert a defendant's due process rights. Irrespective of the media's objectives, courtrooms could become a stage where willingly or unwillingly, participants were forced to perform to a mass audience. Justice Clark warned that some psychological shifts are "so subtle as to defy detection by the accused or control by the judge."[43]

But the Court's critique of television had one major flaw. The justices' observations seemed purely personal: Not a shred of empirical evidence had been presented to indicate whether the camera actually prejudiced court members at all. Indeed, in Colorado, televised trials had been in existence since 1956 without a single complaint that the medium had provoked adverse psychological effects.

The *Estes* decision, in the final analysis, did not provide a clear-cut view on the constitutionality of televised trials. Justice John Harlan, while concurring with the majority opinion, did not agree that television coverage was inherently prejudicial to a defendant's rights. It was the conduct of television personnel and not the mere presence of the medium that prejudiced Estes's rights under the due process clause. Harlan agreed that while television may have "mischievous potentialities for intruding upon the detached atmosphere" of the judicial process, "forbidding this innovation would doubtless [inhibit] . . . states from pursuing a novel course of procedural experimentation."[44]

Still, the *Estes* decision did have a chilling effect on television news coverage of trials and prompted many state legislatures to adopt Canon 35 as part of their own legal code. By 1972, the ABA approved a new code of professional behavior, but the revision still prohibited cameras from covering trials. Recodified as Canon 3A(7), the ABA canon now approved only a restricted use of courtroom cameras for televising a trial for educational purposes or for presenting videotaped evidence. But as the 1970s approached and television became a more dominant source of news and information, the medium appeared to gain more credibility, and media representatives continued to press for greater access to the courts. The potential for the camera's use as an electronic reporter began to meet with less and less resistance, perhaps because of a growing trend in the post-Watergate era of promoting freedom of information and open access to government proceedings.

THE EXPERIMENT IN FLORIDA

The first breakthrough came in 1977 when Florida initiated a one-year pilot project, under the auspices of the state supreme court, allowing televised trials. Following a project review, the court approved the use of television and still cameras in state courtrooms, subject to the approval of the presiding judge. Taken into consideration by the Florida court were the positive comments of Judge Paul Baker, the presiding judge in the case of Ronald A. Zamora, a 15-year-old convicted of murdering an 82-year-old woman. The trial received widespread attention, in part, due to Zamora's defense, which argued that the defendant had been made insane by watching violent television programs.[45]

Sixty reporters and photographers were present on the first day of the trial. Surprised by the large number of news personnel, Judge Baker appointed a local newsman to act as liaison between the bench and the media. Through a mutual agreement, a room adjacent to the courtroom was used to house television equipment and technicians, and pooling arrangements were made among still photographers. Television station WPBT had been given prior permission to operate a single video camera, which fed multiple video recorders in the adjoining room. Baker, who initially had been opposed to the Florida experiment, submitted a report to the state supreme court following the trial in which he concluded that "the pilot experiment must be viewed as a success" because it demonstrated that the courts and the photo-press can work compatibly.[46] The report stated that the television cameras and personnel did not cause any physical disruptions. After interviewing jurors, Baker further concluded that cameras did not interfere with their ability to consider testimony or follow the legal arguments made by counsel.

However, the use of television in other sensational Florida trials immediately after the experimental period did not fare as well as it had in the Zamora case. Following the 1979 trial of Ted Bundy for the murder of two college coeds, the presiding judge endorsed camera coverage of the case. But the defendant himself publicly charged that he had been victimized by media "sharks" and that television specifically posed "a constant threat" to his effort to sustain a successful defense. In another televised case followed nationally in the spring of 1980, five Dade County policemen were charged in the beating death of black Miami insurance salesman Arthur McDuffie. The trial was given extensive media coverage, and trial footage was regularly broadcast on the nightly news. The acquittal of the police ignited three days of rioting in Miami and also led to speculation that the courtroom camera had played some part in the subsequent public violence.[47]

But the state's highest court had already reached its conclusion. The court had examined two post-hoc surveys, one of which was sent to state circuit court judges, the other to trial participants who had taken part in the Zamora trial. Finally, it rejected arguments that criticized cameras, especially those cited in the *Estes* decision, and stated that it could find little evidence to support the charge that television interfered with the orderly conduct of a fair trial.[48]

The court's decision was ratified by the U.S. Supreme Court in November 1981 in the case of *Chandler* v. *Florida*.[49] Noel Chandler and Robert Granger, two former Miami Beach policemen convicted of burglarizing a popular local restaurant, argued before the high court that the mere presence of the in-court camera adversely affected the behavior of attorneys, witnesses, and jurors. The men rested their case heavily on the Court's *Estes* decision, but this time a number of legal organizations supported the state's contention that cameras should be allowed in the courtroom. Filing friend-of-the-court (*amicus curiae*) briefs were most state chief justices and a substantial number of state attorneys general who had now reached the conclusion that cameras could act as a viable press without harming the judicial process.[50]

The Supreme Court's ruling was handed down in the wake of a veritable turnaround within many state legislatures concerning the camera-in-the-court question. The gradual change in attitudes among judges and lawyers was reflected in state legislative moves to allow news camera coverage of trials. By the time the *Chandler* decision was handed down, 29 states had adopted rules allowing courtroom cameras on either a permanent or an experimental basis. Following the decision, more states joined the list, and by July 1993, 47 states had enacted rules permitting some type of courtroom coverage. Even the ABA in 1982 approved a resolution outlining a new Canon 3A(7), which recommends that in-court camera coverage for news purposes be allowed under the supervision of the state's highest appellate court.[51] The association, which had been a staunch opponent of courtroom cameras as far back as the 1930s, could not barricade the overwhelming rush of support for this new courtroom technology.

The Defendants: Claus von Bulow, William Kennedy Smith, and the L.A. Police

THE VON BULOW TRIAL AND THE BIG DAN'S TAVERN RAPE CASE

As television gained widespread acceptance in many state courtrooms, the debate was dramatically reignited in two cases at the turn of the 1980s that became the focus of national attention. While the issues surrounding the cases were highly volatile, it was television itself that incited and fueled another controversy about the medium's role in the courtroom. In the longstanding debate over courtroom television, the Claus von Bulow attempted murder case and the New Bedford gang rape case are notable examples.

In February 1982, Claus von Bulow, a wealthy aristocrat and visible member of Rhode Island's social elite, was brought to trial for the attempted murder of his wife, the former Martha (Sunny) Crawford von Auersperg. Accused of injecting her on two separate occasions with potentially lethal doses of insulin, he stood to inherit the bulk of her vast estate. Although the doses proved not to be fatal, according to prosecutors, it left her in what was described as an irreversible coma, a permanent vegetative state.

Two years later, in New Bedford, Massachusetts, a 21-year-old mother became the victim of a gang rape, a crime that shook the small fishing town as well as the nation. The case would come to be known as the "Big Dan's Tavern" story, named after the bar where the attack took place. It was particularly egregious in that the crime had been witnessed by onlookers who cheered and goaded the rapists on.

In the beginning, there was little to connect the two cases. Von Bulow, a former English barrister and a prominent socialite, traveled in the posh circles of Newport, Rhode Island, worlds apart from the working-class life style of the woman who had been raped. His arrest made national headlines; the Big Dan's Tavern case was relegated to a mere four paragraphs on page five of New Bedford's *Standard Times*. But despite these contrasted beginnings, the destinies of both would be irrevocably linked by the in-court camera.

By the time both cases came to trial, the glaring spotlight of the press had illuminated them as major national stories. But it would be the courtroom visuals, recorded by the camera, that the public would remember. These images fueled the notoriety attached to the personalities and events surrounding the case, stimulating worldwide attention.

The von Bulow case in particular had all the trappings of international intrigue, the participants resembling characters in a dark soap opera. More than 60 witnesses testified in a trial that would continue for 47 days. Each day the courtroom was packed with more than 100 spectators and 38 reporters from the print, radio, and television media. Another 100 reporters were housed in a building across the street. The presence of von Bulow, along with his prominent attorney, Herald Price Fahringer, often incited bedlam among the members of the press. Television capitalized on the case's notoriety even before von Bulow went to trial (prior to the proceedings, a local television station even produced a half-hour special entitled "The von Bulows of Newport"[1]).

For four months beginning in January 1982, virtually every local newspaper and television evening news show carried a daily story on the von Bulow case. Cable News Network (CNN) broadcast the actual trial live to a national audience, while the three major network affiliates reached 300,000 homes in Rhode Island with reports ranging from short 30-second accounts to more in-depth 2-minute stories. London's Thames Television covered the trial for about a month and broadcast a half-hour special on America's "aristocracy" based on the von Bulow family.[2]

The public's fascination with the trial as it chronicled the downfall of one of the state's prominent families led the press to dub it "The Greatest Show on Earth." Television added to the spectacle by broadcasting the defendant's every move. When the verdict was rendered, the camera zoomed in for close-ups of von Bulow's face and hands in an attempt to capture his emotional state. Observers angrily denounced the selective coverage as "immoral" and "inhumane."[3]

Prior to the trial, Fahringer had warned that television coverage of the von Bulow case was "an expedition into the unknown, and danger to our judicial process lurks everywhere."[4] The lawyer had not changed his mind after his client was convicted of two counts of attempted murder. (The verdict was subsequently overturned by an appeals court, and in a second trial, von Bulow was acquitted.) Particularly vulnerable to the camera were jurors, according to

Fahringer, whose independent judgments are at risk in a televised trial "where the pressure is to come up with a socially acceptable decision."[5]

The attorney noted that the prospect of television coverage had altered the method of *voir dire* in selecting jury members. The camera was yet another factor in his determination of whom to select, and prospective members were questioned as to whether their judgments would be affected by being part of a televised trial. Fahringer cited one example of how "this very powerful medium changed human behavior." Barbara Connett, the jury forewoman, had been reluctant to serve because of the publicity the trial would receive and expressed those feelings to the judge on several occasions. Sensitive to her shyness about publicity, Judge Thomas Needham instructed the camera technician to pan from the juror when the verdict was announced. To his surprise, Connett protested, urging that the verdict be televised. That same day, along with other jurors, she held a televised press conference in which she discussed the deliberations that had led to the verdict. "This was a very different person than we had seen in the beginning," contended Fahringer, attributing the change to the effects of being part of a televised trial.[6]

The in-court camera also appeared to raise the level of media attention outside the courtroom. Although journalists would have covered the case regardless, the daily coverage of court proceedings seemed to ignite an already volatile press. The concentration of such media attention, said Fahringer, "placed enormous burdens" on him. He recalled that during the nine weeks of the trial "there was never a movement you make without encountering a reporter." Along with von Bulow, he was a virtual prisoner, "trapped" by the troops of reporters from even leaving the court building during lunch. Even in the relative seclusion of their hotel, swarms of reporters camped in the lobby, waiting for them to exit, each vying for an impromptu interview.[7]

The framing of the von Bulow trial and retrial within the electronic and print media pointed to the often contradictory agendas that exist between the courts and the media. Marital fidelity, the corrupting influence of wealth, and family betrayal—all examined in the von Bulow case—were issues that were used differently to fulfill the needs and expectations of both the media and the courts. Media critics Susan Drucker and Janice Platt Hunold remark that this dichotomy was clearly evident at the von Bulow trials.

Generally, the courts deal with these acts in order to determine if societal norms formalized in law have been violated. The media magnify these acts in order to criticize and reaffirm values. Claus von Bulow was a man charged with both criminalized behavior and conduct that offended the common morality. The legal system found von Bulow was not guilty of criminal acts; a large segment of public opinion found him guilty of moral transgressions.[8]

Beyond the expectations of the media and the courts were the apparent demands of an insatiable public audience, fed by television and the plethora of images coming out of the von Bulow trial. As Susanna Barber notes, in the aftermath of the trial, there was little criticism about the sensational news reporting or the aggressive behavior of the press; rather, critics began to take a closer look at the role that in-court television played and the symbiotic relationship it fostered with its audience.[9]

The camera . . . permitted viewers to see von Bulow's every blink and wrinkle. The camera waits and watches breathlessly, capturing the eternity of suspense the defendant must be enduring. . . . As the axe falls, the audience scrutinizes the face and hands for reaction—a momentary tightening of the fingers, no perceptible change in facial expression, narrated for those viewers who were momentarily distracted at the vital instant or who want their own impressions verified or corrected. Such television reporting may be a substantiation of the premise that Americans are sufficiently committed to voyeurism to prevent a too robust growth of the right of privacy.[10]

As had happened in Newport, Rhode Island, the New Bedford case also gained increasing public attention in the year it came to trial. One week after the alleged crime, a large group of protesters marched through the streets of the city denouncing violence against women. They were joined by sympathy marchers in other communities all over the country. The case contained other sensitive overtones. The city's large Portuguese community, fearing racial backlash, reacted angrily to press reports that repeatedly identified the assailants as Portuguese immigrants. By the time the case went to trial, the enormous amount of pretrial publicity had become a major factor in selecting a jury. But it was the live television coverage that would do the most damage, creating a firestorm of controversy as it related to the victim in the case.[11]

Although television was aggressive in its coverage of the von Bulow case, at the Big Dan's Tavern trial a more serious journalistic sin was committed. When the trial began in nearby Fall River, four electronic news organizations, including CNN, went on the air with live courtroom coverage. Colony Communications, a local cable system, aired the trial gavel to gavel. In a "mistake" that was to overshadow the trial itself, television microphones picked up the victim's name and broadcast it to 44,000 homes in the New Bedford area. CNN also revealed the identity to a national audience.[12]

But the carelessness of the media did not stop there. The broadcast served to make the journalistic policy against such identifications moot in the minds of some editors. The same day it was televised, the victim's name also appeared in local newspapers. Four days later, United Press International exacerbated an already wrongful situation by providing the name to its 1,000 subscribers.

The victim, according to critics of the press, had been raped "for a second time." The media effectively had abandoned a time-honored practice of shielding a rape victim's identity from the public spotlight. Even as critics lashed out against the press, television continued to besiege the woman by airing a videotape of her leaving the courtroom. Although some news organizations continued to be restrained in their coverage, the damage had already been done—and, in some quarters, public anger began turning against the victim. On radio talk shows, callers expressed their disgust toward the victim herself, commenting that she had "asked for it" and "had led the men on." Such recriminations prompted Scott Charnos, the victim's lawyer, to bitterly complain of public insensitivities that hold that "it is more odious to be the rape victim than the rapist."[13]

Near the close of the trial, Judge William C. Young reprimanded the media, declaring that the decision to publish the victim's name was "an abysmal error of judgment."[14] The essential motive of the press, he charged, was crass commercial exploitation. The offending CNN for its part offered a shallow excuse, stating that the microphone had inadvertently picked up the victim's identification and that it was not financially feasible to install a tape-delay system to avoid such mistakes.

In a postscript to the trial, CNN was criticized before a Senate subcommittee for failing to exercise self-restraint. Senator Arlen Specter, a Pennsylvania Republican, said television's treatment of the Big Dan's Tavern trial could "terrorize" other victims and discourage them from reporting sexual attacks. He also voiced the concern that such coverage could inspire "copycats" and pointed to a recent case in Rhode Island in which a 12-year-old boy was accused of sexually assaulting a 10-year-old playmate on a basement pool table after watching the Big Dan's trial footage.[15]

Beyond the specific journalistic abuses at the Big Dan's Tavern trial, a broader critique about television's role in the courtroom surfaced. The medium's ability to provoke the general public regarding the serious issues surrounding the case pointed to television's powerful role as an electronic press. In the New Bedford case, the camera coverage tapped into the public psyche and focused attention on the problems of sexual assault and the rights of victims in an unprecedented way.

Even before the trial had ended, social and political action groups saw the case as a vehicle to move their own agendas into an incited public forum. The Coalition Against Sexist Violence, for instance, attended the trial each day, scrutinizing testimony they believed would help or hinder perceptions about rape. The information became part of a public education program that included radio and television spots as well as workshops, hotlines, and appearances before civic groups.[16]

Columnist Sydney Schanberg commented that the New Bedford case stirred public discussion on the subject that was unequaled in other cases of this nature. "This is true, I think, not only because large segments of the trial were carried live by a national cable television network, but also because the issues in the case forced us all to grope with our notions of right and wrong in a climate where they are so often blurred."[17]

The public spectator is a critical participant in the Television Trial and invariably an uncontrollable agent. In both the von Bulow and the New Bedford trials, the infiltration of mass opinion was an unpredictable factor that possibly weighed heavily on the minds of trial participants. Seven years after the Big Dan trial, in another televised case in Palm Beach, Florida, the specter of public opinion would once again play a significant role.

THE WILLIAM KENNEDY SMITH TRIAL

There were few similarities between the Big Dan case and a sensational rape trial brought to court in 1991. The accused in the trial was not an anonymous mob, but a member of the nation's most prominent political family. The alleged attack did not take place in a blue-collar tavern in New Bedford, Massachusetts, but at a posh estate in Palm Beach, Florida. The common denominator, however, was television and its gavel-to-gavel coverage seen by a national audience.

The charge in the case was straightforward: A 30-year-old local woman accused a 31-year-old medical student she had met at a local bar of raping her at his beachside estate. Clearly, it was a case that never would have exploded on the American consciousness had it not been for two relevant factors. The first was that the accused rapist was a member of the Kennedy family, a name representing a powerful elite that had become a cultural icon, while evoking tragedy and misfortune on a Shakespearean scale. William Kennedy Smith, a nephew of Senator Edward Kennedy and the son of Jean Kennedy Smith, could not shake free of his family legacy that resonated well beyond the boundaries of a small cramped courtroom in Palm Beach. Yvon Samuel of *France-Soir* told *Time* magazine, "I am here because of the Kennedy name. Willie Smith is a nobody."[18]

The case also could not escape the unblinking eye of the television camera. The Smith trial was a made-for-television event, a neatly wrapped ten-day legal fray that "pushes all the country's hot buttons: sex, money, date rape, the almost mythic Kennedy clan and the Palm Beach scene."[19] In short, the Palm Beach trial was box-office television, replete with explosive allegations and explicit language. Stated reporter Jeff Greenfield on the ABC news program "Nightline": "When a member of the most celebrated, controversial family in America battles a charge of sexual misconduct, when the presence of cameras in the courtroom guarantees that we will see the rich and famous in moments of supreme stress, when we will hear live stories of the most private, imaginable matters, we are hooked."[20]

In late 1991, Americans indeed were hooked—and feeding their addiction was the gavel-to-gavel footage brought to them by two emerging cable networks competing for their attention. CNN, which had aired the New Bedford case seven years earlier, had elevated its reputation as a major network in the year following its aggressive coverage of the Persian Gulf war and the confirmation hearings of Clarence Thomas, a Supreme Court nominee who faced accusations of sexual harassment from Anita Hill, a law professor at the University of Oklahoma. The other network, a six-month-old television experiment engineered by Time Warner Inc., called Courtroom Television Network (Court TV), was counting on the William Kennedy Smith trial to thrust it into the national limelight. Both networks would soon hold center stage.

CNN reported that 3.2 million viewers—nine times what the network draws during those hours—tuned in to watch the two-day-long testimony of the alleged victim, Patricia Bowman. Millions of others watched excerpted versions of the testimony during subsequent newscasts. The case transcended national boundaries to become an international event as dozens of journalists from France, England, Germany, Spain, and Italy descended upon Palm Beach.

Places of work and education were soon turned into extended courtrooms, as each day's testimony was viewed in its entirety, dissected and discussed, entrenched in the discourse of the day. Macro issues, such as widespread unemployment and a deeply entrenched recession, took a back seat on the media agenda. As the court tried to make sense of testimony and evidence brought forth during the trial, Americans, involved in a media-inspired detective game, discussed the missing links in the case, ultimately drawing their own conclusions as to the processes of law, the competency of competing attorneys, the guilt or innocence of the defendant.

The case itself revolved around two crucial contentions. Patricia Bowman insisted she had been brutally raped; William Kennedy Smith insisted the pair had engaged in consensual sex. The details of the case were also contentious. According to Bowman's testimony, the pair had met at a chic Palm Beach night club called Au Bar, March 30, 1991, where they talked and danced. There they discussed her daughter's health problems after which Smith introduced her to his uncle, Senator Edward Kennedy, and his cousin, Patrick Kennedy, a state representative from Rhode Island. Leaving the bar in the early morning hours, the woman asserted in testimony, Smith asked for a ride back to the Kennedy family compound where he gave her "a sweet little kiss" and asked whether she would like to see the house. Later, walking along the beachfront property, Smith asked Bowman if she would like to join him for a swim in the ocean, an offer she declined. After his swim, Smith was accused of chasing and tackling her as she sought to leave and then raping her.

Before the in-court camera, Bowman remained a nameless and faceless accuser, her identity blotted out to the television audience by an electronic blue dot devised by CNN—Court TV followed suit with its own computerized "mosaic wipe" that electronically obliterated Bowman's image. (Following the trial, Bowman herself would shed her anonymity by giving an interview to the ABC-TV news program "Prime Time Live.") Along the edges of CNN's blue dot, viewers could still discern her shoulder-length black hair, a tailored suit, and a string of pearls around her neck. During her ten hours of testimony, viewers could also at times see a glimpse of her face (at times, the electronic blip had trouble obscuring the woman's facial features when she shifted position on the witness stand).

Bowman's sometimes tearful outbursts prompted some observers to sympathize with her plight, others to accuse her of "playing to the camera." Harvard law professor Alan Dershowitz surmised that Bowman's emotional testimony was reflective of her understanding that she was reaching a far greater public than was present in the courtroom. "You're playing to a bigger stage, to the world, and your gestures have to be bigger," he said.[21]

Richard Lacayo, a *Time* magazine correspondent, wrote that, for the alleged victim, "the bitterest part of a rape trial is the experience of having her personal life spread before the court, and usually torn apart by the defense. Gavel-to-gavel coverage only magnifies the misery—perhaps even more so in this instance, as the accuser's face is concealed on camera in a way that protects her identity but also turns her into a cipher."[22] Lacayo suspects that "being at center ring in their own media circus" may discourage other rape victims from reporting the crime. His prediction would prove correct. In Palm Beach County, the number of reported rapes dropped dramatically between the time of the reported incident in April and the trial in November.

Following Smith's acquittal, other court observers were fearful that television, in the final analysis, had sent the wrong message to viewers who were also the victims of rape and sexual abuse. Activists who were usually vocal spokespersons for women's rights found themselves backpedaling against pretrial commentary that had all but found Smith guilty of the rape charge leveled against him. Susan Estrich, a professor at the University of Southern California and author of *Real Rape*, stated that the verdict "does not mean every man will be acquitted, or should be." She noted that the Smith trial differed from most rape cases because of the defendant's celebrity. Rape victims should be assured, said Estrich, that most cases receive little, if any, media attention and that few are carried live on television. The conclusion to be drawn from the Smith trial, according to Estrich, was that "the nightmare was not so much what happened in the courtroom as what happened in the press."[23]

Smith's version of the events leading to the rape allegations made against him substantially differed from that of his accuser. He insisted in his testimony that the woman had caught his attention only after brushing up against him at the bar: He said he had the feeling he was being picked up. Soon they danced and started becoming intimate. When his uncle and cousin departed the bar, he said Bowman had offered him a ride home. At the estate, she suggested a walk to the beach in front of his grandmother's house, where kissing led to fondling and eventually sex.

The details of the alleged rape were graphic as it was projected through the camera lens. Inquiries and testimony about sensitive material that once was unthinkable as a fit subject for public discourse became riveting television fare that made even regularly scheduled television soap operas seem tame by comparison. The print press followed TV's lead with even the *New York Times* giving prominent play on its front page to Smith's testimony. The sense of intrusion of privacy had been so great that it later prompted President George Bush to comment "about so much filth and indecent material coming in through the airwaves and through these trials into people's homes."[24] Bush was to find support for his views from unlikely sources. "Hard Copy," for instance, a top-rated tabloid television show with a heavy emphasis on sex, was critical of the press and of the attention and explicit nature of the coverage given to the trial. Other television executives suggested that the lurid testimony broadcast during the Smith trial would hardly deter, but rather would encourage prime-time courtroom dramas to present more explicit story lines and language. "Now there is no turning back," said Dick Wolf, the executive producer of an NBC-TV crime series called "Law and Order." "You can't put something that sounds softened to the viewers after they've seen real-life cases like this."[25]

In their competition with television coverage, some newspapers gave extensive space to the graphic testimony having to do with the circumstances surrounding the alleged rape. The *New York Post*, for example, ran side-by-side accounts of Bowman's and Smith's testimony of what occurred on the beach and lawn adjacent to the Kennedy house. Under a headline that read "She Snapped," Smith's testimony was reported as the following:[26]

Q: And then what happened?

A: She unbuttoned my pants, I took her panties off. . . . We embraced and I could feel her, I put my hands on her . . . she was excited . . . and I asked her if she had any birth control.

Q: What was her response?

A: She said we better be careful.

Q: And then what happened?

A: She sort of sat up and I rolled off to the side and she put her hands on me.

Q: Where did she put her hands?

A: She put her hands on my penis.

Q: And what did she do?

A: She massaged me.

Q: And what were you doing at the time?

A: I was kissing her.

Q: And so what happened?

A: I ejaculated.

Q: After you ejaculate, what occurs between the two of you?

A: I sat up and I asked her again if she wanted to go in swimming and she said you go
   ahead.

After his solitary swim, Smith said he found the woman on the lawn of the
Kennedy estate.

Q: So what then happened?

A: She started pulling at my towel and started kissing and we put the towel down on
   the lawn. . . . She took off her panties and . . . we were necking for a while and
   she was massaging me and I wasn't excited, and she put me inside her and we
   started to and she said to be careful and we started to make, have sex.

Q: And what happened as you were doing this?

A: I got more excited after a while. We were moving together on the lawn and I got
   more excited and I thought I was maybe gonna ejaculate inside of her.

Q: So what happened?

A: Well I held her very tightly and I stopped moving and I told her to stop it and I called
   her "Kathy."

Q: And what were you thinking when you said that?

A: The minute I said it, I knew it was a mistake and I just hoped she didn't hear it.

Q: What was her response?

A: She sort of, she sort of snapped.

Q: In what way?

A: She got very, very upset and told me to get the hell off of her and she hit me with
   her hand.

Much like a race-track handicapper, the *New York Post* also placed its bet on
the trial's outcome following Smith's testimony. Reporter Murray Weiss pronounced that "nothing short of a Clarence Darrow finish by prosecutor Moira
Lasch can prevent the 31-year-old heir from walking out of the Palm Beach
courthouse, crossing the bridge over the Intracoastal Waterway and bouncing
back into Au Bar a free man."[27]

At a time when "celebrity" stories have become a regular item in the daily
editorial news hole, the Smith trial would certainly have been a topic of intense
media interest with or without in-court television. But with the unique perspective that television can bring, with its captivating, close-up visuals and graphic
testimony broadcast by the cameras, the Smith story became an object of
obsessive desires on the part of the media and the public. Elevating the trial
beyond the dimensions of a "high profile" case into a mediated stratosphere, it
magnified personas and particulars without regard to their inherent legal
importance. In doing so, the trial resonated in ways that would not have been
possible without the presence of television. The Television Trial is unique in
the way in which it recreates itself: that is, a media event of the highest

magnitude, one in which the trial participant is lifted to the status of a public figure. The Smith trial was quickly elevated to a symbolic plateau, emblematic of social issues that may or may not have had actual relevance to the case itself.

This new ecology surrounding this media phenomenon is overlooked by camera advocates. They posit the notion that in-court television itself isolates the courtroom, and thus protects it, from the tumult that swirls around the case. In a "Nightline" interview, Steven Brill, the founder of Court TV, stated that "what you have in the William Kennedy Smith trial, if you have a circus, it's a circus that is outside the courtroom. Inside the courtroom is not a circus."[28] Brill's inference is clear: The camera is distinct from the rest of the media, merely a reportorial tool used within the confines of the courtroom.

But such conclusions are clearly short-sighted. In studying the rise of the Television Trial, certain patterns of media behavior and actions have become predictable, laying way the claim that television is a contained courtroom technology. The extension of the camera reverberates far beyond the parameters of the courthouse into a vast public arena. At the Smith trial, the court participants, the public, and the media all confronted this distinct mediated environment.

MEDIA SELF-CONSCIOUSNESS

The Television Trial helps to create a new type of participant—in essence, a mediated media. As millions of Americans viewed television coverage of the Smith trial, the media watched themselves, commenting on their own role and purpose. By its very nature, television cannot avoid its presentational journalism: The storyteller is typically obtrusive in telling the story. But at the Smith trial both electronic and print media were no longer consigned to a secondary role, and instead found themselves at center stage, molding an event, strangely, in their own image.

Typically, as in the case of the Smith trial, the Television Trial prompts the competitive media to carve out even more space on their news pages and time on their programs. When there is little news coming from the trial, that space and time vacuum must be filled. Inevitably, the media find *themselves* filling the void by becoming the prominent story of the day. While this cathartic exercise may be valuable therapy for an angst-ridden media, the result is a narcissistic and unsettling form of journalism.

Paradoxically, the reporting of the media by the media follows the axiomatic practices given to other types of news stories. Critical, controversial "bad" stories make news, so when the press reports about itself, the results are often bizarre and disconcerting. The media-on-media stories at the Smith trial were thematic and representational of similar reports from other televised trials. The basic themes typically had to do with how the media function—or more precisely, how they malfunction.

According to Joe Queenan of *Time* magazine, "the journalistic horde" seemed to be split into two camps: reporters covering the trial and reporters covering the "media event." He writes: "Those who are covering the trial spend almost all their time watching TV, then rushing out to phones or TV cameras to utter the same phrases as their 200 peers. Those who are covering the media circus spend their time interviewing other journalists: reporters from the Miami *Herald* grill reporters from *France-Soir*, while reporters from Italy's *La Repubblica* patiently answer questions posed by reporters from the Palm Beach *Post*."[29]

The media-watching-media coverage bordered at times on the absurd. When a camera crew from the German weekly *Der Spiegel* entered into a makeshift pressroom to film American journalists watching the televised trial, they failed to realize that they were filming a fellow countrywoman at work. As Queenan concludes, "Thus the Germans from *Der Spiegel* having flown thousands of miles to cover the coverage of the trial, ended up with footage of a German reporter from *Stern* [a competing national magazine] watching an American TV, when the trial takes place 300 yards away. Sacco and Vanzetti it ain't."[30]

Village Voice correspondent Mim Udovitch offered an equally wicked eye-witness view of the press parade in her article entitled "Fear and Loathing in Palm Beach." Her conclusion that the case "was a waste of time" for more than 300 journalists camped in and around the Palm Beach courthouse was as much a commentary on the specifics of the case as it was on the overwhelming national attention given to it. "The consensus is that there are more journalists here than news," she writes. "Meanwhile, [presidential chief of staff] John Sununu's resigning, Pan Am is history, [publishing magnate] Robert Maxwell's chickens are coming home to roost, [Middle East hostage] Terry Anderson is free, and here we all are, crouching at the feet of Court TV [correspondent] Steven Johnson when he does a stand-up so that we can stay out of the shot without losing our front row view of the courthouse doors."[31]

Caught in a quicksand of their own design, the media could not extricate themselves from an event that was exponentially spiraling out of control. Television in the courtroom had inspired a "circus" outside of it. "It's almost beyond trite to observe that this trial, of no conceivable importance as a legal landmark, has become a media circus," concluded Jeff Greenfield. "In fact, when a member of the press calls an event like this a media circus, he is overlooking the fact that he, too, is probably one of the clowns."[32]

A JOURNALISTIC FRENZY

Judging from the specifics, the William Kennedy Smith trial was neither a ground-breaking legal case nor a notably significant social forum for elevating national consciousness regarding the crime of rape. In a "Nightline" report, Ted Koppel stated, "Indeed, if you wanted to argue that televising a rape trial raises public sensitivity on the issue, you could find a dozen rape cases on any given day which would do the job more effectively and with far fewer distractions."[33]

The Television Trial, however, as Koppel is well aware, is not concerned with legal relevancy. And the Smith case was no exception. By lifting the ordinary story to the sensational, the camera instigated what could be described as a journalistic frenzy. In effect, the entire media corps at the Smith trial fed off and competed with the visuals propagated by the in-court camera. No longer relegated to stories that merely recited the major testimony of the day, the media pounced on stories having to do with personalities, analysis, and predictions. As journalists were given wider reportorial latitude, stories that may never have been considered a part of ordinary coverage were now highlighted and given undue emphasis. For the public, the task of distinguishing relevant legal information from the banal had become increasingly difficult—and perhaps irrelevant—within this mosaic.

The excesses of the print press, for instance, were not exclusively within the province of tabloid newspapers already known for their sensational content. The coverage of the Smith trial by more traditional newspapers was equally intense. Even prior to the trial, the *New York Times* was sharply reprimanded within journalistic circles for its coverage that publicly identified the alleged victim and then chronicled her personal life with detailed information on her past marriage, her driving record, and her social predilections.[34]

The portrait was hardly flattering and, according to critics, a media assault on the woman's reputation and privacy. Using an unidentified source, the story told of Bowman's "little wild streak," alluding to the alleged victim's propensity for fast cars and parties. It also cited the women's driving record, noting that she received 17 tickets for speeding, reckless driving, or being involved in an accident between 1982 and 1990; her license had been suspended in 10 cases for failing to pay fines assessed in these violations. Bowman's personal life was also exposed, telling of her parents' combative divorce with allegations of physical abuse and, then in 1989, the birth of her own daughter "by a local man she did not marry."[35]

The response from the journalistic community was immediate and furious—and also the substance of a second *Times* report that appeared nine days later. The article cited Chicago columnist Mike Royko, among other journalists, who said the article "was part of an outbreak of galloping journalistic idiocy." *Newsweek* declared that "virtually everyone in journalism agrees that the nation's most highly regarded newspaper has egg on its face." Even the editor of the *National Enquirer* proclaimed that the *Times* was less ethical in its reporting than the coverage given to the Palm Beach case by his supermarket tabloid.[36] The criticism from within the *Times'* own editorial circles was as scathing. Anna Quindlen wrote in her column that the profile appeared to be punitive and irrelevant. And, in another highly unusual move, about 100 staff members, including reporters and editors, issued a petition expressing their "outrage over the profile," condemning the newspaper's decision to identify Patricia Bowman by name and the article's judgmental tone.[37]

Despite this early criticism of its coverage, the *Times'* enthusiasm for the Palm Beach rape story was hardly dampened when the case came to trial in November 1991. Reporters, columnists, and editors were put on full alert: The paper was committed to extended coverage. Entire pages were devoted to news stories, sidebars, features, editorials, and commentaries, reportage typically seen for major national and international events. The *Times'* media critic, Walter Goodman, acknowledged that "every paper was full of it, not just the tabloids, but the *Times* ran an awful lot of stuff on it." The newspaper's interest in the case, originally tied to the Kennedy name, leaped as the trial unfolded via the television screen. The newspaper was no longer competing against other segments of the print media, but with television and the immediacy and visual intensity it brought to trial coverage. "It was something no one had ever seen on television before," said Goodman. "Newspapers can't compete with this anymore. The audience is so fast and so big."[38]

Goodman himself was thrust into a hyperactive role, with different desks at the newspaper calling for his commentary about the media and their role in the Smith case.

I knew I was going to write about it. I didn't know I was going to write this much about it. I cover only news [programs] and documentaries for TV for our newspaper. So when a matter like this comes up, I have to write about it. However the national desk kept pressing me for more stuff. I don't know how many pieces I wrote, but I would not have written that many. I would have written one at the beginning, one in the middle, then a sum-up later. I did a piece in Arts and Leisure—they ran my articles day after day, they really wanted the story.[39]

While the *Times* was dogged in its coverage, the Smith trial was a made-for-tabloid event, and newspapers like the *New York Post* were typographically gleeful in their coverage. Significant news events were even hardpressed to nudge the Smith case from these newspapers' prime editorial pages during the trial's two-week span. When the trial was not in session, the Kennedy family continued to be the topic of inflammatory headlines occasionally attached to preposterous stories—most notably by the tabloid press whose purpose was to keep the Smith trial at the forefront of public attention.

Under ordinary circumstances, December 9, 1991, would have been such an off-day for media coverage of the trial. Nevertheless, though the Smith trial was in recess, the *Post* continued its editorial barrage, featuring a backlog of stories, columns, and editorials singularly focused on the Kennedy family, though not all were directly connected to the Smith case. Its December 10 banner headline read "Teddy the Bully," attached to a sub-headline that the "Cursing Senator Tried to Bribe Son's Rehab Buddy in Vain Attempt to Kill Coke Story." A large photograph of an imperious-looking Edward Kennedy completed the front page. The article itself was based on a *National Enquirer* interview with a man who spent time with the younger Kennedy at a drug treatment center in New Hampshire in 1986 and now was being paid by the tabloid newspaper for his story.[40] The story was just one of a group of articles that dominated the main news pages. Another four-column story carried the headline "Jackie O Fears She's Susceptible to Alzheimer's," a loosely written article based on a conversation overheard by an anonymous source while Jacqueline Kennedy Onassis attended the funeral of her aunt who reportedly had suffered from the disease.[41]

Columnist Amy Pagnozzi used her space to criticize presiding Judge Mary Lupo for rushing through the trial and failing to allow the prosecutors to fully develop their case. She described Lupo as "a Ticking Judge" for her efforts to expedite the case.[42] Another story, with the headline "Judge Boots Reporter for Smiling," recounted that a news-magazine writer was ordered out of the courtroom after Lupo found him smiling during the testimony of an expert medical witness who told the court that with a partially erect penis, Smith could not have raped a struggling female.[43]

The more serious and disturbing article about the trial that appeared in the *Post* that day was written by Joe Nicholson. In the story he characterized the group of men and women who comprised the jury as "a hanging jury—very conservative and tough-minded about criminals."[44] Nicholson described the group as being all-white, Republican, with no-college background—"a prosecutor's dream . . . which may even lower the level of reasonable doubt necessary to convict." The reporter was not satisfied merely to identify and characterize the jury, but sketched odd profiles taken from testimony given during *voir dire*.

- Thomas Sterns Jr., married with four children, a former Army guerrilla fighter who "gave up his brawling habits after he broke too many knuckles." The story described the 62-year-old Vietnam veteran, who had received seven Purple Hearts, as someone who would "go hunting for any man who raped his daughter."
- Mary Kracunas, 63, married with three children, a Roman Catholic convert who describes her parish's late pastor, Rev. Joseph Berg, as "her favorite person."
- J. Darrell Peacock, 54, married with two children, a local utility executive, an Air Force veteran, a Methodist "who says the people he most respects are his father and President Bush."
- Priscilla Roper, 44, married with two children, a Roman Catholic convert, a Bob Hope admirer—and a crime victim, after her car had been recently stolen.
- Doris Welsch, 60, a Lutheran, retired after having worked 30 years with her husband in the refrigeration business. George Bush is her favorite public person.

• Lea Haller, 37, owner of a $2.5 million cosmetic company which donated money to Lt. Col. Oliver North's legal defense fund.[45]

Though such background reports are technically within the public domain, the story not only stretched the boundaries of good journalism, but also may have eviscerated a traditional agreement between the press and the courts. Many state courts have been sensitive to protecting jurors. Rarely have the identities of jury members been published during a trial, and in most states cameras are expressly forbidden from showing visuals of the jury box. The legal system has been strict in its efforts to ensure that jury members are free of public pressures and possible threats that might arise should they be identified. The media thrashed that notion at the Palm Beach trial.

Whatever excesses were delivered by the print press, it was the courtroom camera that led the way. Prospective jurors, for instance, were televised during *voir dire*, often without their knowledge, and sometimes to their embarrassment. One such potential juror, Florence Orbach, told the court that "the worst thing that the Kennedy family . . . from what I've read, that they're very smart, but when they get horny their penises take over."[46] Her remarks were repeatedly broadcast nationally, and an embarrassed Orbach later told Judge Lupo that she was unaware that the camera was recording her remarks. Once the six-member group was empaneled, the jurors became familiar faces to a national audience, leaving open the possibility that jury members would also become an object of press and public scrutiny.

Live visuals of the trial by CNN and Court TV were intended to strip away the subjective filters of the print and other electronic press. But even attempts to separate the subjective and sensational interests of the media from "unfiltered" television coverage fell under the weight of other realities. CNN interrupted its broadcast from the Palm Beach courtroom every few minutes—and often during critical junctures—to air an array of commercials. While such programming was all too familiar for viewers weaned on tens of thousands of commercials in a lifetime, breaking court coverage to sell products eventually distorted and trivialized the trial process. Reacting to the infusion of commercials within the coverage of the Smith trial, critic David Bianculli excoriated the network, stating: "The CNN coverage isn't so much gavel-to-gavel, actually, as gavel-to-commercial-to-gavel, with former CNN Gulf War correspondent Charles Jaco acting more as ringleader than reporter. . . . On this assignment, Jaco is less Ed Murrow than Ed Sullivan."[47]

In an unusual admission, Jaco candidly apologized for the plethora of commercials that had cut viewers off from ongoing testimony, including Bowman's emotional recounting of the alleged rape.[48] But even such frankness could not inhibit the network from continuing to saturate its trial coverage with ads, some of which bordered on the bizarre in the context to trial programming. Following Edward Kennedy's testimony, in which the senator poignantly spoke of the tragedies that had befallen his family, the network ran a promotional advertisement for the movie *JFK*, a graphic retelling by Oliver Stone of the John F. Kennedy assassination.

THE GREAT EQUALIZER

The Palm Beach courtroom seated about 40 spectators, with just 16 seats reserved for the media. Most of the reporters assigned to the story were relegated to watching a broadcast of the event much like the rest of the country. Television in a sense had become the great equalizer, with ordinary citizens and the press sharing equal access to information and courtroom visuals. Television's new-found stature buttressed arguments that court cameras had democratized the news, prompting citizens to draw their own conclusions as to the veracity of witness testimony and the guilt or innocence of the accused. The *Times'* Pulitzer Prize–winning journalist Anna Quindlen stated that "in the 'you are there' department, there are times when television can't be beat."

"They saw the prosecutor, heard the accusations, listened to Mr. Smith," she stated. "Overwhelmingly, polls show, they would have made the same decision had they been on the jury. And in a sense, they feel that they were, that they participated in the process that, we should remember, was always meant to be public."[49]

But Quindlen draws a dubious conclusion and one that is based on a peculiar, if not incorrect, assumption regarding the connection between the public and the courts. While the legal notion of the "public trial" is in fact mandated through the Sixth Amendment, that legal construct is far different from that of the "Public Trial" espoused by Quindlen. Rather, the idea of "publicness" has been linked to the concept of an open court and jury review as contrasted to secret tribunals that proliferated in Europe prior to the framing of the U.S. Constitution. The Public Trial referred to by Quindlen is a modern-day creation of television. The use of this nascent teledemocratic tool is not mandated within constitutional law; rather, it is considered a *privilege* granted by state law and judicial rules and regulations.[50] Whether or not the camera itself is present at a trial, the courtroom remains a forum open to the public and the electronic and print media.

Legal questions aside, Quindlen's central idea that the public is aptly served by watching for themselves the processes of justice is a common rationale among proponents of courtroom television. The medium places the viewer inside a mediated jury box where conclusions about evidence and testimony and ultimately a verdict can be rendered. It so happens, she reports, that most television watchers agreed with the Smith verdict. The democratic process must have worked, according to Quindlen's analysis, since both trial jurors and public jurors came to a uniform agreement. But such allusions are quickly torn apart when public perceptions clash with legal reality.

RODNEY KING AND THE LOS ANGELES POLICE TRIALS

The Smith trial ended almost a year before another sensational trial was aired. When a group of Los Angeles police officers was acquitted of charges stemming from the beating of Rodney King, a black motorist, the city exploded into violence. The verdict triggered the worst riot in the history of the state, resulting in 53 deaths and one billion dollars in property damage.

The incident that sparked the conflagration in Los Angeles occurred on the evening of March 3, 1991, when police tried to stop King's car for a traffic violation. Instead of stopping promptly, the 26-year-old man led the law enforcement officers on a high-speed chase through the streets of the city before being forced to pull over by a squad of police cars. According to police accounts, King was suspected of being under the influence of drugs when he stepped out of his car and refused to submit to arrest. Immediately, he was surrounded by as many as twenty police officers. A group of white officers tried to subdue King with at least three of them repeatedly kicking and using their clubs to strike the unarmed man. King was later hospitalized with multiple bone fractures, facial lacerations, and bruises.

From the beginning, videotape images stemming from inside and outside the courtroom played a dominant role in inflaming public consciousness. An enormous amount of pretrial publicity was inspired by the release of an amateur videotape of the police beating King. By the time the case came to trial, millions of Americans, as well as members of the international community, had witnessed in numbing repetition at least part of the 51 seconds of videotape, with King struck to the ground, cowering under a rain of blows from police batons. The subsequent verdict seemed a *fait accompli* to a nation of jurors. For the black community, in particular, the case was a compelling and graphic representation of the police brutality that blacks have in the past found difficult to prove and to seek redress for within the criminal justice system.

The Courtroom Television Network broadcast the proceedings across the country while local stations carried trial footage on their nightly reports. When the verdict to acquit came down, it set off a firestorm that surged for days on the streets of Los Angeles. The analysis during those troubled days concluded that although television had *proven* the charges against the police, the court system had failed; even worse, the verdict was racist and, in a sense, akin to the very act that was carried out by the police.

Without digressing into the broad social and political issues surrounding the case, the Los Angeles trial proved noteworthy within the context of the camera issue. Fundamentally, it reaffirmed the enormous strength of the visual image in shaping and activating the public mindset—a power that is often unpredictable. On the one hand, videotape images of the King beating were crucial evidence, instrumental in bringing those police officers involved in the incident to trial. Yet, repeated viewing of the beating turned the visual images from a representation of a particular act into a powerful icon that came to symbolize social injustice, police brutality, and institutional racism. Icons can be taken as virtual truths—whether or not they actually are—making it almost impossible to distinguish facts and evidence that may be relevant, but that run contrary to the symbol. The process of law mandates that these legal distinctions be made; it is the undeniable charter of the American courtroom. But when judicial opinion runs counter to emotionally-heated public opinion, fanned by television images, a veritable explosion can occur. And it did in Los Angeles.

Although the four Los Angeles police officers on trial were found not guilty on all charges (except for one about which no decision was reached), the United States Department of Justice pressed federal charges against the officers for intentionally depriving King of his constitutional right to be free from unreasonable arrest. The government's response was seen in some quarters as a *political* response to a *legal* dispute and was criticized for employing a 130-year-old law passed by Congress following the Civil War, a statute originally designed to protect black citizens when state authorities were unable or unwilling to provide protection under state law. Some prominent critics, like *New York Times* columnist William Safire, went on the record to accuse the government of violating the police officers' constitutional right of "double jeopardy"—that is, forbidding the criminal justice system from trying a defendant more than once for the same crime.

The assumption elsewhere, however, was that the original trial—moved to the mostly white Los Angeles suburb of Simi Valley—had failed to vindicate the rights of the victim and, on a larger scale, to address the demands of the black community of Los Angeles. The second trial, beginning in February 1993, would this time be held in the more racially-mixed downtown Los Angeles. And this time, the courtroom camera would not be permitted under regulations that prohibit the televising of criminal cases in federal courtrooms. Such rules, however, did not prevent Court TV from broadcasting extensive live, ongoing analysis of the proceedings outside the courthouse.

Even without the in-court camera, the second trial proceeded under the fearful shadow of mob violence. The symbolic weight of the trial, according to legal analyst George Critchlow, acted as "a lightning rod for collective anger and frustration." Over the course of the six-week trial, the city "was an anxious and tense time bomb, waiting to explode into a new round of mob violence at the prospect of another verdict of not guilty."[51] Los Angeles resembled war-torn Somalia, with thousands of police officers and National Guard soldiers patrolling the streets as political and civil rights leaders tried to help calm the inflamed situation.

The six-week trial ended with jury deliberations that lasted seven days. When the jury returned a verdict finding two of the four police officers,

Sergeant Stacey Koon and Officer Laurence Powell, guilty as charged, Los Angeles and the nation at large breathed a collective sigh of relief—the verdict appeared to curb the potential for mob violence. But a nagging concern still persisted. Was justice achieved or simply bent to mollify racial communities sensitive to the issues in the case? According to Critchlow, "We have to acknowledge that the always difficult problem of balancing the rights of the accused with the need to vindicate the rights of victims becomes even more problematic when the process is magnified through the lens of an ever alert press in an age when information is transmitted instantaneously throughout the world."[52]

These concerns came into play in yet another Los Angeles case. This time, the defendants were two black men who faced serious criminal charges for acts against passersby who were caught in the street frenzy that followed the state court jury's refusal to convict the four police officers in the King beating. The trial of Damian Williams and Henry Watson was immediately enveloped by an electrified social climate that threatened to explode once again into civil unrest and violence. Though not legally connected to the police trials, in the minds of many blacks in the still smoldering Los Angeles inner city, the trials were symbolically linked. Both were products of an inherently racist judicial system that appeared to benefit white defendants and punish black defendants. Reminiscent of the warnings which preceded the first police trial, threats of "street justice" played repeatedly on nightly news reports. Curiously, the media found that they were not immune to the hostility within the black community, and reporting from inner city Los Angeles during the Williams-Watson trial proved to be a hazardous assignment. As one veteran WCBS-TV reporter acknowledged after his camera crew was attacked during a filming, "In all my years as a reporter, I have never seen such anger on the streets."

Videotaped images again played a decisive role and were used as crucial evidence against the defendants who were charged with 12 separate crimes involving eight victims. A number of incidents were captured on videotape by a news helicopter hovering above the scene, including the brutal assault of Reginald Denny, a driver who was dragged from his truck while passing through the intersection of Florence and Normandie streets. State prosecutors contended that these images provided incontrovertible proof that Williams was responsible for heaving a brick into the face of the already unconscious truck driver and then performing a celebratory dance.

The case came to trial in August 1993, sixteen months after the riots, and just two weeks after police officers Koon and Powell were given, as seen by many observers, lenient sentences on federal charges. Court TV cameras extended the spectator gallery of the courtroom into the living rooms and the workplaces of America, bringing the medium's imagistic power to bear on a case already burdened with enormous social and political pressures.

Once again this Television Trial would fail miserably in justifying public faith in a judicial system that appeared to be reacting to combustive social pressures that weighed heavily on the case. After a nearly three-month trial, and three weeks of stressful deliberations, the jury found both defendants innocent of the most serious attempted murder felony charges, and seven other counts, that could have carried a life sentence. Williams, the principal assailant, was convicted of a single felony count of mayhem and four misdemeanor assault charges, while Watson was found guilty of a misdemeanor assault charge.

To blacks in Los Angeles still angry at the court's treatment of the white police officers in the Rodney King beating, the outcome seemed to be judicial retribution. But for others, the punishment of Williams and Watson was a mere wrist slap in light of the brutality of their crimes. More disturbingly, the city's judicial system itself was perceived as being ineffectual, even cowardly, against the forces of urban crime. In response to the verdicts, Los Angeles District Attorney Gil Garcetti told a television audience, "I know the frustration. I know the anger. I know the fear that is in some of your hearts."

Through television, Americans had observed a bizarre symbiosis in these trials in Los Angeles. Disconcertingly, the courts had failed twice, finally evening out the score among racial communities caught in the emotional furies of perceived injustices—a scene painfully played out on the television screen. In the end, the trials of the Los Angeles police officers and Williams and Watson marked a turning point in the relationship between television and the courts. In a peculiar melding, videotape images from the streets as well as the courtroom had come together, portraying a legal process and a social compact that had, for the most part, broken apart, blurring even further the tenuous line that separates mob rule from the rule of law.

The Electronic Courtroom:
The Rise of Court TV

As the story is now told, the Courtroom Television Network (Court TV) originated with a taxi ride in 1988. Traveling through Manhattan, Steven Brill—a 37-year-old journalist with a hard-nosed reputation as president of The American Lawyer Media—overheard a radio report that a sensational murder case would be televised locally. An attorney by the name of Joel Steinberg was on trial for killing his six-year-old daughter, and the media had petitioned the court to broadcast the trial. New York camera legislation had been in place for about a year, but presiding judges in other recent high-profile trials had turned down media requests for camera access. When Acting Justice Harold Rothwax opened the Steinberg trial to television, local affiliates jumped at the opportunity and soon afterward were producing nightly news accounts amplified by actual footage of the day's testimony.

Brill's long-range plan, however, was far different and, in fact, a radical jump in electronic journalism. By cellular telephone he contacted Steven Ross, then the chairman of Warner Communications, and later a proposal was made. Brill's vision: a 24-hour-a-day, 7-day-a-week national cable network entirely devoted to broadcasting trials. It was an audacious plan and an expensive one. The newly constituted Time Warner Inc. was committed to investing $40 million over five years. Several days after their initial meeting, Brill and Ross sealed an agreement. "I sold him on the idea that the new network would be a cross between C-Span and soap opera," said Brill.[1]

It would take months before the channel could become operational. Slated first to start in October 1990 and then in early 1991, Brill encountered legal wranglings with Cablevision Systems, a Long Island–based cable station that had already extensively televised a local murder trial and was planning to develop its own court programming. With the backing of NBC-TV, Cablevision announced that it would begin to telecast "In Court" at the same time that *The American Lawyer* magazine and Time Warner joined in partnership.[2] In late 1990, both ventures merged under the name of the Courtroom Television Network.

The dramatic debut that Brill was counting on to introduce his network to the nation in early 1991 never materialized. Court TV suffered a major setback when it was denied television access to an impending trial known as the Central Park Jogger's case: A group of black teenagers stood accused of the near-fatal beating and rape of a young investment banker who had been jogging in the park. Beyond the terrifying aspects of the crime, the trial evoked bitter racial overtones throughout New York. As their pilot project, the network had planned to cover the entire trial, but was denied permission after the district attorneys' office and the defense attorneys objected. Under the state statute, the presiding judge could rule against the admission of television in cases involving lurid sex crimes and involving children. At the time of their arrest the defendants were under 16 years of age.

The network was jarred by the decision to bar cameras, and Brill was personally furious, believing he was misled by the district attorneys' office. According to press reports, Brill called a high-ranking assistant district attorney and excoriated her in the most graphic language for failing to warn him about the office's change of heart regarding the presence of cameras in the court.[3] In a calmer moment, Brill went on record to state that the judge's no-camera ruling "was undeniably a reasonable exercise in discretion." "The defendants are indeed kids," he said, "and the trial is likely to be filled with horribly invasive testimony . . . and the medical testimony is likely to be just as gruesome."[4]

Even with such lip service, Brill was far from convinced that the camera blackout would make the legal process a fairer one; nor would it serve a community that was very much keyed to the events surrounding the trial. He argued that the ban on cameras had neither shielded the jogger nor protected the defendants from the daily and graphic recapitulations of the crime. Interpretive reports only presented an incomplete, distorted view of the courtroom and the charges brought in the case. "As the case goes on, we'll see, read and hear capsulized accounts of the case that cannot and will not be as accurate as the real thing," he said.[5]

The jogger trial blackout was a disappointment for a network seeking to make a dramatic premiere—but New York State's failure to ratify new legislation permitting courtroom cameras was nothing less than a stunning blow. Virtually no group—whether in favor of or opposed to camera legislation—expected what was, in effect, a no-decision by the state. After a three-year-old experiment, television was no longer a novelty in most courtrooms, and the question before lawmakers did not appear to be whether or not camera legislation would continue, but rather what adjustments, if any, to the current bill would be implemented. The state senate and assembly had each drawn up a bill, though with distinct differences. In particular, the senate version would require that every witness give affirmative consent before being subjected to audiovisual coverage. Most political observers believed that a compromise decision would quickly be worked out, but they were wrong. The camera bill soon was stuck in a political mire, as the state pushed aside a compromised bill. It would take an entire year before a new law would be enacted.[6]

On June 1, 1991, the camera-in-the-court legislation expired, and New York became the first state ever to cut off television from the courtroom through legislative decree.[7] The irony for Brill and his associates was all too apparent: Situated in Manhattan, the media center of the nation, Court TV would be banned from airing criminal trials from its own state.

When Court TV was finally launched on July 1, 1991, it was met immediately with a degree of skepticism. That Monday the channel brought viewers a Florida trial in which a man was accused of killing his mother-in-law 25 years ago, a case that was reopened by the defendant's son; the trial of an Ohio basketball star charged with rape; and the first live coverage of a federal civil trial, an age discrimination case held in a Philadelphia courtroom. Walter Goodman, the media critic for the *New York Times*, warned that "the obvious danger is that in its reach for ratings, the program will drift more in the direction of exploitation than elucidation."[8] Stated *Newsweek* reporter Harry Waters: "The question facing the 24-hour Courtroom Television Network is one of quality rather than quantity: can excess yield success without getting mired in the tedious or resorting to the tabloidish?"[9]

While seeking to attract a national audience, Brill touted the commercial viability of his new channel to cable operators. "The big risk in anything like this is that we'd give a party and no one would come," he stated.[10] As of February 1992, Court TV was in 5.5 million homes in 43 states, and Brill anticipated that within five years more than 50 million homes could be wired for the channel. Preliminary ratings indicated that just over 1 percent of viewers—or about 60,000 people—were watching the network at any given time, but Brill notes that Court TV attracts "a cumulative audience" and that as many as 300,000 viewers followed the network over the course of a day. "That's pretty good," he said. "And it's good comparatively, much higher than CNN [Cable News Network] or Lifetime television or USA network."[11]

The break for Brill's network finally came in December 1991. In a 4,000-word article in *The American Lawyer*, titled "How the Willie Smith Show Changed America," Brill predicted that *Florida* v. *Smith* "is probably going to be the best thing to happen in a long while to the confidence Americans have in the legal system."[12] Whether or not Brill's prognostication would prove correct, one thing was evident—the William Kennedy Smith trial was the best thing to hit Court TV.

As the Courtroom Television Network monitored the trial (it literally provided the live "feed" to a media pool), the news media (also quite literally) watched the network.[13] Virtually all major newspapers across the country carried stories about the network's coverage of the trial. National news programs such as ABC's "Nightline" and PBS's "The MacNeil/Lehrer Newshour" interviewed Brill and examined the impact of cameras in the court. Excerpts of Court TV coverage were shown on all major networks as well as CNN and A&E (not to mention its becoming a favorite parody of "Saturday Night Live"). Even television crews from France, Germany, and Japan prepared reports about America's new courtroom network.[14] With unintended ironic overtones, it was the glossy "Entertainment Tonight," a weeknight celebrity program, that concluded that Court TV coverage "may change forever" the way TV viewers witness justice at work.

The six-month-old pioneering venture finally had access to a trial that would place the network on the national map. That expectation would be fulfilled as hundreds of thousands of Americans began turning to a new genre of television programming: gavel-to-gavel courtroom coverage. In San Francisco, its rating easily surpassed popular talk shows and soap operas, said Brill, who noted that his primary competitor, CNN, more than tripled its usual audience and that Court TV typically outdistanced CNN where both were broadcast.[15]

The network executive acknowledged that while a vast audience tuned in to the trial, some members of the legal community were not necessarily enamored of the coverage. Lawyers, in particular, expressed their doubts about television broadcasts, especially the Court TV commentary that was aired during breaks and recesses. Brill said: "Many complained to me that the TV show sends the message that what they do isn't . . . 'a search for truth.' Rather, it comes off on TV as some kind of game akin to a tennis match or football game, complete with 'color commentators' who trivialize a solemn process."[16]

One critic of the network was Roy Black, Smith's lead attorney. Black acknowledged that complete trial coverage may have some educational benefits to the public—a justification for cameras often cited by Brill—but believed that the presence of courtroom television could probably hamper the work of jury members. Articulating what Brill acknowledges as "the most compelling argument" against Court TV, Black said: "The whole purpose of the trial is not to educate people. It's to decide whether or not a citizen in this community is guilty of a crime and should be punished by going to prison. And the way you determine that is whether the allegations are true or false. We have to pick people who can decide this case calmly and dispassionately. . . . I think it's very difficult under these circumstances."[17]

Black's point of view though was ultimately dismissed by Brill who was less concerned with safeguarding the courts than with bringing a "story" to his audience and, in keeping with his longstanding media crusade, with "demystifying" a legal system exalted within the press and the legal community itself. It is this latter agenda—his moral equivalent of "the public good"—that forms the basis of his journalistic philosophy. The trial itself, maintained Brill, "is not a preordained, truth-producing science, but a game" in which the "players," most notably the competing lawyers, are not the "brilliant gladiators" as depicted by fictional television stories and an "awestruck" press, but ordinary and often fallible human beings. "It is a game that lawyers, in the new age of televised trials, will have to own up to, because the mass TV viewing of trials that the [Smith] case foreshadows will now forever demystify the process."[18]

Another nationally renowned attorney, however, looked skeptically at Court TV's involvement with the Smith trial as less a journalistic enterprise than an attempt by the network's chief executive to expand his power base from *The American Lawyer* magazine into the far reaches of telecommunications. Alan Dershowitz, a longtime critic of the magazine, specifically rebuked Brill for using the channel to consolidate his own power and influence by commercially exploiting the network's position as the "pool camera" in the Smith courtroom. In an essay entitled, "How *Not* to Televise Trials," Dershowitz accused Brill of misleading potential subscribers and advertisers by claiming to hold "exclusive rights" to the trial. "The only 'right' Court TV had was to the pool camera in the courtroom," he said. But according to the network's "raw feed agreement" with other stations, Brill had demanded a per diem payment and a signed agreement that forbid stations from protesting this arrangement. "Since Court TV is the sole pool camera," said Dershowitz, "this is an offer that can't be easily refused."[19]

More disturbing to Dershowitz was what he perceived as Brill's attempt to "monopolize the televising of trials"—a possibility that poses "significant dangers of censorship." During the Smith trial, he said, Court TV dictated what restrictions would be placed on the videotape feed coming from its camera. Under Court TV's contractual guidelines, stations were required, for instance, to follow network policy by electronically blocking the transmission of the face of the accusing witness, Patricia Bowman, and by also withholding her name from public disclosure. "Steven Brill said it was his decision to censor the name and face of the accusor," said Dershowitz. "Whether this information should or should not be disclosed is a hotly debated issue. But it seems abundantly clear that the decision should be made by each network or station for itself. The decision should not be dictated by Brill as a self-appointed censor for the entire nation."[20]

Court TV executives bristle at such criticism, contending that the network was obligated during the Smith trial to obey an administrative court mandate requiring that Bowman's identity be electronically obscured. "[Stations buying Court TV's 'raw' videotape feed] had to adhere to the same rules," explained network executive Merrill Brown, adding, "We strongly believe in the integrity of our signal."[21]

INSIDE THE COURTROOM TELEVISION NETWORK

The channel—co-owned by Time Warner, American Lawyer Media, Cablevision System, NBC, and Liberty Media—planted its headquarters on the East Side of New York City. In point of fact, its operations—executive offices, newsroom, and television studio—are scattered over a six-block radius in the East 30s.[22] The sites have a storefront look, even a year after the network's opening. The executive offices at 600 Third Avenue, seemingly freshly painted, are a maze of cubicles with crates of videotape stacked against the walls. A visitor to the nearby Court TV broadcast station is reminded that he is observing a pioneering effort as he enters a small, no-frills studio. The production staff is surprisingly young and informal, some eight men and women working individual eight-hour shifts. Of the 80 people employed at Court TV, about 50 work in programming. At any time, the network may be airing trials live from three different courthouses and taping several more.

In mid-February 1992, several high-profile trials are reaching a culmination. A buzz of activity and anticipation sweeps over the staff with comments from secretaries to executives speculating on soon-to-be-reached verdicts. Merrill Brown, senior vice president of corporate and program development, interrupts an interview to turn up the television sound tuned to an ongoing murder trial. "Live verdicts are remarkable moments," he exudes. "I can't imagine anything with more clear and explicit drama that's ever on TV, anywhere, than a verdict. The stakes are obvious, the level of unknown is obvious. It's astonishing, everybody gathers in the newsroom, around the monitors, waiting for this moment, all this investment we've made in this case, all this curiosity."[23]

One such case reaching its culminating moment involves the shooting death of a 16-year-old black youth by a Teaneck, New Jersey, police officer named Gary Spath. The officer is charged with second-degree reckless manslaughter in the death of Phillip Pannell. Spath claims he fired in self-defense when Pannell appeared to be reaching for a weapon inside his coat. It is an explosive case, pitting police against community charges of police brutality and racism. As played out on television, the case has had unusual moments. A former police officer, cited for heroism after being crippled by a gunman's bullet, is seen wheeled into the courtroom, angering the trial prosecutor, Glenn Goldberg, who sees the move as a cheap ploy to win sympathy from the court. In another segment, Goldberg holds up to the courtroom—and to a television audience—a red overcoat that belonged to the dead youth. Clearly visible on the right side of the coat is a gaping bullet hole.

Other cases are competing with the Spath trial for air time. Also reaching a close is the pretrial hearing of Jeffrey Dahmer, a case in which the defendant has pled insanity. The court will determine whether the defendant is legally competent to serve a life-term prison sentence or should be remanded to a state psychiatric hospital. The serial killer has confessed to killing and then mutilating more than a dozen young men in Wisconsin. At yet another trial in Indianapolis, former heavyweight boxing champion Mike Tyson stands accused of rape, and while cameras are blacked out, a Court TV reporter is providing regular accounts of the proceedings. Even by network standards, the range of celebrated trials has been overwhelming and leads Brown to believe that the courtroom channel has arrived at a pivotal moment in the history of American jurisprudence.

There's no question of the fact that at this moment in time of history, early 1992, courtroom trials are exceedingly visible—Mike Tyson, Manuel Noriega, L.A. cops. If you listen to a newscast from CNN on the hour, it's courtroom, it's courtroom, it's courtroom. We are also at a point when courts, looking to move cases through the system, are meeting on weekends. So if you turn on the radio news on Saturday, the first story was Tyson meeting on a weekend, the second was Dahmer meeting on a weekend. So there's no reason to believe it's a passing fancy, but we'll see.[24]

Brown concedes that some cases are far too involved to extensively report as part of network programming. The Manuel Noriega trial is a case in point. When the former Panamanian strongman came to trial, Court TV tried to present coverage, but, according to Brown, "it was extremely complicated." "We are trying on-the-hour newscasts to keep people apprised of Noriega, but in terms of spot coverage, we couldn't make it make sense. The issues are too complex, a huge number of documents and people. Keeping track of it in two-minute reports is futile."[25]

Glenn Goldberg, the prosecutor in the Spath case, has been on the air for hours, and the station is reluctant to break away, following a policy that mandates in-depth coverage of the lawyer's final summation. Inside the network's production booth, staffers are bored—they have trained their cameras on the punctilious prosecutor for hours—as is the show's anchor, Cynthia McFadden, who places a friendly two-dollar bet with the program's producer. Goldberg's reputation for long-winded summations is legendary—in another case his closing remarks were reported to have lasted *eight days*—and McFadden was betting that his summation at the Spath trial would extend past three o'clock that afternoon. By 3:30, Goldberg was still analyzing the case for the jury, and McFadden was two dollars richer.

McFadden is an appealing anchor who came to the network after a stint as executive producer of the Columbia University Seminars on Media and Society, broadcast nationally on public television. A graduate of Columbia University Law School, she has a knowledgeable legal mind, but she also understands that her role is to facilitate dialogue among an all-star cast of media commentators that include prominent attorneys, judges, and university professors.[26] Executives at Court TV like to boast, though inaccurately, that they have "invented" a new journalistic entity called the "legal expert," and, in fact, major networks and other cable television shows have picked up on their lead by hiring their own expert commentators during coverage of high-profile trials. Occasionally, Court TV has been "raided" by the commercial networks, as in the case of Starlet Jones, a Brooklyn district attorney who made her debut on Court TV during the William Kennedy Smith trial and was then hired by NBC.

The chief anchor and managing editor of Court TV is Fred Graham, whose homespun quality is evident in person as well as on the air. He joined the American Lawyer Media team in 1990 after a career as an attorney, as a *New York Times* legal writer, and then as a law correspondent for CBS News. A respected journalist during his 15 years at CBS News, his beat included the Supreme Court, the Justice Department, and the FBI.[27]

But the true "star" of Court TV is Brill himself. A Yale Law School graduate who never took the bar exam, Brill, as a young man, seemed more interested in carving out his niche as a journalist. His work began to appear in *New York* magazine, *Esquire*, and *Harper's*, but it was his 1978 book *The Teamsters* that earned him critical acclaim and his book a spot on the best-seller list. Soon afterward Brill found an ideal subject for other investigations—the legal profession itself—a professional world that had for the most part remained outside the hard scrutiny of the working press. Brill became enamored with the idea of an investigative magazine dealing with the world of law and lawyers. With a partner, Jay Kriegal, who later became a top CBS executive, he was able to attract overseas backing to bankroll the $2.5 million project called *The American Lawyer*. Founded in 1979, the magazine shook the legal profession with reports on the often clandestine world of law. Stories began appearing making public the revenues amassed by city law firms and the salary levels of law partners, information that previously was zealously guarded. Other articles examined the business ethics of firms and their treatment of associates.[28]

Although the New York market was at the center of his attention, Brill's vision extended across the country, and during the next decade he established a network of legal newspapers in ten regional markets. Brill's style of journalism earned top prizes in the field and became required reading for many lawyers, jurists, and legal critics. In 1983, a story he wrote helped to free a man on death row. But with the accumulation of power came critics who resented what they perceived as Brill's self-styled journalistic crusade. His attack-type journalism led to accusations that he used his magazine like "a hit list," going after firms as well as individuals he did not like.

Brill also was not especially well liked by his own staff. Over the years he earned a "Jekyll and Hyde" reputation that reached legendary proportions within New York's editorial circles. As described by the *Boston Globe*, Brill was a "brilliant, tempestuous editor, possessed of an almost demonic streak that he frequently used to humiliate and intimidate his staffers."[29] His editorial comments could be scathing, as when he asked one writer he disapproved of if English was his second language. He is reported to have told another writer that she might consider suicide if she could not do a better job for his magazine. His circulated interoffice memorandums that would publicly excoriate his employees: In one instance, he berated a reporter for a grammatical mistake and then threatened to fire the next offender.[30]

Under his heavy hand, *The American Lawyer* has been likened to an editorial version of "boot camp." Still, Brill has his supporters who see his stewardship of the cable network as an outgrowth of a career as a maverick investigative reporter. "His reporting has, from my experience, always been right on the money," said attorney F. Lee Bailey, who is a frequent guest commentator at the network. "Brill changed the legal profession—he cut through all the secrecy of the big firms, and he was the first to do that." Bailey believes that Brill's new television venture "will help to enlighten the public if it is done in a responsible fashion and I'm confident that Steve will handle it that way."[31]

With the start-up of Court TV, however, other prominent legal voices went on record to criticize Brill's latest attempt to expand his media empire. Harvard law professor Alan Dershowitz told *New York* magazine that his running feud with Brill became exacerbated when *American Lawyer* criticized him for writing about his client Claus von Bulow. "Nobody trusts Brill," charged Dershowitz. "I don't think people in the legal profession have faith that anything he touches is going to be objective, neutral or educational. I'm in favor of bringing TV cameras into the courtroom—but there couldn't be a worse person to do it than Steve Brill."[32]

Dershowitz himself is an attorney best known for his involvement with sensational trials and flamboyant personalities—Claus von Bulow, Mike Tyson, Leona Helmsley, to name a few—that have captured the public glare and the media spotlight. He has been an outspoken critic of Brill and what he describes as the media mogul's attempt to turn the practice of law into a crass bottom-line business.

Before the "Brillization" of the law, as it has come to be called, lawyers claimed to be part of a learned profession. We did not always live up to that claim, but at least it was an aspiration. *The American Lawyer* changed all that. Now law firms are ranked not primarily by their professionalism, their ethics, or even their litigation successes. They are ranked by their bottom-line profits. This kind of crass commercialism is already in evidence from Court TV.[33]

Dershowitz contends that few lawyers are willing to publicly dispute Brill, fearing his editorial wrath. Brill also has a reputation for rewarding allies, a "carrot and stick" approach that Dershowitz claims to have experienced himself.

After openly criticizing Court TV, the attorney said he received two "frantic" phone calls and a letter asking him to become a network commentator. "Since I regarded this invitation as an obvious attempt to 'buy off' my criticism, I turned it down," he said. Immediately following the Smith verdict, Brill himself called to warn Dershowitz that if he continued to criticize the network, his own strong interest in bringing courtroom television to America would be damaged. "I responded that Brill's warning confirmed my worst fears, namely that his way of televising trials—selecting the most salacious and atypical ones for maximum commercial exploitation—will be seen as the only way to televise trials."[34]

Dershowitz disclosed that several lawsuits challenging the network's authority to commercially exploit trial litigants for profit were pending before the courts in December 1991. He openly mused: "I wonder if Court TV will cover those cases."[35]

The major obstacle in Brill's path, however, is not negative reviews from his critics, but whether or not his network can reach an audience large enough to sustain it. With just over 5 million subscribers, Court TV will need to attract 10 to 15 million homes to maintain its viability, an increasingly difficult task at a time when the cable dial is glutted. Part of the network's revenues comes from charging cable companies 10 to 11 cents for each subscriber. The rest comes from advertising dollars, which averaged a miniscule $250 a spot in 1991.[36] Ads have not readily poured in, placing pressure on the network to promote and cover more sensational trials to boost ratings and ad revenues. "When you have William Kennedy Smith or Jeffrey Dahmer," he said, "you don't have to do any marketing to get people involved in these stories because newspapers all over the place are doing that for you."[37]

Court TV has set aside eight minutes of each hour for national and local advertising, but it is a goal they have yet to reach a year after starting operations. The advertising industry appears to be sensitive to placing products on a program associated with depressing events or lurid testimony about the underside of societal life. "Selling ads on Court TV does, indeed, raise a gaggle of interesting moral questions for advertisers," suggests *Newsday* business writer Dottie Enrico. "Is it a cheap shot to sell time on shows that zero in on real human suffering?"[38] Compounding the problem is the network's own sensitivity to running ads that somehow undermine a newly developing reputation and public image.

Despite its original plan to offer live comprehensive coverage of trials, Court TV is not entirely gavel to gavel, nor is it necessarily live television. Described as the "CNNization" of the courts, the network soon began to incorporate taped trials in order to make programming more flexible.[39] Likewise, complete coverage of certain high-profile trials was reduced to "crisply produced" two-to-three-hour "Prime Time" trial stories that mixed trial footage with interviews of judges, attorneys, jurors, and other court participants. A series of programs during the day, such as "Yesterday in Court," "Docket Report," and "In Practice," updates previously televised cases and recent verdicts, and even offers a continuing legal education program for lawyers. Brill has virtually implored his audience to become involved with the network to the extent of establishing a Court TV "Hot Line" for viewers' questions and comments. The multifarious nature of the network is described by Susan Drucker, a media critic at Hofstra University: "Court TV shows range from gavel-to-gavel coverage to sound bite journalism. It is slow-paced; it is fast-paced; it is a story playing out in real time; it is glossy highly stylized edited 'trial by story'; it is coverage of an unscripted event with play by play announcers; and it is a continuing legal education."[40]

As part of its program framework, the network features a "Board of Commentators," a melding of lawyers and jurists, already well known to a television audience as participants in other televised legal events or high-profile trials. Prominant attorneys such as F. Lee Bailey, Linda Fairstein, Floyd Abrams, Barry Slotnick, Barry Scheck, Jack Litman, Harvard Law School professor Arthur Miller, and former federal Judge Robert Bork are among a group of color commentators who take turns offering critiques about the progress of ongoing trials. (The attraction of television is sometimes all too evident. Lawyers such as Litman and Scheck, among others, were vocal opponents of courtroom cameras before their stint on Court TV.) The interaction among the network's anchors and commentators, the so-called "play-by-play" analysis, can often be biting. During the William Kennedy Smith case, for instance, prosecutor Moira Lasch was severely criticized by guest analysts for essentially preparing an incompetent state case: ("It's almost impossible to believe this redirect. . . . If the prosecution wins, it'll be almost in spite of itself.")[41]

Brill, however, has been careful to keep his network away from unwanted controversies. Strict in-house guidelines are established to precisely clarify an employee's responsibilities and procedures in dealing with the public and the legal establishment. Brill's television crews have also been careful about being overly aggressive when their coverage might intrude on the lives of crime victims. When Amish survivors of a collision between their horse-drawn carriage and a drunk driver asked not to be photographed for religious reasons, the network showed viewers just their hands.[42]

The network managed to avoid any major mishap until its coverage of its 109th trial in Austin, Texas, in June 1992. The network was taping a trial for later broadcast in which a woman had sued Texas police officers for arresting her during a demonstration for the homeless. A mistrial was called when a Court TV producer, Michele DuMont, told each one of the six jurors outside the courtroom that she wanted to interview them after the trial. DuMont approached the jurors during a recess and, after looking at their facial expressions, realized her mistake. They looked "horrified," she said. The network notified the presiding judge after which he called a mistrial. Judge Steve Russell's letter explained that "A juror looking forward to either being interviewed on TV or being lambasted by another juror on TV might be less candid during deliberations."[43]

As a curious side note, Judge Russell apparently took judicial action in stopping the trial not only to protect the rules of the court, but also to protect courtroom television itself from a possible reprimand by a higher court. Sensitive to the ongoing political controversy over in-court cameras in the state, the judge said he was "disinclined to give the Texas appellate courts an opportunity to tee off on cameras in the courtroom generally. Were it not for the hostility I have observed toward cameras over the years . . . I would have been more inclined to let the trial finish."[44]

As for the network, Court TV broke into its regular programming to report its misconduct. Brill quickly acknowledged that "we screwed up" and voluntarily paid about $500 in court costs.

If anything else, Court TV has inspired an original genre of television programming as well as a unique blend of media criticism. From its early history, television has given rise to an evolving picture of the criminal justice system, its origins still in evidence today in the black-and-white reruns of programs such as "Perry Mason." But the real-life transmission of current trials via a 24-hour cable network has moved away from these stylized and compressed fictional versions of courtroom reality to becoming, as one critic described, "the cinema verité of due process."[45] According to *New Yorker* magazine critic James Wolcott, the genre is distinct from the familiar stereotypes of the fictional courtroom genre.

Where actors portraying lawyers stiffen their necks as if being fitted for halos, the real-life lawyers on Court TV plod through their notes, losing their place as their glasses slide down their noses. At Court TV's slowest, the camera seems to be collecting lint. And yet the cases themselves often exert the dinosaur fascination of a Dreiser novel. Their very artlessness digs deeper into the social and psychological substrata of deadbeat America than the diamond drills of docudrama technique.[46]

Wolcott makes the point that the symmetrical pattern of television courtroom dramas leans toward rational motives and reasonable goals in an attempt to bring order to an entropic world. Real life is different and the courtroom network "is a peephole into a segment of America populated by moral and mental blanks." As an example, he recounts being "hooked" on a Massachusetts trial involving a 16-year-old high school weight lifter who had murderously plunged a knife into his 14-year-old girlfriend and then dumped her body into a pond after boasting to his friends that he was going to kill her. The defendant's lawyer argued that at the time of the murder his client was pumped up on steroids that released what bodybuilders call "roid rage." Illuminating of the moral emptiness that inspired the crime was the "near carnival atmosphere" in town. Authorities were upset at the playful attitude exhibited by local teenagers, including groupies who formed a fan club for the accused. "Late as it was, I couldn't haul myself to bed until I heard the verdict: Guilty," said Wolcott. "Even that outbreak of common sense seemed like a momentary stay. Watching Court TV, you sometimes feel as if the ground has shifted from under the country—that everything outside the courtroom has given way."[47]

While Court TV's avowed goal is to "educate" both the general public and the legal profession, clearly the network has commercial interests in mind as it chooses among the most dramatic trials to boost its appeal. Production decisions to cut between ongoing trials, as well as the very selection of trials to be aired, are reflective of the network's sensitivity to luring audiences more accustomed to mid-afternoon soap operas than dense trial coverage. Between July 1991 and February 1992, Court TV broadcast 76 separate legal proceedings from federal and state courtrooms as well as such disparate proceedings as the parole hearing of Leslie Van Houten (convicted in the 1969 "Manson Family" murders) and the Clarence Thomas confirmation hearings. Of the trials selected, more than half focused on crimes of violence, with 30 trials involving murder or homicide and 14 dealing with assault, police brutality, sexual abuse, or rape.[48]

Trial selections are made at a weekly editorial meeting, and it is a lively interaction of executives and news personnel. A large whiteboard serves as a calendar of events listing ongoing and upcoming trials. Brill maintains that the newsworthy nature of a case and its ability to help viewers better understand the legal process are critical elements in selecting a trial for broadcast. "Balancing the sensational, lurid and gory with the evolution of legal doctrine will be the Courtroom Television Network's ultimate test," states critic Susan Drucker.[49] For the most part, however, the network has clearly leaned on the side of sensational or celebrity-studded dramas.

Among the cases aired in the network's first year was the Pamela Smart murder trial in Manchester, New Hampshire, in which a teacher was accused and convicted of sexually luring three young students into a plot to kill her husband. In *California* v. *Bardo*, an obsessed fan was charged and found guilty of first-degree murder in the shooting death of television actress Rebecca Schaeffer. Live coverage was given to *California* v. *Broderick* in San Diego. Betty Broderick was charged with the shooting deaths of her former husband, a prominent local attorney, and of his second wife as they were sleeping in their bedroom. Broderick was found guilty of two counts of second-degree murder. Some cases, like the Smart and Broderick trials, eventually made the jump to prime-time television movies. The blending of "made-for-TV" with "made-by-TV" movies became more surreal in the Broderick case when viewers found themselves choosing one week between the CBS movie reenactment and Court TV's two-hour "Prime Time" version.

Despite the network's predisposition to present cases that accentuate the grisly and sensational, Brill maintains that Court TV is "going to help people understand the important legal issues that affect their lives—this isn't just entertainment."[50] He notes that most Americans are woefully ignorant of the legal process and that his network can only help in providing a valuable civics lesson. To buttress his point, he cites a 1989 poll that concluded that far more American adults know the name of the judge who presided over "People's Court" (a quasi-legal entertainment show featuring Judge Wapner) than that of U.S. Supreme Court Chief Justice William Rehnquist (54 percent to 9 percent). "Ten years from now, our sense of how some law is working or not working shouldn't be derived from apocryphal anecdotes but from watching that law work in court," Brill said.[51]

He acknowledges that the editorial decision to cover a particular case is often an unpredictable venture. High-profile cases have fizzled; lesser known trials have proven to be surprisingly compelling. When the network sent a television crew to cover the Carolyn Warmus "Fatal Attraction" trial, Brill incorrectly surmised that the case, which involved a love triangle and murder, would attract a large audience. Yet a relatively unpublicized Kentucky murder trial involving a teenage defendant named Tracie English proved riveting to viewers in a preliminary test of the network.[52] Close-up shots were taken of English's tearful and explicit testimony, describing years of sexual abuse by her father, the man she was accused of killing.

But even in that early case, Brill found the network under attack for its apparent cynicism and heavy-handedness. Particularly disturbing to critics were Fred Graham's and Barry Scheck's seemingly insensitive reactions to English's testimony. The anchor could be seen smiling after the network cut back from the emotionally distraught young girl. Scheck, a guest commentator, characterized English's performance on the stand, concluding: "Crying and looking pathetic doesn't make out the position that she's asking the jury to accept."[53] Scheck later said that neither he nor Graham had ever intended to denigrate or mock English, but rather to explain how the court might react to emotional testimony given by the defendant.[54]

But media critics still pounced on Court TV's handling of the English case. *New York* magazine reporter Warren Berger castigated the network for placing additional burdens on a defendant already in traumatic distress. "Though it was a murder and not a rape case," he said, "if English was sexually molested at some point before the crime, wasn't she entitled to some sensitivity from Brill's camera crews?"[55] In response, Brill issued a memo acknowledging that the network had been insensitive and wrong in passing judgment.

These early critiques have not shaken Brill's faith in his network: To the contrary, he exudes an unshakeable confidence that Court TV will become "*the* authoritative source for legal news and commentary in this country and the world."[56] Court TV's major breakthrough may, in fact, be its influence in the newsroom. The network has broken down outdated modes of court reporting, a news beat often treated indifferently by the media. The televised courtroom, says Brill, forces the media to be more accountable for what they report. To drive home the point more forcefully, Brill recounts an encounter he had with a *New York Times* reporter while covering the General William Westmoreland libel suit against CBS-TV in 1985.

Myron Farber was covering the trial for the *New York Times*. He would walk into court every day at 11:00 always carrying a folder with the *"New York Times"* written on it and sit down and ask other reporters what happened. They'd all for some reason tell him. And he'd write down their notes . . . and he would leave at 3:30 in the afternoon. The interesting thing was, all of the cross examination of Westmoreland, for some reason, the real good stuff, happened between 4:00 to 6:00 at night. You read the entire *New York Times* and never knew that Westmoreland was having his head handed to him. There's no way he was going to win the case, they were going to drop the case. It was no surprise to anyone except readers of the *New York Times*. Now if Myron Farber knew he had editors who would have seen the trial on television, his reporting would have been halfway professional.[57]

Brill relishes teaching a few journalism lessons to the venerable *Times*, but the most popular media format to benefit from the televised courtroom may be tabloid-styled programs such as "A Current Affair" and "Inside Edition," which have slotted trial footage into their reports about sexual scandal, murder, and mayhem.

The "television tabloids" have been a thorn in Brill's side since the start of Court TV. Trial judges have been wary about granting access to the network for fear that the same footage used by the network will end up in the manipulative hands of a television-tabloid producer. Critics have charged that such over-zealous programs have continually violated professional and legal codes of conduct; in some cases, this behavior had "bordered on the criminal."[58] "A Current Affair," in one egregious example, paid Anne Mercer, a principal witness in the William Kennedy Smith trial, $40,000 for her story, to be aired before she ever took the stand. "That is definitely going to affect the jury's assessment of the credibility of the witness," said Barry Scheck, the Court TV analyst. "[The television tabloids] are a real corrupting influence and very, very dangerous."[59]

Brill contends that he does not assist the tabloids by selling network coverage to them, although trial footage is available to them from other sources. "They're really pissed at us because we will sell a clip of [serial killer Jeffrey] Dahmer to NBC and we won't to '[A] Current Affair.' And why? Because I think these guys are sleazy, we don't want to sell it to them."[60]

But for all his uncharitable public comments, Brill maintains that even the tabloids' graphic use of courtroom visuals provides a truer understanding of the courts. He maintains that virtually any visual coverage of the courts is a far better representation than traditional second-hand news accounts. "Local news shows that now have blow-dried anchors describing testimony about a mutilation or child beating may instead show witnesses in court describing it. Those sound bites will be no worse than the paraphrases, the trashy reenactments. . . . And they may be better, because any court proceeding puts these gruesome events in a more serious, solemn light."[61]

He also refuses to denigrate an audience that may turn to Court TV merely to watch "real-life soap opera." He insists that virtually all viewers cannot help but walk away from watching televised proceedings with a better sense of the judicial system and their own civic duty. Citing the William Kennedy Smith case, he rhetorically asks: "Can covering a famous family's rape trial, and feasting on testimony about parties and panties and bars and bras, be anything other than a good, long profitable leer?"[62] But such "voyeurs" who tuned in to the Smith trial for its sensationalism, contends Brill, are now "buffs" of the Palm Beach criminal justice system—and also better citizens. As a result, he speculates that local residents may take a harder look at the reelection bid of David Bludworth, the Florida state attorney and Moira Lasch's boss, after the prosecution's "disorganized, often self-destructing presentation."[63] (Bludworth sharply criticized the Courtroom Television Network after the trial, accusing the network of using "Monday morning quarterbacks" and "so-called trial experts" to distort the prosecution's case to the viewing audience.)[64]

Brill also contends that even "lurid gossip reportage" serves a cathartic civic function by opening social issues, once considered an embarrassment, to a public forum. By showcasing the problems of one of the nation's elite families, his network can "give comfort and even guidance" to viewers with the same problems "who can't or won't talk about them."[65]

THE *MOCKINGBIRD* LESSON

Brill's philosophy has not convinced others who view Court TV itself as an outgrowth of a dangerous and unchecked camera experiment that has spread most precipitously across the nation during the last 15 years. Indeed, the network's scope has been far-reaching. By its second anniversary, Court TV had aired more than 240 trials and other judicial hearings from 32 states.[66] While Court TV may serve a nebulous and ephemeral "public interest" by telecasting trial proceedings, critics charge that it may prove hazardous to the legal process and the rights of trial participants.

Marty Rosenbaum of the New York State Defenders Association fought against New York legislation that would permit camera access. He argues that Court TV, using cameras angles, and photographic and editing techniques, distorts the courtroom process, rather than enhances it. The view from the television screen "is not what jurors see."[67] Most important, the running commentary by Court TV's on-air personalities may precariously prejudge a trial's outcome, leading viewers to see the trial as a competition analogous to a sporting event. Ironically, Rosenbaum notes, "jurors are prohibited from talking among themselves [to avoid prejudicing the case], yet on the other hand these commentators declare that 'this one is ahead' and 'that one is behind,' 'he needs a strong summation to win.' We are told not to make a decision here, yet we are promoting a program in which a decision has been made from the mouths of so-called experts."[68]

Other critics, like George Gerbner of the Annenberg School of Communications, also warn of the danger of converting a legal forum into a political one. "When there's a judge who has to be elected or a prosecutor with political ambitions doing and saying things that millions are watching, these actions may become more important than the defendant who is being charged with something, making it very difficult to decide on the merits of the case."[69]

Just what influence Court TV may have on the nation's justice system may be difficult to presently gauge, even as the network stretches its reach. But one point is evident: Court TV is not merely an objective observer, but a self-proclaimed authority that selects, disseminates, and critiques. Its potential influence is far-ranging, turning local legal trials and their attendant issues into an electronic national courtroom, subject to the scrutiny of a nation of viewers and media commentators. Indeed, the legal concept of *jurisdiction*, giving courts the authority to hear and decide a case, has traditionally been linked to geographic location. Court TV overwhelms "the rules of place," catapulting a trial past the very jurisdictional boundaries of the courtroom itself.[70]

Brill's brand of "media imperialism" is not confined to the United States. In 1992, England's Channel 4 purchased Court TV programming for a weekly series. The network also signed an agreement with Ostankino, the Russian State Broadcasting Company, to cover selected criminal trials in Russia and throughout the Commonwealth of Independent States.[71] In March 1993, Court TV's international reach was further expanded with live coverage from the Hague, in the Netherlands, of a hearing before the International Court of Justice. The case was brought against Britain and the United States by Libya, and was related to the 1988 bombing of Pan Am Flight 103 over Lockerbie, Scotland, an event which took the lives of 270 people. Libya asked the court to block the attempt by the two Western powers to force the Libyan government into surrendering two nationals who were charged with planting the bomb on board the aircraft. (The court upheld the rights of the United States and Britain.) In another international trial in May, Court TV aired taped coverage from the trial of two Serbian nationalist fighters facing charges of genocide and war crimes against civilians. Brill contends that his network manifests an increasing global awareness and that the legal landscape is dramatically changing as a result of sophisticated technologies that can take vast audiences inside a courtroom in South Africa or Russia as well as Los Angeles and New York.

Brill likens his electronic courtroom to the small-town courthouse depicted in Harper Lee's novel, *To Kill a Mockingbird*.[72] In Lee's fictional southern town, citizens pack the upper and lower tiers of the courtroom gallery to witness the processes of justice at work, a civic obligation in keeping with an American democratic ethos. With the emergence of Court TV, Brill states that the same opportunity now exists on a grander scale, as television connects to what he calls a "national community" no longer physically or psychologically restricted by geographic markings.

But in his visionary outlook, Brill unwittingly ignores another possibility embedded within the *Mockingbird* metaphor—and it is a fearful one that camera critics warn against. The enormous public pressures and prejudices brought to bear on the fictional case—involving a black man placed on trial, falsely accused of raping a white woman—inevitably resulted in the defendant's conviction and his tragic death. Rather than being an example of the quintessential "open courtroom," the fictional trial may be better understood as an example of law being subverted to the dark demands of a public driven by prejudice and hatred. What *that* lesson may portend for Brill's electronic courtroom—and the exponential rise of an active and vociferous public spectator that it seeks and abets—is a disturbing one seriously worth considering.

The Forty-Fifth State

THE 1987 EXPERIMENT

New York is one of the latest states to join the national movement allowing cameras into the courtroom.[1] But dating from 1987, it has assumed the role of a wary prizefighter bobbing and weaving against an elusive, but powerful, opponent. It is one of the few to continue to seriously question an ongoing television "experiment," refusing to follow the lead of other states that have given camera legislation permanent status. (Of the 47 states allowing televised trial proceedings, only 10 have experimental rules similar to those in New York.) The state legislature has been less than enthusiastic about the permanent installation of courtroom television; instead, it has created a series of "sunset" laws, giving the courts and the medium a restricted time period in which to test their compatibility. New York's move to open its courts to audiovisual coverage leaves only Indiana, Mississippi, and South Dakota as the remaining holdouts.[2]

The New York debate is noteworthy in that it defines the contentious arguments that now only periodically flare across the nation. The ambivalence toward the courtroom was reflected in several emotional and argumentative sessions of the state legislature. Some lawmakers noted that the vast majority of states had cited few problems with the medium as a courtroom observer and pointed to the experience in Colorado where televised trials had been allowed since 1956 without complaint. Furthermore, defendants who had sought to have their convictions overturned because in-court cameras were present found no success upon appellate review.

Proponents asserted that the technology had now progressed to the point where cameras could maintain a quiet profile during a trial, not unlike their presence in many commercial establishments and political forums. Television cameras, in fact, were familiar to the American public, who routinely encounter them in department stores, banks, and office buildings. Cameras have also been trained on legislatures, school boards, county commissions, the Congress, and other public institutions. For some lawmakers, the electronic media will be no more obtrusive, and perhaps less so, than the rows of print journalists and court artists who attend highly publicized trials.

On the other side of the aisle, legislators recited a litany of potential dangers and abuses should television have access to the court. Assemblyman Anthony Genovesi charged that the medium might trivialize the judicial process, rather than illuminate it, by turning trials into a televised sports event with "play-by-play" coverage, instant replay, and a color commentator. Furthermore, legal protections—in particular, witness sequestration rules that forbid witnesses to listen to prior testimony—could be jeopardized. With the availability of courtroom visuals, witnesses could shape and distort their own performance as a reaction to previously televised testimony. "Once the first witness has testified, every witness will be tainted," Genovesi said, "unless you lock up every witness in the beginning of the trial and then keep them locked up from a television."[3] In an even more serious circumstance, certain witnesses may simply refuse to testify at all for fear that the televised exposure might endanger them outside the parameters of the courtroom.

Critics also charged that the medium's presence in the court could possibly corrupt the system in other ways. Assemblyman Robert King speculated that judges might schedule high-interest-level trials for maximum television exposure prior to an election. Defendants who are acquitted could also be unfairly stigmatized as a result of their televised trial, as could victims who are identified during court proceedings.[4]

In spite of the political rift, on January 7, 1987, legislators ironed out a compromise agreement—an 18-month television experiment to begin December 1. Assembly Bill A77-B marked a critical new relationship between the medium and the courts in New York, but still failed to satisfy critics who remained suspicious and even disdainful of this impending media invasion of the judicial system.

In most respects, the bill's provisions were not unlike those of other state laws. The legislation gave the presiding judge broad discretionary power over court cameras and also shielded certain witnesses and jurors from television broadcast. Before being permitted to cover a trial, television news organizations were compelled to file a request with the presiding judge, asking permission to cover court proceedings. That permission was left to the sole discretion of the trial judge, who before ruling, would take into account several factors including the type of case involved and whether the use of cameras would impair the quality of justice, harm any participant in the case, or interfere with law enforcement activity. Defendants, attorneys, witnesses, and jurors were not required to give their consent, and the presiding judge could permit audiovisual coverage over the objections of court participants. The law also restricted the number of cameras and microphones and forbade technical lighting or nonelectronic equipment that emits noise. The placement of audiovisual equipment would be designated by the trial judge.[5]

Certain segments of the trial were also off-limits to audiovisual coverage: covered by this provision were conferences between attorneys and their clients and between attorneys and the presiding judge, as well as any judicial proceeding that was normally closed to the public. In-court cameras were also not allowed to videotape jury selection, jurors, undercover police officers, and victims of sexual crimes. Finally, a trial judge could limit coverage of lewd or scandalous matters or any coverage that would interfere with the fair administration of justice.[6]

Supporters of the 1987 bill received an early setback as judges in two celebrated trials refused to allow television access to court proceedings. In the Howard Beach trial, a highly publicized case that centered on a racially motivated attack on three black men, presiding Justice Thomas A. Demakos ruled that cameras would exacerbate an already emotionally charged atmosphere in the courtroom and that the case was "too highly sensitive to be the subject of the media's experimental coverage."[7] Demakos's ruling was quickly criticized by Assemblyman Saul Weprin, who authored the original camera legislation. "If the judge refused to allow cameras in the middle of a trial there may be something to what he says. But if he's not allowing it because it's 'sensitive,' I think he's wrong. I think there would be less sensationalism if you allow cameras in the courtroom."[8]

Justice Demakos's decision to bar cameras were first overruled by an administrative judge who stated that it was "inappropriate to suggest that the trial is open when only a portion of the media is permitted access."[9] But the New York Appellate Division reversed that decision and ruled that television and still cameras would not be allowed, even to cover closing arguments. The higher court found that the trial judge did not abuse his discretion in banning cameras from the Howard Beach trial, but that the administrative judge had erred in "substituting his discretion for that of the trial judge."[10]

In another case, the Robert Chambers trial, in which the defendant was accused of killing a young East Side woman, Judge Howard Bell ruled that cameras would be banned because of the sexual nature of the crime. In response to media appeals to allow courtroom camera coverage, the high court again upheld the ruling, stating that the trial judge "is expressly accorded broad authority . . . to deny, in his sound discretion, audiovisual coverage in the criminal trial over which he presides."[11]

Despite this early wariness toward courtroom cameras, judicial apprehension appeared to wane. Hundreds of applications requesting audiovisual access to trials were submitted to the courts, and most were approved. By May 30, 1989, eighteen months after the experiment began, some 957 applications had been granted; 84 were denied.[12]

Some critics, however, did not perceive this trend as benefiting the courts: Indeed, they continued to criticize judges who readily accepted television into their courts in the belief that such technology could be controlled without harming the "sovereignty" of the judiciary. A month before the New York law was to expire, Richard Heffner, the chairman of a state-appointed committee mandated to evaluate the camera legislation, publicly condemned courtroom television as a threat to the judicial process and furthermore denounced judges who were deluded by a technology they hardly understood.

I believe that any judge who innocently assumes that the judiciary's traditional sovereignty over the courtroom will be maintained inviolate even as shared—presumably on his or her own terms—with the television camera, fails to appreciate media power, and will come to rue such naivete. . . . Media are the handmaidens of unlimited majoritarianism . . . and the judiciary will likely resist them no more effectively than have other American institutions. To be sure, political realities and media pressures may dictate that "cameras in the court" is an idea whose time has come. But it is a bad idea, not a good one.[13]

1989

Heffner's dire prognostication was quickly realized. On May 31, 1989, just hours before the original experiment was to expire, Governor Mario Cuomo signed into law a two-year extension. A report prepared by the Office of Court Administration (OCA), the state agency that supervised the camera experiment, was a decisive component—and a highly faulty one—in the final decision to renew camera legislation.

OCA analyzed more than 1,100 written evaluations submitted by judges, lawyers, witnesses, and media personnel who participated in televised proceedings. The survey revealed that most judges and lawyers who responded were "favorable or neutral" toward camera coverage. Matthew Crosson, the chief administrator of the courts in New York State, concluded in his public report that "the information gathered during this experiment . . . demonstrates that audiovisual coverage does not adversely affect judicial proceedings."[14] But Crosson soon discovered that his findings, far from resolving old questions about in-court cameras, had created new ones. His statistical survey soon came under fire and was widely criticized as a shoddy and ineffective measuring tool. There was more than a measure of truth to such critiques: The survey results were based on a heavily biased sample that included responses from less than

1 percent of all witnesses involved in televised trials. Jurors and defendants were excluded from the study altogether.[15]

The report was coupled with public hearings at which interest groups argued their positions in favor of or opposed to the continued use of courtroom cameras. Ultimately, the legislature approved an extension of the program, but not before placing further restrictions on camera access to court proceedings. Media organizations denounced the new bill as being overly restrictive and criticized state legislators for "rolling back progress."[16]

Specifically, the bill included provisions that would require the media to apply for access to court proceedings at least seven days in advance and would prohibit the filming or broadcasting of arraignments and suppression hearings unless trial lawyers had consented. The bill also prohibited media requests for audiovisual coverage once a jury has been empaneled, except for verdicts and sentencing, without the consent of the trial lawyers. It would also require that prosecutors and defense lawyers advise all witnesses of their right to request that their testimony not be filmed or broadcast (although the actual authority to prohibit television coverage still rested with the presiding judge). Furthermore, the bill authorized news media to submit videotape copies and transcripts of news reports "to evaluate [their] impact and effect" on court proceedings. (News media bridled against this last provision, charging the state with overstepping its authority and interfering with press rights. Many refused to cooperate with state officials, failing to submit tapes of their news reports.)

The bill still did not satisfy camera critics. Opponents continued to charge that videotape coverage of proceedings subverted the due process rights of defendants, providing a sufficient reason to disband the state's camera experiment. The New York State Defenders Association, which serves 5,000 state defense lawyers, contended that television news reports prejudiced both jurors and the public against defendants. In his testimony before the state legislature, Marty Rosenbaum, the association's director of judicial services, criticized videotape accounts of arraignments where defendants were handcuffed and shackled as an image "that presents a picture of guilt to the public which severely undermines the constitutional 'presumption of innocence.' "[17] In a stinging rebuttal to camera proponents, the defense association's report cited cases in which defendants appeared at televised proceedings with shopping bags over their heads in order "to avoid prejudice from potential witnesses seeing them on television before an identification lineup was conducted."[18] In a Syracuse, New York, case, a terminally ill AIDS patient, charged with violating probation, was sentenced wearing a ski mask in an effort to shield her school-age children from the embarrassment of having her illness revealed on television.[19]

In testimony before the legislature two years later, Jonathan E. Gradess, the association's executive director, would attribute the death of a defendant to the presence of the courtroom camera. As Gradess recounted, Jamie Brame, a suspect in a series of Buffalo area rapes and drug offenses, was brought into court with a paper bag over his head because an identification lineup had not yet been held in the rape investigation. Following the proceeding he was reported to be extremely agitated about being part of a televised proceeding, and six days later he committed suicide by hanging himself with a tee-shirt. In condemning the New York camera experiment, Gradess told lawmakers: "The legislature must know that this experiment has a human face."[20]

1991

Concerns for the rights of defendants did not prevent lawmakers from approving prior legislation, nor would it stand in the way of a new camera bill. Of more importance to state legislators in 1991 was the impact of television on yet another member of the court—the trial witness.

The primary roadblock in renewing the camera experiment was the sensitive issue of witness protection. The Republican-controlled senate strongly favored a provision that would give most witnesses the freedom to refuse televised coverage of their testimony. The Democrat-controlled assembly wanted to continue the law under the old rules that left such decisions in the hands of the presiding judge. Saul Weprin, the principal sponsor of the original legislation in the assembly, acknowledged that should the senate compromise be enacted, "about 90 percent of [witnesses] would say no to cameras if they knew they could."[21]

After nearly four years of state-approved televised trial proceedings, some key members of the legislature and other vested interest groups were not convinced that the experiment had lived up to its promise and believed it was far from a "success"—a judgment repeatedly rendered in newspaper editorials and other media forums. The camera debate had run into a political stone wall, and, as lawmakers wrangled over a long-overdue state budget, the compromise over a newly proposed camera law was left to quietly fade from legal existence. On June 1, 1991, the New York television experiment expired.[22]

It was a political death that stunned media and legal experts who had believed that court television was a fate already sealed in New York. The state's move, in fact, was precedent, marking the first time television ever was removed from a courtroom by legislative action (or inaction) once it had been entrenched.[23]

However, the announcement of television's death in New York courtrooms proved to be premature. In June 1992, the state senate and assembly finally reached a compromise decision: The new bill would extend the experiment, but would severely modify videotape coverage of witness testimony. The provision would specifically give witnesses (excluding the defendant, expert witnesses, and police officers) the right to have their image blotted out with an electronically generated "mosaic" or "blue dot" by broadcasters during their testimony.

Judges would still decide whether to grant camera access to the courts, but would be required to honor requests by individual witnesses to obscure their faces.

Ironically, the idea of the electronic dot compromise had been inspired by the William Kennedy Smith trial. The nationally televised rape trial played a key role in the New York debate, producing an angry backlash against new camera legislation even among former supporters. Senate Codes Chairman Dale Volker, who voted for the 1989 bill, planned to vote against the new one because of the Smith trial "debacle." Having watched the William Kennedy Smith trial," he said, "I think a lot of us feel that every person in that trial was affected by the cameras."[24]

In conjunction with the Smith case, two recent state reports pointed a condemning finger at courtroom cameras and the vast media exposure attached to a televised trial. Northeastern University examined the perceptions and attitudes in March 1991 among New Yorkers toward the criminal justice system. Virtually one-half of the 487 respondents stated that they would be less willing to testify in the presence of television. This figure rose when the survey was conducted among people in high-crime urban areas where the risk of victimization is higher.[25] A second report in April 1992 by the National Victim Center found that 86 percent of American women and 92 percent of rape victims were less likely to report rape to law enforcement authorities if they thought their identities would become known to the news media. Furthermore, the majority of rape crisis counselors reportedly believed that the televised William Kennedy Smith trial deterred victims from reporting the rape to police.[26]

Following the legislative compromise, news organizations criticized the legislation as sharply curtailing their ability to cover a trial, while other groups representing criminal defense lawyers and crime victims endorsed the restrictions. For his part, Governor Mario Cuomo criticized the bill's provisions limiting the ability to videotape witnesses as being "unduly restrictive" and "unnecessary."[27] Nevertheless, on June 23, 1992, he signed into the law Assembly Bill 3823-D. One conclusive point was derived from the state's action: New York's love-hate relationship with cameras in the court would continue until January 31, 1995, the bill's expiration date.

TELEVISION AS EDUCATION

Paradoxically, the lawmakers' primary rationale in drafting the original legislation in 1987 had little to do with "free press–fair trial" rights. Rather, camera advocates posited the hypothesis that visuals emanating from the courtroom could be educational, promote greater understanding of the judiciary, and elevate public confidence in the justice system. The irony was unmistakable: New York had turned to television to provide the civic lessons that the medium had been accused of so sorely undermining in the past.

In spite of this contention, no empirical evidence existed to demonstrate that the in-court camera was a technological teacher of sorts. To the contrary, research concluded that public knowledge, or lack of it, about the judicial process was the same whether court cameras were present or not. A New York University study measured the degree to which state citizens understood even the most rudimentary aspects of the judicial system: The research was conducted just before the state experiment went into effect and then a year later. It concluded that televised coverage of trials had no effect whatsoever on the level of public knowledge of the judiciary.[28]

In retrospect, what the New York legislature had in mind may have had nothing to do with public education, but rather with public relations. During the 1980s, prominent jurists from across the country had espoused a movement to promote a more appealing image of the judiciary. Their belief was that the courts had lost touch with the public and as a result were losing their viability. For some, the answer to the problem was television. Harvard law professors Charles Nesson and Andrew Koblenz, for instance, contended that "judges have become much more aware of their own image problem" and that televising trials would help correct popular misconceptions about their work in the courts.[29] In point of fact, it was this attempt to foster "the appearance of justice" among the populace that moved many states to pass camera legislation.

Jack Weinstein, a former U.S. District Court judge, and Diane Zimmerman, a New York University law professor, stated, "To most people, modern court procedures are more a mysterious rite than an exercise in public governance," in large part due to "an overdeveloped instinct on the part of judges for self-aggrandizement and self-protection against criticism." As the workings of the court become more obscure, public understanding of the problems within the judicial system diminishes. Opening the courts to the public via television would help remove the "mystery" of the judicial process surrounding what they call "the cult of the robe."[30]

But not all lawmakers shared Weinstein's and Zimmerman's beliefs. Televised trial coverage, critics charged, has done little to promote the courts or increase the public's general knowledge about the workings of the judicial system. Assemblyman Anthony Genovesi told the state legislature: "I have never heard anyone give a legitimate reason why we are doing this. It's poppycock to say it is educational."[31]

Richard Heffner, chairman of the state-appointed Advisory Committee on Cameras in the Courts, joined in the criticism, arguing that television had not "enhanced the public understanding of the judicial system," as had been the legislative rationale in passing the original bill. Although his advisory committee had endorsed courtroom cameras in 1987, Heffner was one of a few members to publicly contest their continued use, contending that "public understanding is not achieved simply by claiming it. Nor is it education—or information, for that matter—to be equated simply with exposure." With few exceptions, Heffner maintained, the camera experiment "has really meant more of the same . . . plus visuals. Yes, television has been in the courtroom, but for the most part the courtroom has not been on television."[32]

Paul Smirnoff, the executive producer of Fox News and a longtime camera advocate, took umbrage at Heffner's remarks. Unwittingly, however, he may have driven home Heffner's point more forcefully, noting that the role of the camera was neither altruistic nor necessarily mindful of an imposed civic duty articulated by lawmakers. "We're journalists and we're not necessarily historians or educators," he said, candidly, "We're in the commercial news business here."[33]

Ellen Fleysher, assistant news director for WNBC, took a slightly more conciliatory tone, maintaining that Heffner's criticism was shortsighted and did not take into account the long-term exposure television brings to a vast audience.

I could take a very hard line and I can say to you, "Hey, that's not my job to educate you." But on the other hand, I'd prefer to ask the question, what is education? If you give a child one book, does that mean that child is educated? No! Education comes from a cumulative process over months and years. So it is with this. With one arraignment, are you going to learn the process A to Z? But if you saw Howard Beach, if you saw Steinberg [and other television broadcasts] . . . cumulatively, would you have a better understanding about how the judicial system works? The answer is a resounding "yes," and that can't be debated any way, shape or form.[34]

Just what that "public understanding" represents, however, is a point at odds. In the Television Trial, legal "education" is strictly guided by the rules of the medium and not of law. The criteria for selecting a trial to be televised have less to do with civic mindedness or even journalistic definitions of "newsworthiness" than with ratings—the need to attract a huge public following that is then translated into advertising dollars. Trial footage is turned into selected visuals designed for maximum public consumption: The result can often be a skewed understanding of the judicial system rather than an enlightening one.

In essence, television's educational reality is linked to entertainment values, but, nevertheless, it creates misguided perceptions about actual social life. The vast majority of televised cases involve violence, typically murder, thus creating a social perception that dramatic capital-offense trials predominate the system. Trial participants are also telegenically typecast, like actors, to fit the expectations of the media. John Gotti, a leading organized crime figure, fits neatly into the television world as the "Teflon Don," as does Carolyn Warmus, the "Fatal Attraction" murderess convicted for killing her lover's wife, in Westchester County, New York. Typical cases or defendants that lack the proper credentials of a media figure are seldom seen. Out-of-court plea bargains, the most prominent method for disposing of cases, are never covered by television.[35]

The so-called educational role of courtroom television does not necessarily end once a verdict has been rendered. The Television Trial retains a peculiar afterlife—often short, but traumatic—as part of network prime-time programming. In essence, the Television Trial is merely a preview, and a paradoxical one at that, with the entertainment industry vying for the rights to tell the "real" story, typically through feature-length docudramas.

When John Esposito of Bay Shore, Long Island, was arrested in January 1993 for kidnapping 10-year-old Katie Beers and then entombing her in an underground chamber for 16 days, he apparently never realized that his story would become the next "hot property." His lawyer, Andrew Siden, was not the only interested party at his side during a televised arraignment; so, too, was a representative from Tri-Star Pictures, a Hollywood production company. Siden would wear two hats in the case: one as defense counsel responsible for taking care of his client's interests inside the courtroom and the other as a film agent representing Esposito in negotiations with television and film producers seeking to buy the rights to his story.[36]

No longer constrained by legal restrictions, networks seek to fill a vacuum of public interest left in the aftermath of a trial. Dramatic devices once used by the medium to frame the original trial are now employed with even greater élan in the movie-of-the-week, with thematic plot lines dealing with sex, violence, and mayhem being the typical lessons of the day. The conversion of the real into the surreal may further confuse a public largely knowledgeable about courts and law through the shared information and imagery brought to them by television.[37]

Take, for example, the Nassau County, New York, case of Amy Fisher, a 17-year-old girl who shot and severely disabled the wife of Joey Buttafuoco, the man she said was her lover. Fisher had been the subject of extensive local and national media attention, which featured televised coverage of her pretrial hearings and sentencing. A month after being sentenced to 5 to 15 years in a plea bargain agreement, Fisher became the subject of *three* made-for-TV movies, all premiering in the course of a single week—a curious record in the annals of television docudramas.[38] Viewers, in fact, were left to choose one evening between versions on ABC and CBS, presented in head-to-head competition.

The networks' audience also faced another dilemma of sorts, forced to choose between two distinct story lines. In NBC's "Amy Fisher: My Story," the case was told from the teenager's viewpoint, while CBS's "Casualties of Love," presented her alleged lover's side of the story. Both parties were rewarded with substantial payments for the rights to their respective stories, which, under the heavy hand of the networks, reveled in the lurid and voyeuristic. If television "fact-based" movies have been criticized for their tabloid sensationalism in the past, far less dismissible was the networks' apparent cynicism in presenting material that was not only self-serving to its commercial investment (namely,

Fisher or Buttafuoco), but also, quite likely, founded without a basis in truth. "Both versions can't be right," wrote *Times* critic John J. O'Connor, "yet two major networks evidently proceeded with the projects as if the truth, quite possibly not on their side, was beside the point."[39] (In a third version, the Fisher story was told predominantly from the perspective of Amy Pagnozzi, a journalist who covered the case for the *New York Post* and was then hired as a consultant for the movie, raising another set of ethical questions pertaining to the professional responsibilities of the working journalist.)

Such moral and ethical ambiguities apparently did not faze network executives far more interested in the finite numbers attached to television ratings. They were not disappointed, as the Fisher trilogy amassed huge ratings. Nearly 50 million households tuned in to one or more of the movies.[40]

The permutations of the Television Trial are incalculable, ranging from feature-length docudramas to more inventive genres, such as "reenactments" and "mock trials," programs that jettison the perceptions of crime and punishment into an electronic netherworld ruled by props and sets that serve as vague simulations of the courtroom experience. Cases are scripted for their most sensational appeal, with television's facile righteousness overwhelming points of law. This televised theater is assisted by actors playing the roles of judge, juror, defendant, and the like; some are even real-life trial participants seeking to profit from their public positions.

For instance, Geraldo Rivera, a syndicated talk show host, exploited the Fisher case—branded by the media as the case of the "Long Island Lolita"—by showcasing a grand jury "trial" of Joey Buttafuoco, a man who at the time of the program had not been charged or indicted for any crime. Rivera was determined to enact his version of television justice because, as his senior producer Jose Pretlow explained, "there are a number of people who really felt that Amy Fisher should not be the only one in jail."[41]

Even media reviewers were outraged at the show, accusing Rivera of gross exploitation, turning real-life tragedy into sleaze. "Geraldo's kangaroo court was chilling," stated Steve Bornfeld, the media critic for the Albany *Times Union*. "Buttafuoco, no matter how odious he may strike us, was never charged with a crime. Not with statutory rape of sick little Amy. Not as an accomplice in the shooting. Not even for pimping, if Amy's tale of turning her toward prostitution is to be believed. That leaves Geraldo, self-appointed guardian of truth, justice and ratings, to second-guess the courts. What else is television if not the highest appeals court in the land, with the Swami of Sensationalism presiding?"[42]

Not to be outdone, "A Current Affair" put Fisher "on trial" for the shooting of Mary Jo Buttafuoco in a series entitled, "The Trial That Had to Happen: The People versus Amy Fisher." As an opener to the show, Steve Dunleavy, the program narrator, earnestly pronounced that "the biggest trial in New York criminal history never happened, until now. When Ms. Fisher copped a plea

and went to jail she robbed the public of a trial, leaving behind many un-
answered questions. Tonight we will try to address them and complete the
unwritten chapter."[43]

Ultimately, the lessons proffered by the entertainment industry paint a
topsy-turvy picture of the criminal justice system. For the "A Current Affair"
series, Joey Buttafuoco's own attorney, Marvyn Kornberg, served as a program
"consultant" and also as an on-air "prosecutor," seizing on the criminal culpability of Amy Fisher, who was played by a look-alike actress performing her
part with the requisite anguish and tears. Kornberg's participation in the show
raises serious ethical and professional concerns. While cultivating his own
media persona, the lawyer's participation in a nationally-televised program may
have inadvertently harmed Buttafuoco by calling more public attention to his
client's role and responsibility in the case. Shortly after the airing of the
program, in fact, Buttafuoco was charged with the statutory rape of Fisher by the
county prosecutor's office.

The underlying "lesson" ultimately delivered by the Television Trial is that
the judicial system itself does not work and, even more to the point, that it is
hostile to a genuine model of justice. In an age where media cynicism abounds
in areas such as politics and commerce, the televised courtroom has found its
place. It is here that James Earl Ray, the convicted assassin of Dr. Martin Luther
King, Jr. had the opportunity to "defend" himself and proclaim his innocence
in a "court of law" presided over by "distinguished" members of the legal
community. HBO cable television network, in partnership with Great Britain's
Thames Television, aired "Guilt or Innocence: The Trial of James Earl Ray,"
on April 4, 1993, twenty-five years to the day after Ray was convicted of
shooting the civil rights leader as he stood on the balcony of the Lorraine Motel
in Memphis, Tennessee.

To simulate an actual trial, HBO-Thames journeyed to the Shelby County
Courthouse in Memphis, and induced real-life witnesses to the King killing to
testify before "presiding Judge" Marvin E. Frankel, a former New York district
court judge. Hickman Ewing, once a U.S. attorney in Memphis, and William
Pepper, Ray's longtime legal counsel, played their respective roles as prosecutor
and defense counsel.

During his actual trial Ray entered a guilty plea and was sentenced to 99
years in prison. Beamed into the courtroom by satellite hook-up from his
residence 200 miles away at the Riverbend Maximum Security Institution,
Ray now maintained that he was "maneuvered" by his own attorney, the late
Percy Foreman, into entering a guilty plea in order to avoid being sentenced
to die in the electric chair. Three days after the plea, he fired his lawyer and
asked for a trial; his request was denied. If truth be known, insists Ray, "I was
not a hired killer. I was in the rooming house in Memphis 20 minutes before
he was shot—but I never pulled the trigger. I never fired a shot. I never murdered

King." The culprit, Ray speculates, was the FBI itself, which "orchestrated it all."[44]

A panel of 12 "jurors," selected from neighboring cities, returned a "not guilty" verdict after the ten day trial (which was edited down to three hours for broadcast over HBO). With the television verdict handed down, Ray said he was "pleased that finally an independent jury had examined the state's case and found me not guilty." He urged that all government records connected to the case be declassified and that he eventually be set free from prison.[45]

Television's "curriculum" poses a serious dilemma for the judicial system— and it is one that runs counter to the ideology of the courts. Rather than enhance public knowledge of the judicial system, televised trials only add "audiovisual spectacle" and "dramatic diversions" that "further extend the viewers' already distorted view of the courts," according to media scholar George Gerbner. More problematic is that the medium " 'entertains' the basic values and norms of the community and cultivates conformity to those norms." Gerbner contends: "Popular entertainment and news represent the conventional cultural pressures of the social order. The judicial process, however, represents an effort to adjudicate individual cases according to law. That distinction is crucial."[46]

This is not the first time that such public arenas have served the purpose of affirming the legitimacy of contemporary values. The Roman Empire enjoyed highly publicized confessions, public tribunals, and executions that served such ends. The most popular show in Europe during the Middle Ages was the public execution. Death was the penalty for a great many crimes, and communities gathered to witness criminals led to their deaths by beheading, hanging, and burning; others were drawn and quartered and broken on a wheel. Minor offenders were also subjected to public punishment by some form of corporal punishment, such as mutilation, flogging, or branding. It is worth noting that the very imprisonment of a citizen—a punishment disconnected from public attention and participation—was not instituted in Europe until the early seventeenth century. The idea of prison was twofold: one purpose was to quarantine convicts from the general population (to punish, but also to promote public safety); the second was to safeguard the health and welfare of the prisoner himself from the rule of the mob.

Television has the capacity to make new what was once the order of the day. The potential exists that the Television Trial could one day be accompanied by the Television Execution, the electronic equivalent of an event that was open to public scrutiny in the United States less than 60 years ago. So popular were these events that more than 20,000 people crowded around a gallows in Owensboro, Kentucky, in 1936 to watch a condemned man dangle from a hangman's noose.[47]

In point of fact, the arguments used to promote courtroom cameras (educational value, the "public interest," and so on) were reconstituted in 1991 by a local San Francisco television station that had petitioned the state to televise an impending execution.[48] A nationwide debate ensued after KQED-TV was denied permission by the prison warden to film the state execution of condemned murderer Robert Alton Harris at San Quentin State Prison. The station's attorney argued before a federal court that the television camera would serve the public interest by providing a neutral and far more accurate account of the state's ultimate criminal penalty. But U.S. District Court Judge Robert H. Schnacke upheld the warden's decision, holding that prison authorities could bar cameras from the gas chamber, citing as a rationale prison security. Had the station's petition proven successful, Americans for the first time could have witnessed a state-sponsored execution in their living rooms. Such telecasts would bring full circle a medium that offers "real-life" police arrests, trials, and sentencing as part of its daily programming.

FREE PRESS VERSUS FAIR TRIAL

The language in the original New York bill heralding the in-court camera as a judicial tool for civic education was dropped in subsequent legislation. If television had succeeded in exploiting trial coverage as part of its entertainment-news programming, it had failed to live up to the initial expectation casting the medium as a technological public instructor. Far more complicated to resolve were constitutional issues dealing with the rights of the press and the rights of a defendant to a fair trial. The conflicting interplay between these components of American law moved Supreme Court Justice Hugo Black to acknowledge in a 1941 opinion that "free spech and fair trials are two of the most cherished policies of our civilization, and it would be a trying task to choose between them."[49] Thirty-one years later, Black would continue to characterize the continuing debate as "a civil libertarian's nightmare."[50] The New York camera-in-the-court experiment served only to fuel an already simmering national argument.

The controversy over free press–fair trial rights has squarely placed jurists, lawmakers, journalists, and academicians into ideological camps. Even the very concept of "the press" has been a point of contention. As opposed to the print press, which has historically been protected by constitutional law, the electronic media have not been afforded the same legal rights associated with their typographic colleague. Also, unlike newspapers and other print media, television is a licensed industry, subject to the rules of the Federal Communications Commission, a federal agency mandated to regulate what are "the public airwaves." These distinctions are critical in that they define the legal limits of the medium as an electronic press. The television camera therefore, argue legal analysts, has no inherent constitutional right to be in a court of law, although it can seek special access through legislative or judicial decree.

Fundamental to the question of whether trials should be televised is yet another constitutional mandate that presents its own conflicts. The concept of "open government" gives citizens free access to governmental institutions; the business conducted by publicly elected or appointed officials is open to public scrutiny. Under this umbrella, television has been permitted to enter into political arenas once considered off-limits, including U.S. Senate and House of Representatives hearings. But the legal profession has been more reluctant to embrace television cameras in courtrooms, concerned that the medium might damage the dignity of the proceedings. This extraconstitutional issue is linked with the profession of jurist and the symbolic character of the justice system, and for more than half a century, it has been one of the most difficult to resolve between opponents in the camera debate.[51]

As a branch of government, the courts are obligated to be open to the public, but even the very meaning of "openness" has been a sticking point among legal scholars as it relates to televised trials. An open trial prevents the subversion of the legal process, but some critics argue that "that objective is served by a full transcript, a public presence, and media representatives in the courtroom."[52] They conclude, therefore, that if opening the courts to camera coverage means undermining the judicial dignity of the court itself, then in-court cameras should be barred. Others state, however, that courts have become overly restricted and largely unintelligible institutions, remote even to a well-educated public. An open, televised trial would foster greater intelligibility and serve to restrain breaches in decorum be they judicial bullying, courtroom histrionics of counsel, or unfair treatment of the defendant and witnesses.[53]

Closely related to the notion of open government is the Sixth Amendment right guaranteeing public trials. The amendment was originally conceived to safeguard the rights of the accused by having the public present during judicial proceedings. Susanna Barber, a media scholar at Emerson College, concurs that while "the public's interest in attending trials is motivated more out of curiosity than any notion of protecting the defendant's right to due process, the presumption is still valid and has been emphasized by several Supreme Court rulings."[54] Other legal experts reason, however, that if the law is designed to protect the accused from potential injustices, it is the defendant himself, and not the press and public, who should determine whether or not television should be permitted to broadcast trial proceedings.

Allied with this concept is a serious problem long associated with the media—prejudicial publicity. It is feared that televised proceedings will give rise to a virulent form of prejudicial opinion that could affect the working nature of the courtroom. Since the turn of the century, unrestrained press reports have been criticized for inciting the public wrath, particularly in celebrated cases, but critics charge that television is even more dangerous, creating an unwanted, yet powerful, "thirteenth juror" who holds enormous sway over a verdict. Moreover, should a trial verdict be overturned on appeal, the publicity attached to a case would make it virtually impossible for a defendant to receive an impartial new trial.

In our national democracy, the media reflect and inspire a public dialogue that can be a decisive factor in the resolution of important issues. But the role of mediated opinion in the American judicial system is far different and has proven to be perilous. Several notable U.S. Supreme Court decisions have lashed out against the injection of prejudicial publicity and its subversive effect on the fair administration of justice. The Dr. Sam Sheppard trial in 1954 is often cited as a watershed case. Sheppard, found guilty in Cuyahoga County Court, in Ohio, of murdering his wife, appealed his conviction on the grounds that pervasive media publicly quashed his right to a fair trial. The U.S. Supreme Court ruled in Sheppard's favor and reversed his conviction on the grounds that the trial judge had failed to control flagrant and inflammatory publicity that was impossible for Sheppard to overcome. (In the court's 16-page decision, 4 pages were replete with headlines and stories meant to foment public passions, charging that the defendant was "getting away with murder." Presiding Judge Blythin was also quoted, remarking that this "was an open and shut case . . . [Sheppard] is as guilty as hell.")[55]

In working practice, most states with camera legislation give trial judges the authority to decide whether or not television access to the courts should be granted. Presiding judges often find that they are arbiters in a free press–fair trial argument between strong media groups and trial participants. As chief administrator of the New York courts, Matthew Crosson officially leaned toward the side of television. He maintained that the presence of the camera protects the accused from "unjust persecution by public officials." But with that said, he emphasized that the public itself is "not only concerned with seeing the accused is fairly treated," but also with "seeing that there is justice for the accuser—the police and prosecutors who must enforce the law, and the victims of crime." It is this balance between the rights of the accused and those of the accuser that will reinforce that "justice has been done" and instill a sense of public trust in the judicial process. "Justice must not only be done," he said, "it must be perceived as being done."[56]

New York State Senator Tarky Lombardi, who voted against the state's original camera legislation, argued that "we go beyond the issue of public trials when we bring electronic media into the courtroom, and we ignore what's best for the litigants."[57] The public can already attend trials along with reporters, and the presence of television violates the privacy rights of defendants and witnesses, making them vulnerable to public humiliation and intimidation. The visual intrusiveness of the medium, with its potential to reveal the physical and emotional makeup of court participants, threatens to destroy their dignity and violate their privacy rights.[58]

Proponents of in-court cameras maintain that court participants waive their right to privacy by becoming public figures accountable to public demands. Court decisions appear to uphold the contention that what happens in a courtroom is public property, making the right of privacy "a weak reed to rely upon to prevent a telecast of a trial." The Supreme Court, in fact, while noting an implicit constitutional guarantee of privacy, has yet to use the privacy laws as the single criterion for excluding the press or television cameras. Typical of such court decisions is *Cox Broadcasting Corporation* v. *Cohn*.[59] In that case, the Supreme Court ruled in favor of a television station that was sued for broadcasting the name of a woman who was raped and murdered. The Court held that the press did not violate privacy rights by reporting information that is part of the public court records.[60]

THE CAMERA EYE: THE PSYCHOLOGICAL PERSPECTIVE

Beyond constitutional concerns lie other serious questions having less to do with interpretive rules of law than with psychology and the often intangible connections that exist between television and the human mind. It is arguably the most contentious element of the camera debate—and also the least understood. The danger is that as courtroom participants lose their anonymity in the face of the camera, they will perceive themselves differently and alter their behavior, knowing that their actions and testimony will extend far beyond the confines of the courtroom itself into the public realm and a broader, historical record.

The psychological relationship between the camera and its subjects has long been the grist for both jurists and philosophers. Central to virtually all discussions about the influence of the in-court camera on judicial proceedings is a theoretical question that ascends beyond the legal debate and into a realm of philosophy: Does behavior change as a result of being observed, and if it does, can such change be measured and assessed?

The German physicist Werner Heisenberg is credited with first examining the effect of observation on the scientific process. In 1927, he formulated the "uncertainty" principle, which stated that there are limits to the accuracy to which pairs of physical quantities can be measured.[61] Essentially, in developing a theory about quantum mechanics, Heisenberg postulated that the process of measurement itself disturbs the system being measured. This principle, in its statement of the limits of observation, has been incorporated into the present scientific view of the nature of physical reality.

Heisenberg's theory has been translated into different fields of study, including the social sciences, philosophy, and psychology. It also holds serious implications for communications scholars examining the relationship between media technologies and culture. It has particular value for those investigating the impact of photography and television on human self-awareness and behavior.

Marshall McLuhan was one of the first media theorists to posit ideas about photography and self-awareness. He noted that the development of photography changed notions of human self-consciousness, which alter not only an individual's outward appearance and reactions, but also the critical attitudes tied to his psychological needs. "It is not too much to say, therefore, that if outer posture is affected by the photograph," he stated, "so it is with our inner postures and the dialogue with ourselves."[62]

Susan Sontag expanded on McLuhan's theme in discussing the camera's role in portraying the world and in creating a new level of human self-consciousness. Photographs instill an "idealized image" predicated on the photographic image. "We learn to see ourselves photographically: to regard oneself as attractive is, precisely, to judge that one looks good in a photograph." The fear, explained Sontag, is that somehow the camera will disapprove, failing to return an image that matches the expectations of its subject.[63]

The subject's self-conscious reaction to the camera comes from an awareness that the photographer is an active agent who evaluates the activity before him. Nineteenth-century attitudes view the photographer as "an acute but non-interfering observer—a scribe, not a poet." However, as Sontag noted, "the supposition that cameras furnish an impersonal, objective image yielded to the fact that photographs are evidence not only of what's there but of what an individual sees, not just a record but an evaluation of the world."[64]

In essence, Sontag and others have concluded, there is not simply a unitary activity called "seeing" as recorded by the camera, but a new way for people to view the activity before them, and that is "photographic seeing." Human self-consciousness thus evolves not merely from being "seen" by the camera lens, but also from being evaluated and judged by the photographer himself. Furthermore, media theorists maintain that the interplay that exists between the photographer and his subject often creates a unique self-consciousness in which the subject vies for "control of his image." According to media scholar Halla Beloff, "We no longer want to submit to the camera. We want to control it. We want to use it to produce new images that are necessary."[65]

Roland Barthes, the social philosopher, also noted from a personal view the heightening of self-consciousness before the camera lens. He articulated the subtle transformation that occurs: "Once I feel myself observed by the lens everything changes; I constitute myself in the process of 'posing,' I instantaneously make another body for myself, I transform myself in advance into an image. This transformation is an active one; I feel that the photograph creates my body and mystifies it according to its caprice."[66]

Self-consciousness becomes more acute when television enters the culture. Even attempts to use this powerful imagistic medium as an unobtrusive tool for news gathering have been affected by the "uncertainty" principle. A case in point was the televising of "An American Family" in 1973: Media experts took note of the difficulties of using television as a neutral observer and reporter of human events. The 12-part PBS documentary recorded seven months of the day-to-day lives of William and Pat Loud and their five children. During the course of the filming, the Louds separated (and later divorced), and members of the family revealed personal secrets about their lives (one member disclosed, for instance, that he was homosexual). Using techniques associated with *cinema verité*, the documentary was both lauded as significant anthropology and condemned as indiscriminate voyeurism that transformed the Loud family into instant celebrities.[67]

Critics wrangled over the Loud series for months after it appeared on television. At the center of the controversy was the question of whether the very act of filming altered what happened among family members. Anthropologist Margaret Mead took great interest in the documentary and concluded that the Louds' behavior was not influenced by the presence of cameras. But her point of view appeared to be in the minority. Even the film's director, Craig Gilbert, conceded that "it is undeniable that the presence of cameras affected the family. Although the production crew went about their business as unobtrusively as possible, they were there."[68]

Observations posited by philosophers and media practitioners about the camera and the human psyche have carried over into the legal arena. Jurists have addressed the "camera effects" issue as part of a longstanding debate, critically delineated in the *Estes* ruling, which articulated the potential dangers of television cameras as they affect a trial participant's state of mind. In the 1965 high court ruling, a decision that for the most part halted new camera legislation for a decade, Justice Clark wrote that the psychological impact of television on trial participants was "simply incalculable."[69]

Nearly three decades later, the *Estes* decision continues to echo the fears of camera opponents. Such apprehensions were crystallized in a sensational case that came to trial in New York in October 1988. The murder trial of Joel Steinberg, a wealthy criminal attorney accused of killing his six-year-old daughter, would horrifically connect New York City, as well as the nation tuned to Cable News Network coverage, to the dark and sordid issues that hung beneath the surface of American life. Steinberg's fate would be sealed by a jury of his peers, but another verdict was also to be rendered. The *New York Times* asked about television's role at the trial: "Does the magnification serve the public interest? Perhaps, but the broadcasting of trials is still not a settled question. It's on trial in New York, an extended, interesting experiment that can help resolve the age-old debate over the effect of cameras in the court."[70]

Photo of the Harry Washburn murder trial from the *Waco-Tribune*, 1955. This was the first live, televised trial. Courtesy Steve Reece.

Still photo taken from Court TV air. Courtesy Courtroom Television Network.

Still photo taken from Court TV air. Courtesy Courtroom Television Network.

Still photo taken from Court TV air. Courtesy Courtroom Television Network.

Jeffrey Dahmer. Still photo taken from Court TV air. Courtesy Courtroom Television Network.

Still photo taken from Court TV air. Courtesy Courtroom Television Network.

Still photo taken from Court TV air. Courtesy Courtroom Television Network.

LIVE

Amy Fisher Sentencing
NY v. AMY FISHER
MINEOLA, NY

COURT

Still photo taken from Court TV air. Courtesy Courtroom Television Network.

Part Two

The Steinberg Trial:
A Case Study

The Beginning

On November 2, 1987, at 6:33 A.M., a call came over 911 from a woman who told the emergency operator, "My daughter seems to have stopped breathing." Within minutes, two police officers from the Sixth Precinct responded, arriving at a five-story brick townhouse at 14 West 10th Street, in Greenwich Village, New York. Once the celebrated home of Mark Twain, the building now housed among its present occupants Joel Barnet Steinberg, a 46-year-old criminal attorney; his live-in companion and a former children's book editor, Hedda Nussbaum; and their two illegally adopted children.

Upon entering the third-floor apartment, the police officers' first sensation was that of the strong smell of urine. The rooms were dark; not a single fixture had a working bulb. A wintry chill ran into the apartment through a missing windowpane. Later, in a detailed report, the police would describe what they had found: chairs broken and overturned, clothes strewn about the floor, moldy food that had yet to be cleared from the kitchen counters. The living room was cluttered with an array of objects: books, electronic equipment, television sets, car radios with wires protruding. In a nearby makeshift playpen stood Steinberg's 16-month-old son, Mitchell. Tethered to a playpen post with a four-foot nylon rope, the infant was soiled with urine and excrement, wearing a diaper that appeared to be several days old. Bloodstains were visible on a nearby wall.

From the rear bedroom Joel Steinberg emerged, carrying the limp and naked body of his six-year-old daughter, Lisa. Thin and frail in appearance, the child lay motionless. Police noted multiple bruises on her face and body. When paramedics arrived at the scene, they attempted to revive the failing youngster, but were unsuccessful. Twenty minutes had passed since Nussbaum's emergency call.

Accompanied by her father, Lisa was taken to a waiting ambulance and rushed to nearby St. Vincent's Hospital where she was listed in "extremely critical condition" with a brain hemorrhage and bruises to her head, body, and spine. According to medical authorities, she no longer had brain function. If she survived her traumatic injuries, she would remain permanently brain damaged. But within three days Lisa would be officially declared dead.

During the ensuing hours, Steinberg and Nussbaum were taken to the Sixth Precinct for questioning. Steinberg continued to insist that Lisa had not been injured, but had been throwing up after eating poisoned vegetables. Nussbaum, battered and dazed, dully reiterated her earlier account—Lisa had had a roller skating accident. After four hours of interrogation, both were arrested and charged with attempted murder, first-degree assault, and endangering the welfare of a child.

While Steinberg was placed in a precinct holding cell, Hedda Nussbaum was dispatched to Bellevue Hospital for observation. Severely battered and bruised, she would be transferred the following day to the women's prison ward at City Hospital in Elmhurst, Queens, for treatment of nine fractured ribs, a broken nose, a fractured jaw, and an ulcerated leg that could require amputation. She continued to insist that her injuries were the result of clumsy, accidental falls and that she was not the victim of physical abuse. News accounts reported that Nussbaum continued to express her love for Steinberg.

On November 4, Steinberg was arraigned at Manhattan Criminal Court. That same day his daughter Lisa was given an electroencephalogram. It showed "flat" brain activity. Though legally brain dead, her heart function remained intact. Caught in a medical dilemma, the hospital staff, after reviewing its potential liability, decided to disconnect Lisa's life support system. Fifteen minutes later, the six-year-old stopped breathing. The official cause and manner of death: "Acute subdural hematoma. Contusions on body surfaces. Child abuse. Homicide." On November 6, charges against Steinberg were upgraded from attempted murder to murder in the second degree.[1]

On October 17, 1988, Joel Steinberg was brought to trial for the murder of his daughter.

These early beginnings set in motion a course of events within the criminal justice system, culminating in a four-month trial that riveted the attention of an entire city, if not millions of people throughout the nation. The trial of Joel Steinberg was to become irrevocably linked with the highly charged issues of child and spouse abuse. Though widely discussed, these issues were mere abstractions for many people—the Steinberg case was to change that. Family violence now had faces: a six-year-old child lying bruised and comatose, her severely scarred and beaten 46-year-old mother "so battered," said *New York Post* columnist Pete Hamill, that we "will never forget that face."[2]

The legacy of the Steinberg case was astonishing in that it resonated on different levels for so many people. "It speaks to the responsibility of a battered woman," said author Susan Brownmiller. "It speaks to drug abuse. It speaks to the whole question of private adoptions, attorneys seduced into criminality. It's many things, the responsibility of neighbors and the community. There's just so much this case deals with that I think it's going to stay with us for a very long time."[3]

From the criminal justice perspective, the Steinberg trial also held a legal fascination. "It's child abuse, it's battered women—and it's also a mystery," said Harold Rothwax, the presiding judge in the case. "There are two people there—which one did it? Evidence is circumstantial, there's no direct evidence. It's not who's lying or who's telling the truth. It's really like putting together the pieces of a puzzle."[4] The underlying question of "Who was responsible?" was answered by the plethora of observers connected to the trial. In Rothwax's courtroom, a writer from *Vanity Fair* magazine prepared for her upcoming article entitled "The Trial of Hedda Nussbaum." Meanwhile, Mayor Edward I. Koch's self-proclaimed "verdict" had been widely quoted in the media: Joel Steinberg should be "dipped in oil."

The charge of culpability in the death of Lisa Steinberg had a broader sweep, and criticism during the trial was leveled against the state's adoption procedures and even against the community at large for failing to notify the city authorities despite overwhelming clues of child abuse and wife battering.

Trying to make sense of these disparate pieces was television. An experimental New York State law allowing the television camera inside the court gave the American television audience an inside view of courtroom proceedings. Actual trial footage became an important resource for television reporters, and night after night, the Joel Steinberg trial played on local, national, and international television. Local television programming was preempted by trial coverage that could also be seen across the globe as far away as Australia. Gavel-to-gavel coverage of the week-long testimony of Hedda Nussbaum and the dramatic sentencing of Joel Steinberg proved to be as engrossing to a huge television audience as it was to the 86 spectators inside the courtroom.

The television coverage itself became a source of controversy. Critics charged that the imagistic-based medium worked to reduce the significance of the trial to a shadowy soap opera, with a fixation on personalities, psychological idiosyncrasies, and courtroom drama. Erika Munk in the *Village Voice* stated: "The craziness of American TV is exactly this fixation on individual psychological reactions, and this fixation is part of what makes it so hard for Americans to see a case like Steinberg's as part of a social pathology."[5] At times, television coverage bordered on the surreal. As part of

WCBS News' extended coverage of Steinberg's sentencing, the defendant's former chief counsel, Ira London, served as a television commentator, making a smooth transition from the courtroom well to the television news set.

While audiences were being transfixed by television images of the Steinberg case, new questions arose as to the appropriate use of the in-court camera, its role in providing a visual documentation, and its impact on the courtroom proceedings themselves. Critics claimed that the use of the television camera created a new type of public trial, in essence, a media trial, where courtroom participants now became actors playing on a world stage, responsible not only for trial testimony, but also for out-of-court press conferences and for media commentary and analysis. Proponents claimed, however, that television was invaluable to the case, since it provided a historical record of one of the most sensational trials of the decade as well as greater public access to the courtroom and the workings of the judicial process.

The Steinberg trial was a standard by which to examine the American justice system when television is allowed to invade the inner workings of the courtroom. From the vantage point of those individuals who participated in the trial, this case study investigates the psychological web of the Television Trial.[6]

The Trial

On October 17, 1988, Joel Steinberg, charged with the murder of his six-year-old daughter, entered the eleventh-floor courtroom in the Criminal Courts Building in lower Manhattan. So began one of the most sensational trials in the history of New York City.

The courtroom, modest in size, seemed a staid setting for a trial that over the course of four months would reveal startling testimony of child and spouse abuse and of homicide. Tall wooden doors swung open to a room approximately 60 feet long and 40 feet wide. Divided into two primary areas, it seated about 80 spectators who, upon entering, were required to have bags and briefcases carefully searched before passing through a metal detector that guarded the front entrance.

More than half the available seating was reserved for the press, many of whom regularly attended the trial. During key testimony and proceedings, such as Hedda Nussbaum's testimony, Judge Harold Rothwax's charge to the jury, and Steinberg's sentencing, journalists would line up outside the courtroom as early as three hours prior to the start to be guaranteed a seat. During more routine testimony, courtroom seating became more available to the general public.

The courtroom itself was embellished by ornamental design and classical motifs. On the front wall, behind the judge's bench, hung a painting set in a floor-to-ceiling frame. Untitled and anonymous, it depicted a blind female Justice holding aloft what appeared to be a cross embedded in a crystal ball; kneeling beside her were two barefoot children—a girl holding a dove, a boy with a sword.

To the casual observer, the courtroom had the feel of a sanctuary—a quiet retreat from the confusion and noise emanating from the streets below. But after a day of testimony, the illusion disappeared, and it became obvious that the courtroom was not acoustically designed with either trial participants or the attending media in mind. Street sounds easily penetrated its tall, arched windows and often disturbed the proceedings. Though both the witness stand and the judge's bench had microphones, testimony was sometimes obscured by noise—city traffic, police sirens, and street life. Early in the trial, instructions from Judge Rothwax were barely audible, prompting a request by the media that a microphone be installed at the bench. But voices, even when amplified, did not carry well, particularly to spectators seated in the back.

To watch Joel Steinberg in person, in fact, was discomforting. Throughout the trial, he appeared nervous and in constant motion—scribbling copious notes on a legal pad or fidgeting in his chair. His face would twitch noticeably, and every so often he would turn toward the spectators and stare at someone he recognized. On one occasion, according to columnist Pete Hamill, Steinberg noticed Murray Kempton, who had written an unflattering article about him for *Newsday*. He glared intently at the journalist in hostile recognition. "At that moment," said Hamill, "Kempton began to understand what had happened."[1] On television, a viewer could not clearly discern the edges and angles of Steinberg's physical appearance, but in person the facial tics and the nervous gestures were visible and constant.

Each of the major participants in the trial had a distinct style, and their interaction in the courtroom was interesting to watch. Judge Rothwax presided over the case with a stern hand. His comments could be bitingly sarcastic, directed toward those attorneys he felt had failed to properly present evidence or had abused legal protocol. Steinberg's chief counsel, Ira London, was frequently the target of these tongue lashings. In the first month of the trial, Rothwax was often critical of motions made by the defense, which sometimes led to angry confrontations within the courtroom.

The situation became further exacerbated after Judge Rothwax discovered that London was making out-of-court statements to the press about ongoing proceedings. Rothwax promptly issued a gag order forbidding the attorneys to discuss the case outside the courtroom, a ruling that was subsequently overturned by the court of appeals. London persisted in giving hallway press conferences, while Rothwax remained angry and critical of the defense lawyers. He noted in an interview conducted in his chambers during jury deliberations: "I've been very critical of the defense attorneys throughout the process for giving hallway interviews to the cameras at every break and during the day during lunch hour. I remain very critical of that. . . . I find it demeans the dignity of the process and endangers the integrity of the process."[2]

If the trial had a media "star," it was London, who always appeared neatly coiffed, dressed in expensive, tailor-made suits. Among reporters, he earned the sobriquet of "spin lawyer." Ignoring Rothwax's criticisms and inciting the judge's wrath, London continued his eleventh-floor corridor meetings with reporters. He said that his use of the media to make public pronouncements was designed to help dispel misconstrued perceptions that his client was a "monster," a perception that could leak its way into the court and negatively affect the outcome of the trial. London disclosed that he had used this tactic successfully in two other cases. "The public's perception of Joel Steinberg was so poisoned, was so inflamed, was so negative, that for one year we decided to remain silent," he said. "When the trial started, it was my plan to begin to change the public perception in the case. I think the public perception of a case does, in some way, influence what occurs in a courtroom."[3] In a curious twist in the trial during sentencing, newly appointed defense counsel Perry Reich and Felix Gilroy charged that London had engaged in publicity tactics that only served to harm Steinberg's case.

London followed a similar pattern each day. The trial would break at about 5:00 P.M., whereupon he and co-counsel, Adrian DiLuzio, would immediately make their way toward a designated space in the court house corridor to meet with reporters. There they would "spin" the day's testimony, offer interpretations of court proceedings, belittle the accounts by prosecution witnesses, and reassure the press that a different story would surely be presented in Steinberg's defense. These interactions were noted in a *New York Times Magazine* article that likened London to a "diligent maitre d'who works the room." The lawyer, in fact, spoke frankly to reporters about the long-term benefits of being involved with a high-profile case. "What lawyer doesn't like publicity?" he asked. "I never thought it was going to be as intense as it was, though. I never thought it would be this big."

Co-counsel Adrian DiLuzio, a former Philadelphia prosecutor whose combative courtroom style was in marked contrast to London's low-keyed performance, summed up his own courtroom philosophy. "I don't have any sympathy for any witness," he said. "Every witness is my enemy. . . . They're my enemy up there because the prosecution is my enemy and they are the extension of prosecution."[4]

While both defense attorneys continued to meet with journalists outside the courtroom, the prosecutors avoided the press, a practice they would adhere to throughout the trial. The scenario became commonplace: Camera lights would illuminate the corridor, camera crew operators would be given specific instructions by their directors, and television reporters would besiege London and DiLuzio with questions. Skirting quickly past the scene were assistant district attorneys Peter Casolaro and John McCusker. It was clear they were considered off-limits to the press, and not a single journalist approached them for an interview.

Casolaro, a top senior trial attorney in the Manhattan district attorneys' office, was assigned to the case to offset the less experienced McCusker, who had been with the case since it broke in November 1987. "I'm sure you never saw John and me give a press conference," Casolaro noted in an interview following the trial. "You probably never saw us on television except in the courtroom and that was broadcast. You probably never saw us quoted in a newspaper except what we said in court because we didn't give interviews to the press. It's our feeling that the case should be tried in the courtroom and not in the press."[5]

According to the prosecutor, though London had become chief counsel just shortly after Steinberg's arrest, his relationship with his client continued to be strained. Steinberg would often be seen diligently working during court proceedings, sometimes offering his notes to his lawyers or even going so far as to suggest legal strategies during direct and cross-examination. This may have resulted in defense moves that often appeared confused and misdirected. London continued to shift the focus of his arguments throughout the trial. Initially, he contended that Lisa Steinberg had died from choking on tainted Chinese vegetables. The defense would later blame Reye's syndrome, careless paramedics, and a roller-skating accident for the child's death. Finally, it was conceded that a homicide indeed had been committed. The killer, however, was not Joel Steinberg, but Hedda Nussbaum.

In critiquing the defense attorney's performance, Casolaro noted that the defense seemed ill prepared to deal with the complexities of the case, a situation that was compounded by their client, who insisted on taking an active role in the courtroom. "I think the problem they had with the defense was that Steinberg was probably a difficult client and that they were never quite sure of what evidence they had to rebut because they didn't know how it would come out," said Casolaro. "They knew a lot of our evidence, but they didn't know it as well as they should have known it probably. And so they made some wrong decisions."

More than 50 witnesses were called during the trial, a number of them experts in their respective fields. The key witness for the prosecution was Hedda Nussbaum, who for the previous year had remained a patient in the Four Winds psychiatric hospital in Katonah, New York. The district attorneys' office had dropped the murder charge against her with the condition that she appear as a witness against Steinberg. Nussbaum spent hundreds of hours honing her story with the prosecutors, and during her week-long testimony, in a slow and methodical manner, she detailed the lurid life style she had shared with Steinberg. She also directly implicated him in Lisa's death. Her testimony was carried live on all three network affiliate stations, coverage that was unprecedented in the one-year-old New York State "camera in the courtroom" experiment. Nussbaum's accounts of the events leading up to Lisa's death transfixed many television viewers, but for other observers it was her ravaged physical appearance that proved most disturbing.

The press itself was another major participant in the trial, a small army of television, newspaper, radio, and magazine reporters who followed the case daily. As evidence of the intense media interest in this case, one needed only to observe the plethora of journalists and technicians at work. During jury deliberations, the crush of journalists and technicians working outside the courtroom in the hallway corridors prompted a threat from an administrative judge, Milton Williams, to remove all television and radio personnel and equipment unless the area was carefully maintained and remained unobstructed. The media quickly adhered to the judge's order and were allowed to stay.

While hundreds of child abuse cases are reported annually in New York City (107 children died from parental abuse and neglect in the city in 1987), the Steinberg case was unique. Tony Guida, a reporter for WNBC-TV, made the observation: "You don't expect a wealthy white lawyer living in Greenwich Village with his book editor wife to kill their daughter."[6] While he found these social and racial distinctions "morally repugnant," such characteristics are nonetheless determining factors in the "newsworthiness" of an event. From that standpoint, the Steinberg case, was one of the most sensational trials covered by the local press during the decade.

In a less celebrated case, journalists might commonly attend only highlighted moments: the opening remarks, key testimony, and sentencing. During the Steinberg trial, news reports were constant, appearing virtually every day in all major metropolitan newspapers and on local television news. The Cable News Network (CNN) continually broadcast segments of the trial to a national audience. Midway through the trial, the first of several books on the Steinberg case was published. Susan Brownmiller's *Waverly Place* was a fictional account of the Steinberg-Nussbaum relationship. Shortly after the trial ended, a nonfiction paperback book written by Sam Ehrlich, entitled *Lisa, Hedda and Joel*, was published. The book was a detailed accounting of the trial and the major participants in the trial. Major magazines such as *People*, *Vanity Fair* and the *New York Times Magazine* also published a sweep of articles relating to the case. The Steinberg trial was no longer a major local news event, but rather an international story that reverberated from New York to California, and across the globe to Europe and Australia.

THE DISTRACTION FACTOR

During the Steinberg trial, both the presiding judge and the journalists were particularly sensitive to the use and placement of the courtroom camera to assure that the medium would not interfere with or inhibit proceedings. From one perspective, the camera experiment could be viewed as an alternate trial: Not only would Joel Steinberg be tried and judged by his peers, but the efficacy of allowing television into the courtroom would also be monitored and evaluated by both the legal system and the press. Prior to the trial, Judge Rothwax opposed the television camera's use, recognizing its potential to distract courtroom proceedings. He noted: "I thought it would affect the actual proceedings of the trial, that it would make people self-conscious, less secure people would play to the camera, and that it didn't add anything to the proceedings."

Judge Rothwax shared the view, held earlier by other legal scholars and jurists, that the physical presence of the news photographer and television camera operator and their equipment could potentially impair the quality of justice and interfere with "the dignity of the court." Despite these reservations, however, Rothwax willingly allowed the still and video cameras into the court, although it was within his power to exclude them under the state's newly enacted camera legislation.

Presiding judges in other notorious cases in New York, most notably Judge Howard Bell in the Robert Chambers murder trial and Justice Thomas Demakos in the Howard Beach trial, had raised objections, denying media requests for the installation of cameras. Rothwax maintained that although he had trepidations, he would be remiss by imposing restrictions without first exploring how the medium operated within the courtroom setting. He explained, "I shouldn't allow my personal feelings to interfere anymore than I would in any other situation where I might personally disagree with the law but my job is, as judge, to apply the law."

Prior to the trial, Judge Rothwax met with David Bookstaver to discuss the appropriate placement of the cameras. Bookstaver, an administrator for The New York Broadcasters Courtroom Pool, had the delicate task of supervising broadcast personnel and news photographers. Recognizing that his camera crews would be operating under the scrutiny of lawmakers, media critics, and journalists interested in the television experiment, he readily took measures to ensure that they would not violate court orders.

The limitations on the use of cameras in the court were carefully spelled out by state law. Judge Rothwax reminded Bookstaver that the television and still cameras would not be allowed to photograph the jury or focus on sidebar conversations between himself and the attorneys. Steinberg's private conferences with his lawyers would be off-limits to protect the privacy of those conversations. Cameras would also be prohibited from photographing courtroom spectators.

During pretrial hearings, the cameras were permitted in the well of the courtroom, giving the television technician and photographer a clearer view of the defendant and the witnesses. Since the jury was not present during these proceedings, there was no danger of the cameras panning to them inadvertently, a move expressly prohibited by state law. Once the jury was empaneled, however, the cameras were moved from the courtroom well. Judge Rothwax and Bookstaver decided that both the television and the still cameras should be placed at the end of the jury box, to the front of the rail divider that separates spectators from court members. Cameras would now stand almost directly behind the lawyers during direct and cross-examination, thus requiring camera operators to shoot "over the shoulder" of attorneys in order to have a clear shot of witnesses testifying on the stand. Both the defense and the prosecution were asked on several occasions to change positions so that the cameramen could photograph from a clearer angle.

The position of the cameras allowed the technical staff to pan the courtroom from the witness stand, to the judge's bench, and to the defense attorneys' and prosecutors' tables. Their placement also made it virtually impossible to accidentally photograph or film jurors seated in the jury box, but it also limited other types of shots as well. While the camera crew had a full frontal view of witnesses and the judge's bench, it was forced to focus on the backs of lawyers during questioning or take profile shots of Steinberg himself. According to Bookstaver and Judge Rothwax, this camera position was the best possible under the restrictions dictated by law. Rothwax explained that he could have placed the cameras in the rear of the courtroom, "but this also runs the risk that you are going to see the audience [which violates state rules]. This position was unobtrusive to the jury and a natural place to put it. They didn't have any problem with it and I didn't either."

Most participants agreed that, for the most part, the television camera and personnel were not obtrusive or "distracting" to the courtroom process. Bookstaver, for instance, assessed that the technology had indeed become "ordinary," virtually an expected fixture within the courtroom. He recounted: "I heard a comment that if the camera wasn't there, it would be missed. It's a fixed ornament, part of the courtroom. It doesn't move. The jury came in the first day, looked at the camera maybe for the first ten seconds. It doesn't do anything. There's nothing there to watch that's interesting. They can't see a picture. It's a box with a man standing at it."[7]

Judge Rothwax himself became a convert during the trial, stating that cameras had become "a part of the courtroom furniture." He noted that camera operators remained in their positions throughout the day, setting up equipment prior to the proceedings and removing it after the day's business was concluded. Rothwax regarded the photo-personnel as less conspicuous than other press members seated in the spectator section, who would often leave the courtroom to meet deadlines or to consult with editors or news directors. "Ultimately I concluded there was no basis for distinguishing between a camera and a reporter," he said. "If anything, a camera is less bothersome, it stands still, it doesn't move around, it doesn't make noise."

Although the television camera operated noiselessly, Judge Rothwax conceded that he was distracted in the earlier trial sessions by the single still camera that emitted a clicking noise each time it operated. Admittedly being very attuned to courtroom noise, he requested that the still camera be muffled, explaining, "I'm not going to hear clicks in the courtroom. I'm a little nutty that way." Several times during the trial, Rothwax told a court officer to instruct the still photographers "to muffle that sound or they're going to have to leave." After he complained on one occasion, a photographer loosely wrapped a coat around his head and camera to serve as a self-styled "muffler."

Jurors mostly concurred with Judge Rothwax's opinion that the television camera was minimally distracting during proceedings. Although it may have added to an initial sense of nervousness and apprehension, the jurors became virtually unaware of the camera's presence during the course of the four-month trial.

Helena Barthell, like other jurors, contended that although she had noticed the presence of the still and video cameras, jurors had not been informed that they would be part of a televised trial when originally empaneled. Some jurors believed that the cameras were in place for courtroom purposes only and not for public broadcast. In recalling her initial impressions, Barthell said: "It took a while before it sunk in because while I saw the television camera, I just presumed that they were videotaping it the way they videotape people's testimony when you take a deposition. . . . I didn't realize that this was something that was going to the outside. I thought when I first saw the camera, they're videotaping for accuracy."[8]

Most jurors remained unaware of exactly how the electronic media functioned within the courtroom. Some said they were given virtually no instructions by the court as to their use. Others recalled that they discovered the trial was being recorded and broadcast only after unwittingly watching snippets of court testimony on the news. Allen Jared, listed as juror number 12, sat closest to the videotape camera, but still maintained that he was unaware that it would be operating continuously throughout the trial. He realized the trial was being televised only weeks later after learning that Hedda Nussbaum's testimony was being broadcast live through most of the day by all local network affiliates. "I still don't know if they were on from the time it started every day until the very end or if they turned it on at certain times," he said in the trial's aftermath.[9] This lack of communication between the court and the jurors may have resulted in the confused and hazy recollections some jurors had regarding their initial impressions of the television camera and its role in the trial.

But such indifference was shaken during an episode in the midst of deliberations that startled them. Camera crews were instructed to tilt the camera downward each time jury members entered the court. Jurors noticed, however, that the television camera was trained on them as they exited a side room leading into the court. Barthell remembers being shaken by the incident, as were other jurors concerned about retaining their anonymity in the case. "It really kind of startled me during the deliberations that the camera seemed to be focused right on us," she said. "I was really wondering, are they filming us now? That made me nervous." One juror approached the court clerk who reassured them that they were not being videotaped.

Attorneys in the case maintained that the consuming nature of the trial mandated that they focus their complete attention and concentration on the proceedings. Though initially aware of the camera, once the trial was under way they quickly forgot about it. Both London and Casolaro recalled that the only time they became conscious of the television camera was when they inadvertently blocked it because of its location behind the courtroom lectern. "The only time I am aware of the camera is when I'm cross-examining," said London. "I know they like me to stand in a certain place so they can get a clear shot of the witness. So I try sometimes to stand a little bit away from the jury rail."

Casolaro recalled one moment during the trial when a camera operator was attempting to film a witness who was being shown a videotape of Steinberg and Nussbaum as they were led into the Sixth Precinct following their arrest. Because Casolaro was sitting on the court rail, the technician asked him to shift his position to give the camera a clearer shot. He promptly complied with the request. "I remember that," said Casolaro. "I was certainly aware of blocking the camera. I know that people didn't want to see the back of my head."

For the most part then, participants confirmed an opinion often cited by camera advocates. The presence of the technology did not distract trial members to the point where they were *consciously* aware of its presence. In point of fact, the days of noisy motor drives, harsh lights, and cumbersome equipment have given way to a more streamlined technology capable of operating quietly and inconspicuously. The development of the light-sensitive videotape camera, for example, make cameras virtually noiseless and capable of operating in low light levels. The still and the videotape cameras at the Steinberg trial, except for a few instances, proved to be a quiet and inconspicuous technology. The in-court camera had not deprived the defendant, as cited in the *Estes* decision, of the "judicial serenity and calm" to which he is entitled.[10] But these observations proved to reveal only a small part of a much more complex relationship that existed between the court "actor" and television at the Joel Steinberg murder trial.

The Self-Consciousness Factor

The use of television in the Steinberg trial provided evidence that audiovisual technology could be an unobtrusive tool for broadcast journalists and news photographers in a courtroom setting. Although, as some courtroom participants noted, television and still cameras could distract in inappreciable ways, generally they were stationary and noiseless, quiet and motionless observers. At this trial, television personnel and photographers, too, operated in a restrained and professional manner.

But the presence of the television camera in the courtroom raised questions that are, as yet, unresolved. Although advances in television technology have made in-court cameras virtually inconspicuous, critics are still convinced that their presence affects the performance of court participants in subtle, yet significant, ways, touching on a deeper psychological level that is not easily detectable. In the landmark *Estes* decision, Supreme Court Justice Tom Clark argued that "distractions are not caused solely by the physical presence of the camera and its telltale red lights. It is the awareness of the fact of telecasting that is felt by [court participants] throughout the trial."[1] This philosophy was the basis for his conclusion that television should not be permitted into the courtroom.

Legal theorists and lawmakers have long argued whether Clark's observation was in fact accurate. For the most part, it appears as if they have rejected it, as evidenced by the overwhelming rush by almost all states to televise the trial process. We sought our own answers as we urged trial participants to closely explore their own psychological mindset during those stressful days in late 1988. Did court television, in fact, have an inhibiting, prejudicial, or psychological impact by making them more self-conscious of their actions and role in the courtroom?[2] And, if so, what did it mean for the way in which justice worked in the case against Joel Steinberg?

THE PUBLIC AS COURT SPECTATOR

The intended purpose of the original New York legislation allowing television into the courts was to educate the public about the judicial system and its procedures. Though it is dubious that the medium in fact served such a function, it was evident that camera coverage intensified the level of public opinion about the issues and personalities involved in the Steinberg case. In effect, television broadened the parameters of the courtroom to encompass millions of viewers and provided a direct link to proceedings via the camera lens. While the press would have been present irrespective of the presence of the camera, television was singularly responsible for providing an intimate and first-hand look at testimony and the interactions of trial participants.

Crucial questions still remain as this new "public spectator," now knowledgeable about the trial primarily through television news accounts, becomes an additional factor—a "thirteenth juror"—to be seriously considered by members of the court. Already embroiled in a highly controversial trial, were participants influenced by the specter of public opinion that hung heavily over the case? Were they, in effect, prompted to evaluate how they were being perceived?

For some participants, this public spectator assured the integrity of a fair trial. Chief defense counsel Ira London viewed the camera as a means to bring public pressure into the court, a factor that would benefit the fair administration of justice. The invisible, but palpable, presence of a mediated public at court proceedings could magnify the responsibilities of participants, making them more accountable for their actions.

Imagine this trial taking place with no spectators, no one in the courtroom. When a judge and a prosecutor know that no one is looking over their shoulder, their conduct tends to become more excessive in whatever direction it usually goes. For example, if you have a prosecutory judge, and we have many, he will tend to be more excessive. Same with the prosecutor. He'll tend to bend the rules for himself more. He'll tend to misrepresent things more. The moment you put two spectators in that courtroom, in the back of their minds there are two people sitting there that are watching [them] and they can't go crazy. Put 200 people in the courtroom and they're going to watch their p's and q's. Put a national audience in the courtroom and they're going to be very careful that they don't take away a defendant's rights and become excessive in their prejudices. I've never had a trial with Judge Rothwax although I have known him for many, many years. I can't say how he might have been without the cameras and the large audiences. But certainly it puts him on guard that he's got to be careful.[3]

But others regarded the public spectator as a shadowy and intimidating presence, detrimental to the deliberate and impartial court processes that exist to ensure a fair trial. The Steinberg trial, they noted, was not immune from the prevalent and powerful strains of public opinion inspired to a large degree by the television camera. Cameras in the courtroom could place an additional burden on participants compelled to compare their performance to the indirect demands of public opinion. Warning that such public opinion could be the ultimate weapon used to undermine the right of fair trial, prosecutor Peter Casolaro contended:

I think a lot of times it will become a matter of strategy where a defense attorney will want a case on television because he knows it will scare off the prosecution witnesses, or a prosecutor will want a case on television because he wants to put more public pressure on the jury to come up with a particular verdict. And I would hate to see it become another strategic tool that would be used to influence the process rather than let the evidence decide the case. And I'm afraid that can happen.[4]

Evaluating the psychological "effect" that the public spectator had on the court participant is complex. Each individual held a distinct attitude toward being scrutinized by the camera and, by extension, a huge television audience. Many participants acknowledged that they were affected by the presence of television to some degree. In some cases, the camera served to heighten self-awareness, making trial members more conscious of how they looked and performed. Others expressed concern about how their testimony would be translated outside the courtroom, within a vast public arena. Regardless of whether this shift in self-perception was deemed helpful or not, the point remained clear: The public spectator, electronically tied to the courtroom scene via the camera lens, was a factor to be reckoned with.

JUDGE HAROLD ROTHWAX

Judge Harold Rothwax's reputation preceded him as he took the bench at the Steinberg trial. All the lawyers in the case professed their utmost respect for Rothwax, describing him as a "strong" and "brilliant" jurist. Though none of the prosecutors or defense attorneys had tried a case before him, they were acutely aware of his reputation as a judge who exercises firm control over court proceedings. Both prosecutors agreed that Rothwax's behavior during the trial exemplified his reputation as a "no-nonsense" judge with a low tolerance for legal inefficiency or delays. "He's very good and very stern, very strong with the lawyers, that's always been his reputation," said Casolaro. (His reputation was not diminished after suffering two broken wrists early in the trial when the bicycle he was riding to court was sideswiped by a passing automobile and he was thrown to the ground. Rothwax ordered the trial to continue after being treated in the emergency room at Bellevue Hospital and took his place on the bench with his arms in two plaster casts.)

Defense attorney Adrian DiLuzio criticized Judge Rothwax's "persona" for "going beyond that which is necessary at times," but characterized him as "a brilliant guy" and "a very personable man." He noted that Rothwax had been vilified in certain legal circles as "the evil prince of darkness." "But to watch him for two hours and fifteen minutes give a charge that's straight down the middle, that's fair, that emphasizes the issues, I think creates public confidence. People say, 'hey, even Joel Steinberg gets a fair trial.' "[5]

In his chambers adjacent to a room that housed the jurors, then in their fifth day of deliberations, Judge Rothwax evaluated television's impact in the courtroom. Already familiar with the workings of the camera, Rothwax had presided over three other televised court proceedings. Despite a personal opposition to camera use in criminal trials, Rothwax saw "no basis for exclusion under the statute" and allowed television and still cameras to be present during the Steinberg trial. As the trial progressed, he would reverse his original opinion, explaining that the camera was merely another type of court reporter and one that had little meaningful effect on the judgments and behavior of participants. It was his contention that the camera, like the print media before it, acts simply to record events as they happen. When carefully used and precisely regulated, legal processes are protected, and a fair trial is ensured. The nature of the medium itself is benign and neutral, without serious psychological effects on trial participants. The camera, he claimed, did not generate intense public interest, but served only to mirror the public involvement that already existed prior to the trial.

We're all alive and conscious, we all know [the television camera] is there. There is nobody who conducts this case who does it without an awareness of the public interest in it. Cameras don't meaningfully add to that. Take the camera out of the courtroom and there is still intense public interest in the case of which we are still aware. So it's not as if cameras bring the public into the court; the cameras are reflective of the public interest developing in the case.[6]

Judge Rothwax noted that his initial awareness of the television camera quickly faded as he focused on the complexities of the trial itself. The camera's presence broadened his supervisory functions only slightly when he would occasionally remind camera operators not to photograph Steinberg in conference with his lawyers, or jurors, or sidebar conversations between lawyers and himself. He would, however, order the still and television camera shut down in response to a complaint by a 16-year-old witness that she was nervous testifying in front of them. But the former critic of in-court cameras was now a strong proponent: "Because a witness here and a witness there will be nervous is not a reason to remove the cameras from the courtroom," he said. "It just means that if that is going to affect that witness and affect the proceedings then shut the camera off for that witness. Don't close it for everyone because one witness is bothered by it. You regulate, you don't prohibit."

Barry Scheck, the attorney for Hedda Nussbaum, disagreed, charging that Judge Rothwax and others could not help but be influenced by the presence of cameras. Though Rothwax's daily legal judgments might be unaffected by the camera, Scheck surmised that he seemed determined to keep tighter control over the proceedings in the Steinberg trial than he would have in a nontelevised trial. The judge was "on his best behavior," according to Scheck, a fact that could be directly attributable to the presence of television cameras. He noted: "To a large degree, what the camera in the courtroom does is, it forces the lawyers and the judge to be on their best behavior because they know they are being scrutinized more carefully than they have ever been before in terms of the public's perception of their performance."[7] As a criminal attorney experienced in televised trials, Scheck perceived that the camera has a marked effect on trial participants who have become "very, very conscious that every action is going to be picked up by, not only the jury, but the public."

Though praising Judge Rothwax for his courtroom behavior, Scheck feared that other judges might not be as professional under the pressure of presiding over a televised trial. "What I worry about," he said, "are those judges who do not have the finely developed sense that this judge had and will not react well. I think it changes behavior. It just so happens in this case, I think it changed it for the better, not for the worse."

Witnesses also concluded that Judge Rothwax's courtroom appeared different from others in which they had testified. Dr. Azariah Eshkenazi, a leading expert witness for the defense, said that Rothwax "was himself except that he stuck to the rules very excessively."[8] As an expert witness, it was customary for Eshkenazi to attend courtroom proceedings when other witnesses testified, but "in this particular case, I had to wait all day in the witness room," he said. According to Eshkenazi, Rothwax also exercised tighter control with witnesses in other ways. They were given less latitude during sidebar discussions with attorneys and were forbidden to remain on the stand. Instead, they were instructed to wait in a chair next to the jury box. Eshkenazi surmised: "They followed the rules by the book. I don't know if this was the particular judge, or it was the cameras, but I never had this problem before."

From Dr. Douglas Miller's perception, "it was clear" that Judge Rothwax was "camera conscious." As an example, he cited an incident in which Rothwax instructed the camera crew to stop filming a conference between Steinberg and his attorneys. He feared that "somebody might read Mr. Steinberg's lips on the videotape if it were broadcast and that would be a violation of his privacy," said Miller.[9]

Another witness, however, charged that Judge Rothwax's iron grip over the courtroom—instigated by a keen awareness that the camera "was watching"—

seriously affected the fairness of the trial. Marilyn Walton, a longtime associate of Steinberg and a defense witness in the case, criticized the judge for "making all those asinine comments [to the press] in his chambers" and for being irresponsible with respect to guaranteeing Steinberg a fair trial.[10] Blaming the in-court camera for his behavior, Walton accused the judge of using the trial as a vehicle to "boost his career" and image. "He's right up there with [television personality] Judge Wapner now," she said. During her testimony, she claimed that Rothwax would cut her short, demanding that her answers be more concise. She said: "How can you shorthand the truth? It was important in my estimation that the jury hear the background of what was going on so that they would know *why* this incident occurred, not just that it occurred."

Jurors commended Judge Rothwax for maintaining a disciplined courtroom, but several observed a noticeable change in his behavior midway through the trial. Stern and unyielding in the beginning, they noted that Rothwax appeared more lighthearted and less confrontational as the trial progressed. Concurring with other participants, they speculated that he tempered his demeanor after a report depicting him as angry and argumentative with the defense lawyers appeared on the evening news. It was a dramatic example of the underlying threads that tie together television and the trial participant. (The incident is fully explored in Chapter 11, "Mediated Feedback.")

THE SENTENCING

The case transcended local boundaries, and Judge Rothwax found himself the focus of national attention, most notably during the televised sentencing of Joel Steinberg. The sentencing was broadcast live on all major local stations and reached millions of homes outside New York City through the national Cable News Network (CNN). Up until that moment, Rothwax acknowledged that he had been mostly a background player in television's frame of the courtroom. Television viewers would finally have their first opportunity to watch the judge in the trial's dramatic final stages. A significant and culminating moment, the sentencing brought issues concerning cameras in the court-room to the forefront. The heated debate that ensued between Rothwax and Steinberg's attorneys regarding the camera and its perceived effect on the judge's decision-making abilities, as well as on the defense's legal strategy, came to a culminating moment.

The proceedings were marked by Steinberg's impassioned plea that he was a devoted father, innocent of his daughter's death. It was also dramatized by the emotional confrontations that continually erupted between Rothwax and Steinberg's newly appointed defense attorneys. Perry Reich and co-counsel Felix Gilroy joined the case after Steinberg dismissed Ira London and Adrian DiLuzio following his conviction. Steinberg expressed privately that he was particularly incensed that London did not wage a more aggressive defense, seeming instead more interested in promoting his own career. His new lawyers would make the camera issue the substance of a legal motion. In a notable confrontation, Gilroy criticized Judge Rothwax for endorsing the use of the television camera in court, a tool that he charged had hoisted the weight of public opinion onto the judge's shoulders. "That particular position has been frozen before the court," Gilroy argued before the bench. "Now the court is almost in a position where it's mandated to give this defendant the maximum sentence."[11] The courtroom camera had damaged his client's due process rights, and Gilroy called for the judge's removal from the bench, a move that surprised and infuriated Rothwax.

Judge Rothwax bristled at the notion that his forthcoming sentence was influenced by the presence of the cameras. After angrily denying Gilroy's motion, he disdainfully criticized the lawyers, warning them to be more diligent in presenting their motions before the court. During one testy exchange, Rothwax bitingly remarked: "I have read your entire motion and its supporting documents. You should therefore proceed on the basis that I am fully familiar with your points and the points of the district attorney unless you feel it's absolutely necessary to repeat those points in front of the camera. It is not necessary from my point of view. If, however, you wish to be heard, I will, of course, allow you to be heard, mindful that there is a camera in the courtroom."[12]

Judge Rothwax continued to quash one legal motion after another and seemed to grow increasingly impatient with Reich and Gilroy's tactics. During one motion in particular, the lawyers criticized a presentencing report for allegedly containing several factual errors about Michelle Launders, Lisa's natural mother, and her responsibility in handling her daughter's funeral. Rothwax, outraged, denounced the claim, stating that it verged "on the bizarre and the grotesque."

The palpable level of anger during the sentencing was unusual even for a case that had had a history of confrontations between the judge and defense counsel. Reporting for WCBS-TV news, Mary Murphy commented that she "had never seen anything quite like this before" during the trial.[13] Ira London, in his newly acquired role as a WCBS news commentator during the sentencing, described Judge Rothwax as "a live wire," who was visibly agitated and acerbic. "He's much tougher than he was on us even at his toughest. I think he is upset with the legal issues they've put before him. What upsets him is a presentation in court, by lawyers in a major case, of issues that he feels are not phrased the way legal issues should be."[14]

Reich had a different accounting for Judge Rothwax's belittling attitude. Rothwax, he contended, was not the same person he had known in previous cases. Conceding that the judge was "impatient with attorneys in general," Reich noted that during the sentencing Rothwax was clearly cognizant of the courtroom cameras and the large television audience watching the live proceedings. As a result, charged Reich, the judge had taken a much harsher stance, a view that Rothwax steadfastly denied.

Reich insisted that the judge had not displayed the same temperament he had known in previous meetings.

Even the first time I appeared in front of him in this case, at the bench he was a decent guy and he told me, "I'm going to do this and this and this." I knew because he was cognizant of the camera being on; he just decided to blow my doors down for no reason, and he was wrong. I think Rothwax decided to come out with the attitude that he did because he knew he was playing to an actual audience. We felt he was acting like Judge Wapner.[15]

Reich called the Steinberg sentencing "a Roman circus." "It was Good Friday and I was waiting for the crowd to yell, 'bring us the lions,'" he said. Because of the emotional tension instigated by the television camera, Reich maintained that he was forced to reevaluate and finally change his initial legal strategy. Fearful that certain arguments would inflame a national audience and elevate public opinion against his client, Reich omitted statements that dealt with sensitive issues even though he regarded them to be relevant.

In an interview following the sentencing, he cited legal documents and courtroom statements that purportedly contained implicit anti-Semitic overtones. According to Reich, one such statement appeared in Steinberg's probation report and intimated that Steinberg had "defrauded Catholic women of their children." "They said it was outrageous that here was a lawyer of this sort making representations that the children would be placed with good Catholic families," he stated. "Now in context, the implication was what it was." Reich claimed that similar derogatory overtones were also present in the prosecution's summation to the jury. "They said he was this kind of lawyer, that kind of lawyer and I think Adrian DiLuzio objected on the grounds that the only thing left out was [that Steinberg was] a Jew lawyer."

A request for a nonpublic presentencing hearing was denied by Judge Rothwax, and Reich claimed that he was forced to abandon his original intention to make the objections public during sentencing. "You saw the judge tried to make a fool out of me with respect to the Michelle Launders thing," he said. "But I felt it was important to give a measured response." Without the presence of the camera, Reich contended that he would have moved to make such objections part of the record. The presence of television was inhibiting because "there are certain things you don't want to rip the country open on, not without a strong foundation." He explained, "Say I would have gotten up and would have said on the Michelle Launders thing, 'Judge, look, let's be blunt. This statement here is that you're saying he's a Jew lawyer.' Had there been no camera I would have made that comment."

Reich said that he discussed this point with Steinberg the previous week at the Brooklyn House of Detention. Steinberg was also troubled that such legal arguments might act as a "lightning rod" and "set off some bigots who would say afterwards, 'Well, gee, that's right, the guy's a Jewish lawyer, he did this.'" Such national exposure would only serve to hurt his client's chances on appeal and, Reich noted, would "create a debate on something that really isn't necessary."

In response to Reich's charges that he "played to the camera" and that legal motions were stifled by the presence of the cameras, Judge Rothwax angrily denounced such charges as just another example of the unprofessional and "sleazy" behavior on the part of the defense attorneys. To the accusation that court documents and statements by the prosecution contained anti-Semitic inferences, Rothwax said, "I think it has no validity, whatever. I mean I'm Jewish, I wouldn't be tolerating anti-Semitism in my courtroom. I think that's ridiculous." The judge said that he had read the probation report thoroughly and had heard all of Casolaro's summation, and he categorically rejected the claim that any anti-Semitic allusions were contained in them. "I think it's symbolic, it's evidence of their recklessness with regard to these kinds of accusations, that I'm playing to the camera, that Casolaro is anti-Semitic, I mean it's a recklessness, almost a lack of professionalism bordering, I would think, on a lack of ethics in the way they conduct themselves. They make reckless charges, and if they make enough of them, I guess they figure they're going to stick."

Judge Rothwax also emphatically denied that his reaction to the attorneys during the proceedings, which he described as "mindfully angry," was influenced by the camera or by the knowledge that a large television audience was watching. "My own feeling is they were doing much more playing to the camera than I was," he countered. Recalling events that led to the tense exchanges, Rothwax said:

I had brought them up to the bench before we actually got under way, and before we were on camera, and they had made some stupid arguments in their motion to vacate the verdict, an argument such as I ought to have a hearing going into the factual accuracy of the probation report because they said that Lisa was buried in Michelle Launders' family plot. In fact, she was buried in a Catholic charity's plot. Or that the probation report said that Lisa had been illegally adopted when their point was that she hadn't been adopted at all. These points seemed to me bizarre and grotesque. They seemed to me stupid points, and I said to them in our off-the-record conference, I said it would seem to me better for you to submit the papers and I'll simply deny your motions without having any extended discussion. We don't have to discuss them. I think it's an embarrassment for you to make these arguments. I assume they made the arguments because Joel Steinberg wanted them to make them, not because as good lawyers they thought they were good arguments to make. They were bad arguments to make, foolish arguments to make. And they declined, and I assumed that they declined because

Steinberg wanted them to make the arguments. Now I gave them that option and they rejected it. They wanted to go on the record and argue everything. Under those circumstances I was determined to respond. I wasn't going to permit them to make a record without responding for the record.

During the proceedings, Judge Rothwax said he was "extremely alert and alive" to the lawyers' motions, carefully responding to all remarks made to the bench. He took notes to ensure that no single point was overlooked. He was determined that "they were not going to make a mockery of these proceedings and the points they made would be responded to and addressed." Visibly angry when denying the defense motions, Rothwax became further incensed at a surprise move by the defense team that called for his removal from the case. He regarded this motion as a blatant attempt to deliberately embarrass him in open court. While acknowledging that the lawyers were within their rights to call him to recuse, Rothwax said that they had subverted courtroom procedures by making the motion unannounced, with no advanced notice given to the judge and the prosecution. "I just felt that was really below the belt," said Rothwax. "Those kind of tactics got me going with these guys. I just felt that they were sleaze and I wasn't going to put up with it."

Judge Rothwax believed that the lawyers' actions were "a conscious play to the camera, without question." "I just decided to resolve it in a cold fashion," he said. "I don't know if I was a 'live wire,' I was coldly angry at them." A strong supporter of the use of in-court cameras, Rothwax now faced the dilemma of dealing with lawyers whom he charged were "reckless" with the truth. When asked if such grandstanding would damage the integrity of the court in the eyes of television viewers, Rothwax replied: "I think they did more to damage themselves than anything else." He was, in fact, pleased that the television audience was able to witness proceedings that were "not perfunctory or ritualized, but extended" and conducted in "a serious, sober, conscientious, carefully procedural way."

Judge Rothwax also dismissed Reich's assertions that the defense counsel deliberately quieted the tenor of their remarks and excluded inflammatory statements because of the presence of the camera. The judge believed them to be disingenuous, stating that Reich and co-counsel Felix Gilroy "were about as blunt as they could be without being held in contempt." He warned that had the lawyers been more aggressive, they would have been cited for contempt. Their argument that the cameras should be banned so that lawyers can become involved in a "a real no-holds-barred, bare-knuckle contest" is a persuasive reason for cameras in the court. Rothwax believes that the courtroom is an environment where "civilized discourse" should be the rule of practice. If television worked to restrain Joel Steinberg and his lawyers from running roughshod over the proceedings, he said, then this was a persuasive argument for allowing it in court. He said: "If cameras make people more civilized, more polite and more related to the issues, and less personal, and less angry, then that's all to the good."

CONCERNS OVER WITNESSES

When informed that courtroom television and still cameras would be permitted to record and broadcast the Steinberg trial, prosecutors Peter Casolaro and John McCusker admittedly were concerned that the cameras would affect the nature of trial testimony. "I didn't like the idea," said Casolaro, "because I was afraid it would make not only me, but witnesses, self-conscious."

Casolaro's initial impressions were later confirmed to some degree. In one incident, a 16-year-old girl, testifying for the prosecution, pleaded with the attorney to shut down the cameras when she testified. Extremely nervous and self-conscious, she said that the cameras would affect her testimony. Judge Rothwax complied with her request and instructed the camera operators to stop filming during her testimony—the only time during the trial that cameras ceased operation during testimony.

McCusker, too, had reservations about the camera, fearing its potential to give the court proceedings "a circus-type atmosphere" that could discourage witnesses from testifying. He credited Judge Rothwax's professionalism for "keeping things in line." Still, the prosecution was forced to contend with discomfited witnesses who were reluctant to testify in a televised trial. "There were a number of people who mentioned to us they didn't want to be televised," he said. "But it never got to the point where they wouldn't testify if they were televised."[16]

According to both prosecutors, the "unique" nature of the Steinberg case distinguished it from other criminal trials in which in-court cameras might prove more inhibiting to witness testimony. They explained that most persons taking the stand in the Steinberg trial were "expert" witnesses, already accustomed to courtroom proceedings and indirectly linked to the events for which Steinberg was charged. Furthermore, Judge Rothwax was diligent and sensitive in monitoring the use of the camera. This may have acted to assuage the fears of witnesses uncomfortable with providing testimony in a televised trial. Other trials might have a judge who is less forceful as well as different courtroom personalities who may be more vulnerable when performing in a televised trial.

The assistant district attorneys both realized the inherent dangers that television posed to witness testimony. Casolaro pointed to the upcoming trial of Gene Gotti, an alleged figure in organized crime and brother of John Gotti, as a case in which cameras could have a serious inhibiting effect on witnesses.

[The Steinberg trial] was a different kind of murder case. The witnesses were a different kind of people than you usually have in a murder case. Most of the witnesses I have, I'm sure they would not testify if there were cameras in the courtroom and the people back in their neighborhood knew they had testified. Confidentiality is really important with the average murder case and the average witness because they have to go back and live in the neighborhood with the defendant's friends. That was not true in this case. So I'd be worried if that kind of case became a big publicity case and there would be cameras there. I think I would worry a lot more. The kind of witnesses we had here are not the kind of people who are afraid to face the public generally, whereas the average witness in the average murder case is.

EXPERT WITNESSES

Many of the 39 prosecution witnesses and 13 defense witnesses in the Steinberg trial were considered to be "experts" in their respective fields of medicine, pathology, psychiatry, and law enforcement and were central to both the defense and the prosecution. Some had been witnesses in other trials and were already familiar and comfortable with the courtroom setting; several had participated in other televised trials. Other witnesses were less experienced and admittedly emotionally involved with the tragic circumstances surrounding the case.

Reactions to television varied enormously. But for most witnesses, the presence of the camera changed *something*, even if such behavior modifications were deemed positive. Some stated that being a participant in a televised trial did not measurably alter their responses, which were carefully reviewed by attorneys well before the case went to trial. Still, the awareness that their testimony would be televised heightened self-consciousness among virtually all witnesses regarding their roles. For some, these feelings resulted in improved concentration, while for others it had a disquieting effect and increased their level of anxiety. Though it would appear that the camera did not overtly alter behavior in most instances, some witnesses readily admitted that as part of a televised trial they were diligent in their preparation, more conscientious about their performance, and more aware of the importance of their role. Yet others had difficulty singling out the camera as the primary factor in shaping their courtroom behavior. Regardless of the cameras, these witnesses would have felt the enormous pressure intrinsic in such a sensational and highly publicized trial.

Still other witnesses were well aware that their testimony was seen as part of a larger framework that existed outside the courtroom. Nervous and apprehensive about their roles in this sensational trial, the camera proved to be an intimidating, if not inhibiting, presence. For some, however, including Hedda Nussbaum, a key witness, the camera was seen as an instrument to reach a larger audience with a social agenda distinct from the issues of the case. They admitted "playing" to two audiences, the spectators and trial personnel in the courtroom and the viewing public.

Dr. Douglas Miller, a neuropathologist at New York University Medical Center, was a key medical witness for the prosecution at the Steinberg trial. His testimony was considered vital to the prosecution, which charged that Lisa Steinberg was beaten to death by her father. Prior to taking the stand, Miller said that he felt slightly "amused" upon learning the trial would be televised. "I don't have any real ambition to be seen on television on the nightly news," he said. "Since this was such a celebrated case, it was inevitable that it was going to be on television—so I was a little amused by that." According to Miller, he had been informed by the prosecutors prior to his appearance in court that whatever the press thought about Hedda Nussbaum's testimony, his was the most crucial in the case. He said that he entered the courtroom convinced that his testimony would be a determining factor. "It was clear that when the defense was saying this wasn't homicide, I was clearly going to say that it was not an accident, not food poisoning; this was clearly head trauma, homicide."

But Miller later conceded that the presence of the camera and the awareness that his testimony was being broadcast nationally placed additional pressure on him. "It would be less than completely honest to say that all of us are so self-confident that we don't worry about what we might do," he said, "and I suppose if I had screwed up in some glorious way, then that certainly wouldn't be good for me to look like a fool on national television."

Other witnesses admitted having a more difficult time than Miller. The sensational aspects of the case, as depicted on television, made them wary of the medium's purpose in the courtroom and their relationship to it. Such awareness raised self-consciousness and anxiety. Dr. Mary Elizabeth Lell was one expert witness who recalled feeling "somewhat self-conscious about it." As the chief pediatric neurologist at St. Vincent's Hospital, Lell in her testimony provided the first medical evidence that Lisa's death was caused by a strong blow to the head and was not the result of an accident. Initially she said that she felt uneasy about appearing on camera. "You'd just as soon give the testimony and not have the sense that you were also being viewed every minute," she said.[17] Gradually, her awareness about being videotaped diminished as she focused her attention on the questions being posed to her.

Still, Lell was apprehensive and distrustful about having the television camera trained on her during her testimony. Disturbed over the sensational and "repulsive" treatment the case was receiving on television, she was concerned that her own involvement might be used to further "dramatize" the lurid aspects of the case. On a more personal level, as a pediatric medical expert she was especially anxious about the possibility that children might be exposed to televised testimony that detailed the horrific aspects of child abuse.

Because she believed that television had helped sensationalize the case, the camera's presence only served to remind her of "the reasons for it to be there." As a result, Lell noted that she was very conscious to testify in a deliberate, professional manner. "[The case] had gotten so much publicity, so much dramatization," she said, "that I really felt at this point it was much more important to deal with the facts than to stir up more dramatic effect."

Virtually all witnesses were aware of the significant impact of the Steinberg trial. In Lell's case, she was sensitive and self-conscious about the ability of television to choose selective portions of her testimony to add to the massive publicity surrounding the case. Other witnesses were less "television conscious" and more oblivious to the way they interacted with the medium. Dr. Patrick Kilhenny, though initially unaware that he was being videotaped while testifying, acknowledged that the camera's presence would have made him more nervous had he focused on it. Having played a significant role in evaluating Lisa's condition when she was admitted to St. Vincent's, Kilhenny thought it was imperative to present incriminating medical evidence as well as a personal and unsettling exchange between himself and Steinberg so that the jury could see him as "the criminal he is."[18] Watching news accounts of his testimony that evening, he was angry that television coverage had not stressed that point more strongly.

Besides Kilhenny, other witnesses were also concerned that their testimony was extending beyond the boundaries of the courtroom. But for one witness, the extension represented danger. Defense witness Marilyn Walton was much more critical and concerned about participating in a televised trial, sensitive to the fact that her testimony would be reaching a national audience. Like several other nonexpert witnesses at the trial, she feared the possibility of repercussions. An entertainer by profession, Walton claimed that she worked with "some very rough people." Furthermore, her friendship with Steinberg led her to suspect that many of the people she had met in his company were also criminal types. "Many of Joel's 'friends' were his clients . . . he was a *criminal* lawyer!" Knowing that they had access to the coverage of her testimony only made her angry, yet fearful and inhibited:

I was so conscious of it that at one point I finally refused to talk anymore. The judge asked me over for a bench conference. It was apparent to me that this court and its judge had no regard or consideration for my well-being and that I would have to protect myself from confusing and misleading dispersion of information in the form of questions from the prosecution. I was now a singer, and some of the people I sang for—people who owned and operated these clubs—were downright dangerous. Others were dull-witted and dangerous. That meant that the most innocent remark, action, or reaction had the capacity for being misunderstood, arousing baseless suspicion, or complicating perceptions of me. The most innocent act could have generated a paranoia in some which might have been costly. I didn't want to become a casualty of a mistaken impression.

REACTION

Many court participants perceived varying degrees of nervousness and self-consciousness among witnesses. They attributed such behavior to the pressure engendered by an intimidating triangulation of massive public interest, media coverage, and cameras in the court. Juror Allen Jared said several witnesses were visibly nervous, possibly because their testimony was being videotaped. "I would assume that having the camera in the courtroom did affect them," he said.[19] From his vantage point, Jared believed that the camera "was a definite factor" that exacerbated the emotional condition of at least two witnesses who were already nervous and apprehensive about testifying. He cited Hedda Nussbaum as one witness who appeared to be directly influenced by the presence of the in-court camera, a perception shared by Nussbaum's lawyer, Barry Scheck.

"I just think [the television camera] made it more difficult for her to testify," said Scheck. "It was hard enough for her to get up there in front of all these people in the courtroom, and him [Steinberg], and everybody and the jury. But then to have the conscious awareness that all America could see her, I'm really sure put tremendous pressure on an already quite fragile woman."

Jared and other court participants singled out a second witness, Marilyn Walton, as someone who consciously appeared to "play" to the camera. Her performance on the stand was described by Jared and other participants as embellished and "flamboyant," as if she were directly playing to an audience beyond the courtroom walls. Shrugging at Walton's protestations that the camera had, in fact, inhibited her on the stand, Jared said, "I think she enjoyed having [the television camera] there. It's sort of hard to describe . . . the way she held herself, the way she dressed, the way she sat. She did her best to smile a lot. She tried to show a lot of personality, I thought. She is a performer as well, so I think she was quite pleased that television was there."

Prosecutors Casolaro and McCusker also perceived Walton's mannerisms and dramatic language as being indicative of her awareness of television. "You have the situation where the woman is an entertainer by occupation," said McCusker, "and I certainly got the impression she enjoyed being there and did play up to the camera. I think that the other people who were affected were probably a little less animated and a little less forthcoming."

While the camera may have induced Walton to overstate her testimony, Casolaro said several prosecution witnesses reacted differently, becoming more recalcitrant and nervous about testifying in a televised trial. Witnesses are invariably uncomfortable testifying in any murder trial, he said, but placing television into the judicial process made his job more difficult. Said Casolaro: "I think some of the witnesses were affected by it, but I don't think it changed their answers. I think it just made them more self-conscious than they'd already be."

McCusker noted, however, that even if witnesses remained consistent in presenting testimony, their courtroom personality often was altered by the camera. Even subtle, nonverbal changes in the performance of a witness can have a marked effect on the way that testimony is being received and translated by the jury. He said: "Jurors do pick up on body language, the way that a person answers a question, and the fact that the person is, or is not, aware of the media coverage."

Ira London was aware of two defense witnesses who "clammed up because they got so nervous," but could not evaluate whether it was the in-court camera or the emotionally charged trial environment itself that caused this reaction. Patricia McAdams, a nurse at St. Vincent's Hospital, and an unnamed superintendent were both visibly shaken at having to testify, said London, adding, "We had to force it out of them." In another instance, an expert witness for the defense requested a videotape of his testimony, presumably to critique his own performance.

Most court participants were able to distinguish between the performance of expert and nonexpert witnesses, observing that the medical and law enforcement experts seemed more assured and less self-conscious than did their counterparts. According to Judge Rothwax, "I think they were aware, as we were, that it was a case of great public notoriety and again, I don't think the camera made a difference on that." Juror Helena Barthell, however, noticed some marked distinctions in the performances of expert and nonexpert witnesses, attributing this difference to their level of court experience, as well as to the presence of television and the high visibility of the trial. For the most part, nonexperts were perceptibly nervous and uncomfortable, while experts seemed more self-assured. She observed, "The police officers seemed like this was very routine. For the doctors, many of whom had testified in other cases, it was pretty routine. It was the people like the janitor, and the neighbor, and the toll booth collector, people like that, this was their first time and they seemed terrified."[20]

THE LAWYERS

For the principal attorneys, the Steinberg trial would mark their first experience in a televised trial. But the defense attorneys and prosecutors differed as to the benefits of having cameras in the courtroom. Ira London and Adrian DiLuzio regarded television as another safeguard for their client's right to a public trial, while Peter Casolaro and John McCusker opposed it as an intrusive medium that could alter behavior and ultimately prove detrimental to the trial's outcome. The lawyers professed, however, that after the novelty of working in a televised trial subsided, they gradually lost self-consciousness about appearing before the court camera.

Casolaro contended that he was no more self-conscious during the Steinberg trial than he would have been in a nontelevised trial. Always careful in addressing the court, and realizing that his performance could be reviewed by the court of appeals, he claimed that television was not a factor, either in his preparation or in his courtroom activities. Unlike other lawyers in the case, Casolaro said that he was not concerned that the trial would reach a national and international television audience. The only time he admittedly felt pressure was just before the start of the trial and also during jury deliberations. "Most of the pressure I felt was when I was sitting here in this office, waiting," he said. Even before the television camera was admitted into the courtroom, "the case was very, very big. . . . I don't know whether it became more important because it reached a bigger audience. It may have made it more well-known."

Ira London, however, admitted to having a different experience. Describing himself as a "disciplined" lawyer, London said he soon became comfortable working before the camera. But there was at least one major juncture in the trial where he felt enormous pressure and became acutely self-conscious. When Hedda Nussbaum took the stand, London suddenly realized that his cross-examination would be seen not only nationwide, but also internationally, playing on television as far away as Australia. This awareness called to mind the "awesome" responsibility he had in the case and the possible ramifications such coverage could have for his reputation.

There were some moments [before cross-examining Nussbaum] where I said to myself, my God, no other lawyer in this country has gotten up to cross-examine the principal witness in a murder case live, on national and international television. It was a thought, and it made the cross-examination of her a little more awesome than it was. If Hedda was accepted as a credible witness, the case was over, we knew that. When I got up, and the fact that it was going to be televised live throughout the world, we laughed about it. You know, my God, Adrian, I would say, if I fluff, they're going to see it all over the world.

Prior to his cross-examination London was nervous and "a bit twitchy." He described it as "doing a turn on stage or anything that someone does in front of an audience." Once involved with the questioning, however, he contended that the camera faded into the background and he was able to concentrate on his work. "I've learned to focus on what I'm doing," he said. "I don't focus any attention to myself. My attention is on what I'm doing, and the witness. And with Hedda, I was committed to getting inside her head."

DiLuzio also acknowledged that as a "professional performer" in a televised trial he was concerned about how he would be received by a media-oriented public. In the Steinberg case, it would not be a "small community that's going to pass judgment" but a large, vast public who would make decisions based on media accounts of the trial. He admitted such concerns heightened his anxiety. "I think any lawyer who says he doesn't have any anxiety is either crazy or a liar," he said.

Of serious concern is whether such "media self-consciousness" played a part in significantly altering the behavior of participants during the trial. Though lawyers admitted to varying degrees of self-consciousness before the camera, did that state of mind somehow influence or change the normal patterns of behavior in the courtroom?

Both London and DiLuzio said that the prosecutors performed as expected, seemingly unconcerned with the camera. The prosecutors, however, perceived the defense attorneys as appearing media conscious at times, acting for the benefit of the camera. McCusker observed that they "postured for the cameras quite a bit." He said, "I know my perception was, when Ira, for example, asked a witness to look at a particular exhibit, he would make a point of giving the exhibit to the person and turn it to face the camera." At other times, "there were little things that came up during cross-examination particularly that were meant to play on the evening news that night."

McCusker believed that London and DiLuzio would purposely select "sound bites," short, provocative statements or questions designed to create dramatic effect and to attract television coverage. He cited one incident as an example of the defense team's deliberate ploy to reach a television audience. London had been cross-examining Hedda Nussbaum, trying to attack her memory of the events leading up to her daughter's death. Facing a recalcitrant witness, he finally asked, "Have you placed a sanitary cordon of forgetfulness around that night?" It was a poetic phrase that differed from London's normal speech patterns and mode of questioning. The question was repeated again later that afternoon: Had Nussbaum placed "a sanitary cordon of forgetfulness" around the night Lisa was killed? (Jan Volk, a reporter covering the trial, discovered that London had taken the phrase from Primo Levi's *The Drowned and the Saved*, a book he had recently read.)

Casolaro had a different interpretation of the defense attorneys' actions, explaining that they "defended their case the best they could with a difficult client." He did not perceive London's and DiLuzio's behavior as falling outside the boundaries of normal courtroom interactions. But he remained doubtful that lawyers in other cases would resist the temptation to grandstand before the camera in order to enhance their reputations. Casolaro maintained that lawyers dealing with one-sided cases might "try to save face" on television, rather than working in the best interests of their clients. Even in closely contested cases, he contended that the potential for lawyers to play to a television audience as proof that they are highly skilled could be troublesome and detrimental to the workings of the court. Casolaro noted, however, that Steinberg's lawyers "were trying to do more than save face, they were trying to get the best verdict they could get."

REACTION

According to Judge Rothwax, the lawyers were not grandstanding. Although he had been extremely critical of the defense attorneys for conducting hallway interviews with the press at almost every break in the proceedings, inside the courtroom he concluded that they behaved professionally and did not appear to conduct their defense for the purposes of television. "They may have done that out in the hallway, but they could have done that whether there were cameras in the courtroom or not."

Judge Rothwax concluded that the essence of a lawyer's performance is geared toward persuading a jury; the camera serves no greater purpose than to mirror that performance. "Attorneys and judges are always before the public, they're always in front of the jury, they're always aware of their impact on the jury, and they're always playing to an audience," he said. The camera's presence merely gives them a chance to see themselves as others see them and "to refine or hone their performance to greater effectiveness or greater persuasiveness."

But Barry Scheck disagreed. He perceived both the judge and the lawyers to be media conscious, and this awareness changed the way they behaved in court. "They were not conscious on a daily basis, but I think television coverage in general affected their behavior," he said. "I don't know if it was any greater than you would have had in the ordinary high-profile, publicized trial. But I think to some degree, it's got to be a little greater."

Other participants had mixed perceptions about the lawyers and whether or not they consciously altered their performance knowing they were part of a televised trial. Jurors, for instance, were uncertain whether the trial lawyers were being overly theatrical on occasion to dramatize their case for the jury or for television.

One witness who was emphatic in describing her perceptions of the lawyers' performance was Marilyn Walton. A close friend of the defendant and a defense witness in the case, Walton had publicly maintained that it was not Joel Steinberg, but Hedda Nussbaum who had been responsible for Lisa's death. She was openly critical of the prosecution during the trial, charging that Peter Casolaro had deliberately orchestrated Hedda Nussbaum's testimony in order to appeal to a national audience. Accusing the prosecutor of making leading statements as he questioned Nussbaum, Walton said, "He was carefully guiding Hedda to say things, and they were out and out lies!" She insisted, "It wasn't the jury he was trying to convince"; he was attempting to win public sympathy for Nussbaum "on the assumption that she is a battered woman." In creating Nussbaum as a victim in the public's mind, instead of a culpable participant in the killing of Lisa Steinberg, Walton claimed that the prosecution now had "every wife in America suddenly look at her husband and say, 'that son-of-a-bitch, and if you *ever* do that to me. . . .' "

Walton also accused Steinberg's own lead counsel, Ira London, of posturing for the cameras "so that his entire line of questioning and defense strategy was fractured, without point or direction." She said that the lawyer "appeared to have lacked the most basic resolve to defend his client" by failing to aggressively counter the prosecution's principal witness, Hedda Nussbaum.

London never embarked on questioning that called Hedda to account for her own cocaine addiction, her own alleged participation in child pornography, her own alleged activities in sado-masochistic sex, her alleged initiation of a three-year-old Lisa into sexual perversions with adult males. I believe the presence of the cameras made Casolaro and London hypersensitive toward appearing to the female population as "verbal" or "emotional batterers" of Hedda Nussbaum. So as not to appear as "brutal men," a close and hard examination of this woman was left wanting, the truth of what really happened to Lisa was lost—all because no one wanted to appear negatively before the cameras.

THE JURY

Jurors were relieved that the state rules that governed in-court cameras did not allow television personnel to film them, unlike some other states that allow camera coverage of *voir dire* as well as sitting jury members. Given such leeway, they believed the cameras would have made them more self-conscious and would only have distracted them from performing their duties in court. Helena Barthell, for example, said that she would be more concerned and preoccupied about her appearance instead of diligently following the proceedings. "I'd have to worry, did they catch me slouching, or maybe I should put makeup on," she said. Another juror believed that filming the jury for television would undermine their anonymity and possibly make them more vulnerable to outside influences or threats.

The jurors were supported by Judge Rothwax, who now endorsed the use of courtroom cameras, but opposed widening their range to include shots of the jury. "To show pictures of the jurors is to increase public pressure on them over a long period of time," he said.

Still and videotape photography are distinctly different from the artist sketch, and although court artists are allowed to sketch the jury, Judge Rothwax maintained that in "the drawings you can't identify anyone." He explained: "You see someone over the air—their neighbors, the grocery store, the cleaners—you increase the number of people who are going to be aware of the jurors in this case, who can run up and talk to them and [say] 'Kill the monster,' or that kind of thing. That imports dangers into the process that are not necessary for the purposes the cameras are there for."

Barthell, while opposed to allowing television to film jury members, was open to the idea that the court camera could help safeguard the judicial process by keeping jury members alert and attentive. She disclosed that several jurors had trouble staying awake during testimony that was often lengthy or highly technical. These jurors would fall asleep intermittently, said Barthell; during one session, she counted four jurors sleeping at the same time. "Three jurors wore sunglasses more than they didn't wear sunglasses. And they never wore them in the jury room." Jurors would openly admit falling asleep in court, contended Barthell. One incident was particularly upsetting, when she observed a juror asleep during the testimony of Dr. Douglas Miller, a key medical witness for the prosecution: "[Jury members] were teasing her in the jury room, like 'Boy, you slept through everything today,' and she said, 'Well, obviously I didn't miss much 'cause when I woke up he was saying the same thing as when I fell asleep this morning.' I just was like, oh damn, I can't believe these people could sleep through this. To me this was not a boring trial."

Barthell was very concerned that such behavior could lead to a mistrial. She believed that Judge Rothwax noticed these jurors "because we'd have one guy whose head would be tilted back and his mouth open catching flies." Rothwax could not help but notice their inattentiveness, she said, recalling that at one point during the proceedings he called a break, discreetly admonishing the jurors for "looking restless."

Barthell believed that in-court cameras could have perhaps prevented such mishaps. "I often wondered if the jury was being filmed would they be on a little bit better behavior?" she said. "I suspect they would." She acknowledged that jurors would be much more alert to testimony on the days the television sketch artists were in court. "If every Friday the camera's going to be there [and film the jury], I'm sure that every Friday everyone would be bright-eyed and bushy-tailed," she said.

In a follow-up interview, Judge Rothwax questioned Barthell's observations, emphasizing that "if jurors keep their eyes closed for any period of time, I tell them to keep their eyes open." He added that most of the case dealt with testimony that was dramatic and engrossing. It would be unlikely for a juror to fall asleep at a trial as spellbinding as the Steinberg case, and he contended, "You have to be awfully tired to sleep through that case."

Judge Rothwax also discounted Barthell's suggestion that allowing the camera to film the jury might make them more attentive to the proceedings. "It would be questionable in my mind that jurors who were not alert would suddenly be alert if a camera was focused on them," he said. "My own feeling is that if you're not alert, you're not alert, you're not conscious, and you don't react that much. So I'm not sure I accept that."

PUBLIC OPINION AND JURY DELIBERATIONS

The most worrisome concern that faced jurors was the overwhelming cacophony of public opinion. If jurors were diligent to avoid discussion of the case with close associates, could they also separate themselves from the surrounding public milieu that was saturated with media comment about the trial? Fearing that the integrity of jury members might be compromised by the clamor of public commentary, Judge Rothwax repeatedly reminded the jurors to divorce themselves from news accounts and discussion of the case outside the courtroom. While most jurors appeared to follow instructions conscientiously, the scope and magnitude of the Steinberg case made it extremely difficult for them to be completely unscathed by public opinion.

Even before the trial began, jurors were exposed to the massive pretrial publicity. During the proceedings, several admitted that it had been impossible to avoid banner headlines proclaiming Steinberg's guilt. Even those who insisted that they were untainted by media coverage remained very aware that the case was being closely monitored by a large public audience. Sensitivity to the burgeoning media attention increased after jurors learned that television was transmitting the trial to a national and international audience. When Hedda Nussbaum's testimony was televised in its entirety over the course of a week, jury members were astounded. According to Barthell, "When I heard that Hedda's testimony was preempting soap operas, preempting regular broadcasting, I said, 'Holy mackerel, this trial is much more important than I would have thought possible.' "

Still, some jurors maintained that public opinion, and their general awareness of the media, had little effect on the outcome of the trial: Knowing that a vast public was scrutinizing their actions did not place additional pressure to reach a verdict. Barthell acknowledged, however, that there were instances during deliberations where she feared the jury might be appearing foolish before the attending media and felt it necessary that the panel look more decisive and in control of their actions. Illustrating her point, she told of one incident in which jurors, upon entering the courtroom after hours of deliberation, were asked by Judge Rothwax whether they wanted to listen to extensive read-back testimony that night or resume the following day. The jurors struggled with the decision and could not seem to make up their minds. The protracted confusion prompted Rothwax to send them back to the jury room to come to a decision. Barthell recalled being concerned that "we're looking like fools here" and was anxious that the press was perceiving them as being not only indecisive, but also inept.

In front of the press and media, we can't even come to a decision on whether we want to hear something tonight or tomorrow. They're probably laughing in hysterics at us because there was this undercurrent and murmuring . . . that we were acting so indecisive. And the judge even said, "It is not appropriate to be discussing this out here, would you like to go back to the jury room?" And some people were saying yes, let's go back, others were saying no, no, just say tomorrow, just say tonight. Finally the judge doesn't even wait for us to give an answer and says go into the jury room, come back with your answer. And when we left to go into the jury room, Joel was grinning ear to ear. We are thinking the press is loving this, they're laughing at us. We're looking like a bunch of idiots. So we finally came to some decision and went out and told our answer. But two or three days later, the same thing happened again. But this time the judge didn't give us a chance to make fools of ourselves. He said go into the jury room and let him know.

During the lengthy deliberations, Barthell found herself empathizing with news reporters camped outside in the corridors awaiting the jury's decision. She remembered feeling "these poor guys, I wish they could go home and get some rest, because I knew early on that we're going to be here a while." But she insisted that the jury was not coerced into reaching a verdict quickly because of the widespread media attention given to the case. Indeed, the lengthy eight-day deliberative process was turbulent and at times marked by personal confrontations and recalcitrance.

In a prepared statement to the press following the verdict, Jeremiah Cole said, "I want to stress the extreme difficulty we had at arriving at a unanimous verdict. First, it became apparent that some jurors would never vote guilty on the first-degree murder count. Secondly, some who voted yes [on murder in the second degree] began to have doubts."[21]

According to jurors' accounts, the group was divided into three factions: four members had initially voted for second-degree murder, five were undecided, and three believed that it was Hedda Nussbaum who had committed the crime. The first vote on the murder count was 8–4 for conviction, which later reached 10–2. Jury members had finally resolved that Nussbaum could not have killed her daughter and that Steinberg had recklessly struck Lisa; he had further endangered her life by failing to seek immediate medical assistance. But several jurors remained doubtful about an important element in the murder charge: that Steinberg had demonstrated "depraved indifference" toward Lisa's life. The prosecution had failed to prove conclusively that Steinberg was fully cognizant of Lisa's life-threatening injuries when he delayed summoning medical assistance.

Barthell feared that rising emotions might forestall a verdict. She had strongly believed in Steinberg's guilt on the second-degree murder charge, but "I didn't want a hung jury because I thought that was a terrible thing, a terrible waste of time and money and he could walk the streets free."

On January 30, 1989, after nearly 70 hours of deliberation, the jury came back with a conviction of first-degree manslaughter. Jurors conceded that the decision had been a compromise, not satisfactory to everyone, but one that served the interests of justice.

At the end of the trial, major participants conjectured whether the overwhelming media attention to the case had hovered over the jurors and affected them during deliberations. Judge Rothwax believed that their verdict stood as proof that the media and public opinion had not influenced them. "You would have expected Steinberg would have been convicted of murder and he was convicted on manslaughter," he said. "I certainly don't think that the jury felt themselves pressured by the media, I don't think so at all. They really went about it in a very well-organized fashion, they deliberated for eight days. If they were feeling that kind of pressure, you would have expected a verdict much sooner."

But prosecutor John McCusker differed with the judge's assessment. The glaring sensationalism, aggravated by the intense media coverage surrounding the case, may have in fact influenced the outcome of the trial. But rather than working against Steinberg, he speculated that mediated public pressure could have had a converse effect on jury members. The jury was much too solicitous toward Steinberg, said McCusker, and may have "bent over backwards" to compensate for the negative publicity against him. That sensitivity may have also been reflected in the jury's decision not to convict Steinberg of murder. "I think that in some ways, [media coverage] in the long run may have hurt us because the jury was very conscious of the public's attitude," he said.

McCusker conceded that he had difficulty gauging the extent to which the jury was exposed to media coverage. "But when you pick up newspapers and see profiles of the jurors and caricatures of the jurors, and that type of thing," he said, it seemed likely that "they were quite aware of the attention that they're getting and the attention they are going to get after the verdict."

In March 1989, Joel Steinberg was sentenced to a maximum term of $8\frac{1}{3}$ to 25 years.

The Hedda Nussbaum Testimony

The testimony of Hedda Nussbaum was an extraordinary event. From a legal perspective, Nussbaum's detailed accounting was the prosecution's linchpin in a case based primarily on circumstantial evidence. Of the four people who lived at 14 West 10th Street, she was the only direct link to the events surrounding the night of Lisa Steinberg's death, other than Joel Steinberg himself, who was silent for fear of self-incrimination. From a societal perspective, her battered appearance on the stand rudely awakened a city ensconced in wealth and status to the harsh realities of familial abuse. From the perspective of the New York camera experiment, the gavel-to-gavel coverage of her testimony would demonstrate television's inherent power as a news medium and its potential to impact the courtroom environment.

In the seventh week of the trial, Hedda Nussbaum took the stand, and her testimony became a media event. Prior to her appearance, local stations had provided daily coverage of the trial using selected clips on the nightly news. But Nussbaum's testimony marked a turning point, with three network affiliates preempting local soap operas and talk shows to broadcast it live to millions of New Yorkers. Sam Ehrlich, a writer, stated that television's response to the Nussbaum testimony "was an unprecedented translation of private trauma into public drama."[1] WCBS broadcast six days of her testimony; WNBC and WABC were more sparing, but still provided extensive coverage. Roger Colloff, vice president and general manager for WCBS, said, "Child abuse, spouse abuse, drug abuse—just all sorts of things came out during the course of that testimony. It came out over a long period of time and wasn't neatly wrapped in a tiny little package with a bow tied around it."[2]

In the aftermath of the Steinberg trial, a telephone interview with Nussbaum was conducted via her lawyer, Barry Scheck. Nussbaum was still a patient at Four Winds Hospital, a private psychiatric center. Her part in the tragic circumstances surrounding Lisa's death had divided public opinion. She was alternately viewed as a victim herself, a battered woman who literally bore the scars of physical and mental abuse, or as a criminal who may have had responsibility in her daughter's death. Said Susan Brownmiller, "To me the primary issue is child abuse and unfit parents who just did not understand that in babies begin responsibility and that's why I hold them both morally culpable."[3]

Along with Joel Steinberg, Nussbaum initially was charged with second-degree murder. But a month prior to the trial, the district attorneys' office dropped the charge in return for Nussbaum's testimony against Steinberg. The prosecution contended that having been a victim of physical and psychological abuse herself, she was incapable of either harming her daughter or intervening in her defense. In the early part of the trial, Judge Rothwax would describe her as "the single most important witness in the case."[4]

Though 13 months had passed since her arrest, on the witness stand Nussbaum still bore disturbing signs of the physical torture she had endured. Although she had undergone reconstructive surgery, her nose remained flattened and bent, her upper lip was misshapen, and her cheeks were visibly scarred even under the heavy pancake makeup. Though spectators in the rear of the courtroom could not clearly discern the deformities, on television Nussbaum's image was a grim reminder of her violent history. "I think the television image particularly repeated that strongly," said columnist Pete Hamill. "That's why I said in one of my columns that we'll remember that face forever, we'll remember it because of the repetition."[5]

THE TRIAL

Despite her physical condition in the courtroom, Nussbaum had vastly improved since the night of her arrest on November 2, 1987. A five-minute videotape, recorded at the Sixth Precinct station house that evening, was played for the jury. Jurors noticeably winced at the sight of Nussbaum on tape. A mass of bruises covered most of her body. The cartilage in her nose had completely collapsed, her face was severely swollen and clumps of her hair were missing. Her lip had been split, her ribs had been broken, and her right leg was enlarged and gangrenous, a physical state that caused one juror to audibly gasp.

A courtroom packed with spectators as well as a huge television audience watched transfixed as Nussbaum took the stand. In a flat, monotone voice, Nussbaum recounted the events leading up to her daughter's death. The first session was brief, lasting just 80 minutes with a short recess midway to allow her to regain her composure. Her testimony would span two weeks and cover a decade of depravity and abuse—a family life gone out of control, shattered by drug abuse, sadism, and beatings. Steinberg had so systematically abused her physically and degraded her emotionally that she was no longer able to function with any normalcy. Keeping her isolated, he caused her to lose her job as a book editor for Random House along with the last remnants of her independence and self-worth.

Nussbaum told the court that the relationship had become so damaging that she had contemplated suicide. The abuse had continued to escalate over the years and had nearly killed her. In 1981, Steinberg's violence had resulted in a ruptured spleen that required surgery. In subsequent years the beatings and cruel punishments had become habitual, and Nussbaum testified that Steinberg often "made me sleep on the floor or in the bathtub if I had displeased him." Several days into her testimony, she would admit that Lisa had also been abused shortly before her death.[6]

Though the details of Nussbaum's life with Steinberg were horrific, the prosecution's case was based on the "bizarre" events of November 1, 1987—events that left six-year-old Lisa beaten, comatose, and barely clinging to life. Nussbaum told the court that Lisa had entered her father's bedroom to ask if she would be accompanying him to dinner that evening. Moments later, she heard a thud, and Steinberg emerged with his daughter, unconscious in his arms. Nussbaum testified, "He said he had knocked her down but she didn't want to get up again," and recalled that Steinberg was upset with Lisa because "the staring was just too much. He said this staring business has got to stop." Lisa had been "talking in negatives, using words like 'can't' and 'won't.' Joel had been saying I was staring and the children were staring at him, that we were trying to hypnotize him."

According to Nussbaum, she attempted to revive the child by giving her artificial respiration, but "Joel said, 'Don't worry.' And he promised he would get her up when he came back. But she didn't wake up."

"I looked at the phone we kept in the bathroom," she continued, "and I started thinking, 'Should I phone 911?'"

"But I said, 'No, no, Joel said he would take care of her,' and I said to myself I should not be disloyal and not be distrustful. So I didn't call. I expected him to get Lisa up because he was a healer. I believed he had the power of healing."

"What led you to believe that?" asked Casolaro.

"Because once I had a bruise on my face and he rubbed it and it went away," she replied.

When Steinberg returned from dinner around midnight, Nussbaum said that he suggested they smoke cocaine. Lisa, meanwhile, still lay comatose on the bathroom floor. The couple continued to freebase cocaine until 4 A.M. while the child remained unconscious, her condition now grave and rapidly deteriorating.

Nussbaum said at one point that she attempted to diagnose Lisa's condition by consulting a medical manual. She stopped at the word "coma," but discounted it because "it sounded too permanent" to her. Two hours later, at about 6 A.M., Steinberg called to Nussbaum that the child had stopped breathing. Nussbaum remembers entering the bedroom and seeing "Joel frantically trying to revive her." She asked if she should summon help, but was told by Steinberg, "No, give me a chance first" as he tried to administer cardiopulmonary resuscitation. When his attempts failed, Nussbaum said, "He told me to call 911 and I did." Lisa was subsequently rushed to St. Vincent's Hospital where she died three days later.

Though Steinberg was on trial for the murder of his daughter, his life style with Nussbaum was also being scrutinized, extensively analyzed, and tried by the media. Author Susan Brownmiller, who wrote *Waverly Place*, a fictionalized treatment of the Steinberg-Nussbaum relationship, said, "What attracted me to the case from the beginning was the interconnection between Steinberg and Nussbaum. That without their bizarre relationship—and it was a reciprocal and very entwined relationship, it wasn't a one-way street—Lisa Steinberg would have been alive."

Such analysis and commentary within the press put greater emphasis on the question of Nussbaum's own culpability in Lisa's death. Following his cross-examination, Ira London concluded that "the public perception did a total turnabout. Before she took the stand, she was the darling of the feminist movement; people felt sorry for her. There isn't any doubt that when she left the witness stand, people saw her as a mother who sold her child's life out."[7]

Still, the strength of the prosecution's case rested with Nussbaum's testimony. In hundreds of hours of interviews her testimony would be carefully screened by the district attorneys' office. It would be further restricted by Judge Rothwax's legal mandate that there be a certain order to the direct examination. The prosecutors had been instructed that Nussbaum must first testify about the fatal night of November 1, 1987, and only then would she be allowed to provide a truncated history of her relationship with Steinberg. On the stand, Nussbaum seemed methodical and deliberate in her responses, taking long pauses in an apparent struggle to recall events exactly as they happened. But according to defense attorney Adrian DiLuzio, she was also deceptive and "infuriating . . . the worst kind of witness."

It made me angry because I perceived her as a person who was manipulating reality. She was the most deceptive witness you could ever imagine. She was the kind of witness who was capable of lying while telling the truth and I can give you a perfect example. The question Ira [London] put to her, referring to a letter that we wanted to question her about: In 1978 you went to summer camp, isn't that correct? Answer, no, I didn't go to summer camp. Question: Miss Nussbaum, weren't you a counselor in 1978? Yes, I was. Well, then didn't you go to summer camp in 1978? Well, no, I didn't go to summer camp, I was a counselor at summer camp. Well, isn't that the same thing? Well, I suppose so. Nothing she said was a lie, yet her initial answer was a lie because a truthful witness would have said, yeah, I went to summer camp, but not as a camper. You'd get a forthright answer. The question that raises is, for how many other questions did we fail to act properly enough within the constellation of what constitutes truth?[8]

But her attorney, Barry Scheck, and the prosecuting attorneys held a different opinion, praising Nussbaum for her ability to withstand enormous public pressure to present testimony that was sound and believable. "Hedda exceeded all our expectations," said Scheck. "She was devastatingly credible. Certainly that seemed to be the reaction the defense attorneys had when they suddenly tried to switch to an insanity defense. Given where she started, it's extraordinary."[9]

Ironically, Nussbaum's accounts, so extensively covered by the media, were rejected by some jurors in their final deliberations. In postverdict interviews, several jury members said they were skeptical of Nussbaum's testimony, believing it had been tainted by her own self-interests in the case. The fact that she appeared rational on the witness stand, responding to the extensive interrogation in a thoughtful and coherent manner, belied the image promoted by the prosecution: that Nussbaum was submissive, unable to discern reality, and virtually psychotic during the months leading up to Lisa's death. According to Scheck, television propagated this misguided perception of her and helped to shift public sentiment against her. "The way that she testified reflected a considerably recovered woman," he said. "The image of that is so powerful that people kept on thinking, the woman I saw on the witness stand was the woman who was there that night."

Scheck noted that his client was limited in the scope of her testimony to that which had been carefully structured by the prosecution, a situation that undermined her own personal trauma within the courtroom and in the mind of the public. "The emphasis that was put on her testimony in terms of the material selected, the order that it was selected, was designed to make people think she was a pretty good reporter who was reliable and credible and who you can trust. What was de-emphasized was the extent to which on the night in question, she was plainly psychotic, and that she was suffering from extraordinary delusions."

There were 35 areas of abuse and criminal action that occurred in her years with Steinberg of which the jury would remain unaware, said Scheck. In one such instance, while the couple freebased cocaine, Steinberg had allegedly taken a blowtorch to Nussbaum's face. The burning left her face scarred and heavily pockmarked. "It would have gone a long way in putting in context exactly how all this could have happened to her," said Scheck, "and how she could have been reduced to the point she was on the fatal night in question."

In the trial's aftermath Scheck would criticize the press for not focusing more intently on the Steinberg-Nussbaum history. He contended that the torments Nussbaum had suffered had made her, in effect, another victim in the case.

You don't see in the media any real understanding of what happened. And what happened? The systematic way that all these things were taken away from her, her family, the way the drugs destroyed her mind, how she lost her support system, how he took work from her, destroying her manuscript, helping in losing her job, the way that the level of the intensity of the beatings increased, the implementation of the system in which she had to ask for food before she could eat and then was punished, or deprived of food for other things that were supposed to be wrong, how she had to ask permission about where she should sleep. She had to sleep on the floor, she couldn't get a cover. The systematic use of this kind of punishment and this imprisonment of her . . . really amounted to . . . captivity, to brainwashing.

TELEVISION AND HEDDA NUSSBAUM

Hedda Nussbaum had various reasons for electing to testify. From a legal standpoint, she was bound to an agreement with the district attorney to provide detailed information about the case in return for immunity from prosecution. But according to Scheck, his client was motivated by a second agenda. She was candid about her personal history and the circumstances surrounding her daughter's death because she felt her testimony would help the cause of other battered women who find themselves trapped in a destructive familial environment that can be life threatening. Said Scheck: "It might serve as an example that a person who was as terribly beaten and imprisoned psychologically as Hedda was—her terrible situation—could still find the strength to come forward and testify. That seemed to all of us very, very important and one of her very strong motivations then, and now, is that she can be of use to people in her situation. It's something that she feels she owes Lisa, something she feels she owes all those who have been supportive of her."

Scheck noted that initially Hedda was uncomfortable with the idea of testifying in a televised trial, but chose not to litigate the issue before Judge Rothwax. She realized, however, that through television she could reach a broader audience—one that would extend far beyond the confines of the courtroom. On the stand, she testified that she was, in fact, keenly aware of coverage and how her testimony was being disseminated by the media and interpreted by the public at large. Although Nussbaum was intent on exonerating herself from Lisa's death, Scheck maintained that "Hedda was painfully aware that, like it or not, she had been placed in a position of being a symbol." Numerous letters from other battered women and women's rights groups supporting her strengthened her resolve, and they decided, said Scheck, not to oppose the in-court camera. Instead, they would use the medium as a vehicle in which her plight as a victim of domestic violence could be brought to public attention. "It was our conscious choice that her best chance, really, to affect people given the situation she was in, is to let it be televised. And that's how the decision was made."

Nussbaum said that she had regularly watched herself on television. While her reactions to seeing herself varied, she maintained that she was more concerned with the opinions offered by the newscasters and the segments of her testimony they singled out for broadcast. She remembered being upset and angry by one news account in particular. In it, WNBC-TV news reporter Tony Guida remarked that Nussbaum's testimony seemed rehearsed and illustrated the point with a clip that showed her hesitating before giving an answer. According to Nussbaum, the inference was that her pauses were part of a well-planned performance, rather than being a sincere account of her recollections. Scheck agreed with his client's assessment:

The notion is that a spontaneous answer can be a less rehearsed answer. When she looked at that, she was upset because it was illustrating, in her mind, exactly the opposite and that when she was asked questions, she struggled very hard to give as precise and as honest an answer in each and every instance. When she was asked, "Can you recall something for which you were testifying out of your own experience, precise dates, and lots of events for the last two decades?" she tried very hard to remember and to be careful and try to give an answer to the question. She was trying to be thoughtful and that was characteristic of her testimony in general. She regarded this as the exact opposite of being rehearsed, so she thought that [Guida's report] was an example of a misinterpretative news report.

During the length of her testimony, Nussbaum and her lawyer would watch the nightly television coverage of the trial from her hotel room. According to Scheck, Nussbaum told him that she was pleased her testimony was being broadcast regularly and that she was anxious to watch other witnesses testify because "she wanted to see for herself everything that was preceeding it." She was disappointed to learn, however, that hers was the only testimony to be given such extensive coverage.

Nussbaum acknowledged that her curiosity and concerns extended beyond the actual testimony to how she appeared in the courtroom and notably how she looked on television, a fact she had revealed during Ira London's cross-examination. Media observers noted the change in Nussbaum's manner and dress during the period she was on the stand. On the first day, her appearance seemed rather severe—her gray hair cropped short and her dress plain and drab. Later, as she appeared more confident and animated testifying, Nussbaum began to dress in brighter clothing. For several days she wore brightly colored scarves that she would occasionally adjust on the stand. Court participants took note of her new apparel. Said Helena Barthell: "I think she was just trying to look pretty. She was just trying to look a little more groomed."[10]

But at least one fashion blunder had been made, according to her attorney. Referring to a flamboyant Korean Olympic scarf that seemed a favorite of Nussbaum's, Scheck called it "a mistake" that distracted and diverted attention away from her testimony. "It was a bad choice," he conceded. "I got scolded by Jack Litman [the defense attorney in the Robert Chambers murder trial], who asked, 'How can you let her go on camera with that scarf? It was very distracting.'"

Media observers also commented on Nussbaum's efforts to appear more presentable before the television camera. Susan Brownmiller described Nussbaum's attempts to "soften" her image:

The first day she looked like a prison matron. People were saying she looked tough and hard. What they didn't know was that her body was stiff from her injuries, so the total effect came across as tough and hard. But after that she softened her image. It was obvious to all of us [that] she had watched herself on television and had gotten a little bit of media advice from her friends between the first and second day.

Court members also noticed Nussbaum's distinctive mannerisms on the stand. But opinions differed as to whether these gestures were a "play" to the camera or merely representative of her physical demeanor. Jury Shirley Unger commented that each time Nussbaum sat, she would pull her skirt down in a deliberate manner; when she read a document, she would carefully remove her eyeglasses from a case and then methodically replace them. "She seemed to be a person who was very mannered in terms of her gestures," said Unger.[11]

Steinberg himself believed that Nussbaum's presentation and mannerisms were affected by the presence of the camera. He describes this in Chapter 12.

Prosecutor John McCusker had closely observed Nussbaum during the hundreds of hours of interviews prior to the trial and said that he noticed a marked change in her behavior once she entered the courtroom. He observed that she was "very conscious of the way her testimony was being received by the public and by the media" and that her "body language" on the stand was noticeably different than it had been in his office. "I don't think the substance of what she said was in any way affected by the media coverage," he said. "I do think that the way she conducted herself, her affect, the way she answered questions, was influenced by the media coverage." Explaining that such overt changes in a witness's physical posture can make a significant difference in the minds of the jurors, McCusker added, "I think oftentimes a witness's affect, the manner in which she presents herself, is as important as what she's saying."[12]

Peter Casolaro, who conducted the Nussbaum direct examination during the trial, disagreed with McCusker and others who claimed that she had played to the camera while testifying. He took particular exception to one charge that he believed was unfounded. At certain points during the questioning, whenever she was uncertain of how to respond, Nussbaum would characteristically close her eyes, squint, and then look up in a long, extended pause that seemed to indicate she was struggling for an answer. Some participants felt the gesture was a deliberate overreaction. But Casolaro maintained, "She was always like that from the first time we talked to her. In fact, a lot of our interviews were so long because we'd ask questions and we'd get that same pause and wait for the answer. She did that all the time. So if people interpreted that as body language, that she was playing to the camera, that's a mistake."[13]

Judge Rothwax warned that the camera was not the only variable in the courtroom that could have made Nussbaum self-conscious. He raised the possibility that her sister and lawyer, who were also present, may have been more influential than the presence of television. "Even if the camera's not in the courtroom, her sister and her lawyer are going to be saying, 'Look, this is the way you're coming across or this is the way you're behaving and you ought to modify your behavior.' "[14]

Nussbaum herself stated that the only time she consciously tried to change her body language was when she entered the courtroom. Suffering from degenerative osteoporosis that stiffened her hip and legs, Nussbaum said that she was uneasy about her awkward gait and made a concerted effort to compensate by attempting to present a more natural, flowing walk.

The extensive television coverage of Nussbaum's testimony was significant in that it had a dual effect. While revealing to a vast television audience the history of her relationship with Steinberg and all its tragic overtones, it also enabled her to turn inward, to closely examine herself at a crucial time in her recovery from severe trauma. Television, according to Scheck, acted as a mirror and reawakened Nusbaum to her own physical state of being. This self-discovery may have affected her performance and heightened her awareness of her courtroom appearance. Scheck recounted one poignant and revealing incident that occurred after he and Nussbaum had returned to her hotel room following the first day of her testimony. After watching herself on television and then staring at her image in the mirror, Nussbaum began to cry. She was upset, Scheck recalled her explaining, because she suddenly realized the full dimensions of the physical abuse she had suffered. She knew at that moment that she would never again be the same.

As a teenager she would look in the mirror a lot. She was very pretty. She would almost all the time enjoy looking in the mirror. In mental hospitals they do not have mirrors and they keep them out of the rooms. She had been in mental hospitals [for the last year]. So [her emotional outcry] was, in part, a reaction to seeing herself on television. But she suddenly realized that even though she was told over the ensuing months that she was looking better and better after having a number of operations, plastic surgery for her nose and her eyes—that just as she physically improved and became better nourished, it suddenly hit her that first evening that she had been terribly scarred. Even though she might have been looking better, she was never going to look the same way that she had before Joel began beating her. She began to think, maybe I'm not improving as much as I think I am. It was a very sad moment for her, and I don't know whether that would have occurred to her as forcefully if she hadn't been watching herself on television.

Nussbaum was not the only person affected by the presence of the camera. While she was taking center stage inside the courtroom, her lawyer was besieged by reporters, the photo-press and other media in the hallway corridors. Scheck disclosed that he spent many hours talking to the media off the record on behalf of Nussbaum. Though he was initially reluctant to discuss her testimony with the press, he candidly admitted that he was compelled to take a more visible public stance to counter accusations made against his client. With Ira London criticizing Nussbaum's court performance in his hallway conferences, Scheck believed that he had no choice but to present his case to the media as well. "He's attacking my client and I felt I had to defend her," he said.

According to Scheck, the cameras in the courtroom had directly inspired a more aggressive press, eager to report "spins" from lawyers in the case. The extraordinary live television coverage given to his client's testimony had created tremendous competition between both the print and the electronic press "for something new and different." This resulted in media more willing to report the "unbelievable number of leaks" of confidential materials, many of them associated with his client.

Scheck found himself constantly trying to diffuse inflammatory television reports based on these leaks. In one instance, he criticized a television news account that had disclosed Nussbaum's confidential psychiatric reports in which she purportedly stated that "she has to think about herself now" in the aftermath of Lisa's death and her subsequent arrest. According to Scheck, this segment of the story was out of context and not indicative of Nussbaum's true state of mind. Just beginning to come to terms with the "overwhelming losses" that she had suffered, her words, said Scheck, merely echoed the statement made by a psychologist who was helping her cope with the tragedy. "These statements were put out of context and put us in a terrible position," he contended.

In addition to such leaks, Scheck said that television was working against Nussbaum in other ways. Interpretations of her testimony in the form of sound bites helped to create misguided impressions "that did not necessarily reflect what was going on." Daily newscasts drew inferences and conclusions often counter to the actual content of Nussbaum's testimony. Television had, in essence, created a paradoxical situation. While allowing an audience to view her testimony in its entirety, it also reduced it to short and often decontextualized snippets of information that were easily digested. "If somebody had watched [her testimony] all day, they would have gotten a different gut feeling than having watched the sound bites on the 6 or 11 o'clock news," said Scheck. "I think the primary problem with trying to make the argument that the Nussbaum case was the greatest example in the world of cameras in the courtroom is that the coverage is just as influential with its sound bites and its attention to conflict."

WCBS–TV AND THE NUSSBAUM TESTIMONY

An interesting sidebar to the Nussbaum testimony was the behind-the-scenes decisions by major local stations as to how they would report the event. By airing the testimony live, stations broke new ground in the camera experiment. Of the three network affiliates, WCBS pursued the Nussbaum testimony most aggressively with gavel-to-gavel coverage. The other major stations, WABC and WNBC, prompted by their WCBS competitor, broadcast several hours of coverage, but declined to go gavel-to-gavel. "We gave it about 75 percent of what CBS did," said Michael Callaghan, managing news editor for WNBC. In hindsight, he added, he was disappointed that the station was not more aggressive. "Frankly, I would have liked to have seen us give the Steinberg case more coverage than we did."[15] Still other local syndicated stations opposed committing any of their resources to such extensive coverage. Paul Smirnoff, the executive producer for Fox News, explained:

Blowing out what we believed would have been eight hours of programming a day would have been financially difficult for us. On top of that, our audience during the day is a little different from the [major stations]. As opposed to having soap operas and therefore adults watching, our daytime audience is often children and in the long run it would cost us a great deal in terms of animosity from parents. That's a problem. We discussed it and decided not to go for it.[16]

For six days between December 1 and December 12, 1989, WCBS-TV was the most aggressive station in New York, airing 18 hours and 31 minutes of live testimony, which included Nussbaum's complete direct and cross-examination. The coverage was particularly difficult in that WCBS was required to preempt local programming. It was a move that would irritate network executives, anger some television viewers, and result in lost advertising revenues for the station. Programming problems also had to be overcome, such as filling "dead time" when the camera was required to shut down during certain court proceedings.

"Did we know what we were getting into, that it would run over six days and would preempt 18 hours?" asked Steve Paulus, assistant news director. "We probably didn't think that out as well as we might have. If we would have thought about it, we would have taken it nonetheless."[17]

The first critical decision made by the station's management was whether to air the live testimony at all. WCBS executive Roger Colloff recalled that there was little debate among the top executive managers. They felt the trial was important, with strong reverberations for many family viewers. "Anybody who ever had kids knows what this is all about," said Colloff. "[This case] involved the entire family. It involved a husband and wife, it involved a child who is dead, a child who was abused. I mean there are just all sorts of implications." Previously, judges in high-profile cases such as the Howard Beach and the Robert Chambers trials had limited or banned the use of the in-court camera altogether. The Steinberg trial provided the station with a unique opportunity to telecast extensive live testimony, since the courtroom experiment was legislated in New York State.

According to Colloff, broadcasting Nussbaum's testimony had tangible benefits for special groups, as well as the general audience, that were now able to see courtroom proceedings in an extended form. "We got a number of calls from hot lines that handle physical abuse," he recounted, "and they reported that their call volume was up dramatically during the period of time the Nussbaum testimony was carried. Clearly, it seems [to be] the reaction of women in similar situations . . . taking action as a result of hearing Hedda Nussbaum describe what had happened."

Paulus recalled that the station was unclear in the beginning about how much air time to allow for the Nussbaum testimony, and a decision had not yet been made whether to go gavel-to-gavel. "We took direct questioning," he said. "We had to take cross-examination in terms of fairness. Once we went ahead and aired some of her testimony live, the feeling here was that we had to take the cross-examination. That's why we stayed with it gavel-to-gavel."

The station received some complaints from devoted soap opera fans angry at the preempting of their favorite shows, but, said Colloff, "There's always a risk in doing something like that, but I think we felt that the risk was outweighed by the potential benefits that the broader audience would view this." Paulus contended, however, that despite some criticism, the television audience was intrigued by the coverage. "People loved it," he said. "People would call and ask when it was going to be on. The irony is that we were preempting 'People's Court' to show live courtroom proceedings." He added that he does not imagine that the television audience "took the real stuff for the fake stuff," but were intrigued by Nussbaum's engrossing testimony. He noted that ratings during the live coverage were occasionally higher than for regularly scheduled programming. But "it didn't make us any money since it wasn't sponsored."

Colloff was quick to note that the loss of revenues from preempting regular programming was never a factor in his decision to air Nussbaum's testimony, although he had to contend with network executives who are "never thrilled when you preempt network time." He explained: "Some of it was local time but a lot of it was network time we preempted. They weren't thrilled about it, but neither did they argue. I think they understood the importance of the trial. There really wasn't any way for them to say you shouldn't do this. There wasn't an effective counter argument to our saying we think this is an important thing to do in the New York metropolitan area." Encouraged by the response to the Nussbaum telecast, WCBS later ran live broadcasts of Judge Rothwax's two-hour charge to the jury and the sentencing of Joel Steinberg.

Despite general public acclaim for airing the Nussbaum testimony, the station was criticized in the press for the type of coverage that accompanied the court proceedings. Since the camera had to be shut down during bench conferences and various breaks in the proceedings, the station had to fill long lapses in the direct television feed with "instant analysis" and "play by play" commentary by newscasters and legal "experts." During one such segment, a doctor who had treated Nussbaum at Mount Sinai Hospital elucidated on her testimony. Such coverage lent fuel to press criticism that the medium could operate only in an entertainment mode that ultimately reduces public discourse to a "sporting event" with "winners and losers."

"We took some flak in the press because we did what was described as 'play by play,'" said Paulus. "I think that was unfair because we had no alternative. The camera in the court went off, and we had to, in essence, kill time." The breaks in court proceedings could be lengthy. On December 2, 1988, during Nussbaum's first full day on the stand, WCBS aired her testimony from 10:28 A.M. to 12:45 P.M. and resumed coverage at 2:21 P.M. Paulus said, "We can't jump in and out of regular programming, and it would be impossible. We had to do [commentary]. There was no other way. I mean we could have gone to dead air, [but] the very nature of the process forced us into analyzing the proceedings."

In spite of this criticism, station executives maintained that court proceedings fit into the constraints of the medium and that Nussbaum's testimony, in particular, proved to be absorbing television. "I think in this case it was riveting television," said Colloff. "People had seen her face so much and she still obviously bore the scars of what she'd been through. This was the face of a person who had been through hell. And that was evident in both what she was saying and in just looking at her, just the physical abuse she'd been through."

Feedback: Television's "Mirror"

Televising the Steinberg trial gave court participants a chance not only to view their performances in their roles as lawyers, witnesses, and judge, but also to evaluate how others appeared as they were reconstituted by television. We examined whether this televised "feedback"—this public "mirror"—somehow changed the way in which major trial participants saw themselves and their place within one of the celebrated cases of the decade.

The feedback effect is not without a theoretical history. Some theorists believe that the way a person responds to his surroundings has a direct relationship to the feedback he receives from others. Social psychologist Erving Goffman has employed a dramaturgical metaphor to discuss the manner in which each person presents himself in everyday social relationships. Like the "actor," individuals use certain techniques in order to sustain a "performance" and control the impressions formulated by others. He writes: "When an individual plays a part he implicitly requests his observers to take seriously the impression that is fostered before them. They are asked to believe that the character they see actually possesses the attributes he appears to possess, that the task he performs will have the consequences that are implicitly claimed for it."[1]

Goffman notes that in daily social interactions each individual must adjust his behavior to conform to what he describes as a "definition of situation," the expectations that others may have of his performance. "This constitutes one way in which a performance is 'socialized,' molded and modified to fit the understanding and expectations of the society in which it is presented."[2]

Televised trials present a unique and complex communications transaction. Unlike Goffman's theatrical model representing typical interpersonal relationships, television allows participants to interact with their own performances by eliminating the distinction between actor and audience. No longer a distinct entity, the court participant becomes a viewer, scrutinizing his own remarks, body language, and the nuances of the performance as broadcast on television. As an actor–audience member, he can evaluate and redefine the situation and alter his behavior accordingly.

Jurists and lawmakers historically have understood the significance of this type of direct feedback and have concluded that viewing news accounts of a trial can have a detrimental effect on court participants. In virtually all states, for instance, legal regulations forbid jurors from following news reports of their trial, fearing such reports will influence their judgments and deliberations. The use of in-court cameras presents a unique dilemma for the legal system. While enabling a large audience to keep abreast of a particular trial and become more familiar with the workings of the judicial system, it also allows court members to view actual proceedings in which they are participants.

The consequences of direct feedback have been clearly documented in legal writings on the subject of cameras in the court. They suggest that court participants who watch media coverage of a trial are in danger of altering behavior, attitudes, and judgments to fit a self-styled image that they wish to project on television. Even jurors, under court instructions to ignore news coverage of a trial, may be induced by a highly accessible medium to follow these court proceedings on television. It would follow that such television coverage could affect a juror's judgment and influence his or her vote. Witnesses testifying during consecutive days are vulnerable as well. Televised coverage affords them the opportunity to watch their own performance and the performance of other witnesses. Such feedback could prove harmful to their subsequent performance in court. Similarly, judges and lawyers might be tempted to alter behavior to conform or change images that appear in televised accounts of the trial.

The Steinberg trial was distinguished for the extraordinary coverage given to it by the press. But the case was further highlighted by the presence of the in-court camera, giving a large television audience an intimate view of trial proceedings. Besides opening the court to greater public scrutiny, it gave participants the chance to scrutinize their own actions and the actions of other court members. The manifestations of this public mirror could prove to be dramatic and revealing.

WITNESSES

Besides Hedda Nussbaum, other major witnesses in the Steinberg trial watched television closely to monitor their courtroom performances. Azariah

Eshkenazi, the director of the Forensic Psychiatric Service of New York, was an important expert witness for the defense. He had examined Hedda Nussbaum and found her mentally competent. The defense attorneys attempted to use his testimony to counter the prosecution's claims that the physical and emotional traumas that Nussbaum had sustained rendered her incapable of inflicting injuries on her daughter.

Eshkenazi recalled following television coverage of his testimony closely in order to "critique" his performance in court. Watching television critically better enabled him to determine his effectiveness. "I'm concerned, being a foreigner, that I speak too fast with my accent," he said. "I was concerned with the jury understanding me because they can't stop me and say, 'Doctor, I did not understand your accent.' "[3]

For many witnesses in the trial like Eshkenazi, television served as a reflection by which to judge appearance and the manner in which testimony was being projected. They also acknowledged that the medium's interpretation of their testimony was something that could not easily be overlooked and that such coverage could affect them.

Dr. Aglae Charlot, the medical examiner who performed the autopsy on Lisa Steinberg, also watched the television coverage of her testimony and could not help but notice the "unflattering" way in which television projected her image. "The way I appeared on the screen is completely different from the way I really look," she said.[4] Charlot, however, was more encouraged by the way television coverage handled her testimony and by the fact that "I came across very well because [television] picked up the really exciting part of my testimony." She had contended in her testimony that Lisa's death was not an accident, but a homicide, a crucial point in the prosecution's case.

Charlot was perturbed, however, when at one point during her four days on the witness stand, she saw television coverage of Ira London mischaracterizing her testimony during a hallway interview. Upon a request made by the defense lawyer in court, Charlot was required to turn over "personal notes" to London. "The very next thing he did was to take them to the press," she said. London proceeded to offer misinterpretations of her writings, claiming that her notes contradicted her testimony on the witness stand. Charlot explained: "Mr. London is not a physician, and there is some specific medical language he did not understand. But he just went to the press and said what he had totally misunderstood and that's what came out on television that night."

Angry and unsettled about London's press comments, Charlot felt frustrated that as an expert witness she was obligated to withhold comment to the press during the trial. "So, unfortunately, I could not have access to the press and say that it was totally wrong," she said. "I felt that this was not fair, that he could go to the press and I couldn't myself."

Another medical expert, Dr. Douglas Miller, stated that as a practicing physician he had experience analyzing himself on videotape. While attending medical school, videotape allowed him to evaluate how well he interacted with patients. He conceded, however, that participating in a televised trial was a different type of experience that caused him to take mental note of his appearance and mannerisms. "It's always a little bit of a different feeling to see what you actually look like on videotape as opposed to what I look like in the morning when I shave," he said. "I look different." But Miller believed that he would have demonstrated the same concern about his appearance had the trial not been televised because "there's an image we have to uphold and so we put on our best suits and don't wear loud ties."[5]

Prior to giving his testimony, Miller recalled watching excerpts from Ira London's opening arguments, in which the jury was told that Lisa Steinberg's death was not a homicide. Though he had been prepared by the district attorneys' office that such a claim would be made, television coverage confirmed that speculation, and Miller was determined to rectify the inaccuracies in the court record. "I knew how wrong that was from the start," he said.

After testifying, Miller said he watched the testimony of another expert medical witness who had been diametrically opposed to his conclusions. He found himself disagreeing with some of the points raised by a defense witness, Dr. John Plunkett, as to the cause of Lisa Steinberg's death and noted: "I don't talk to the television much, but if my wife was there, I probably would have said, 'That's wrong.'" Miller disclosed that the prosecutors had questioned him about what he had seen on television of Dr. Plunkett's testimony. "They wanted to know if there was anything else to ask," he recalled. "But actually they had much more information on what he'd said than came across on the news."

Still, Miller's interactions with television may suggest an ominous shift in courtroom procedures. Traditionally, witnesses are sequestered from the court during the testimony of other witnesses to avoid possibly compromising their own performance on the stand. But with television, a witness, now able to watch other testimony contradicting his own, may become more determined to adamantly present a point of view that refutes court statements he finds objectionable. While such rules have often been relaxed for "expert" witnesses, as they were in the Steinberg case, in most states, as well as within federal jurisdiction, witness sequestration rules are in effect and enforced.

Other witnesses, however, were more disenchanted by the way in which television coverage failed to accurately or comprehensively report their testimony. Dr. Patrick Kilhenny, a resident physician at St. Vincent's Hospital who was one of the first to examine Lisa Steinberg, had notified police after suspecting child abuse. As a witness for the prosecution, he was disturbed after watching coverage of his testimony. Recalling his initial encounter with Steinberg at the hospital, he charged that television news accounts "had left out a lot" and failed to put his testimony in its full context. "It didn't portray what a real criminal this man is," he said. "They just said he was smiling when I told him the bad news, which was odd. In other words, it portrayed him as an odd person. He's more than that. I think he's a criminal."[6]

Prior to testifying, Kilhenny said that he watched other witnesses on television. He was "unsure" if it affected the nature and content of his own testimony, but he recalled being very aware of their accounts. "You're not going to forget everything until you sit down and calm down a bit," he said. "It's a very stressful situation and you want to make sure that you're keeping your story straight."

Marilyn Walton was also "mortified" about television's treatment of her testimony.[7] Describing herself as a professional singer and a former law client and friend of Steinberg, she testified for two days, charging that she had seen Hedda Nussbaum being physically abusive to Lisa when the child was two years old. Her testimony was highly publicized because she had given previews of it a week earlier on a television news program. But despite her apparent exuberance in giving interviews to the press outside the courtroom, she said that she was furious that her testimony could be recorded by the in-court camera, arbitrarily edited, and then broadcast. She recalled that, after viewing clips of her testimony that evening on the local news stations, "I wished I could have dug a hole in the ground and hid." Walton was incensed by one WCBS report in particular, in which the prosecution had branded her "a liar." She had watched the report after testifying. Had she done so earlier, Walton acknowledged it would have compelled her to alter or edit subsequent testimony.

It was this type of admission that confirms the fears of critics of courtroom cameras. The feedback of images from this powerful mass medium may prove to be inflammatory, making participants, most notably witnesses, more sensitive to how they are being projected to a vast public. Even in the case of a witness who appears to relish the visibility attached to a sensational trial, the courtroom camera can be intrusive, and even disturbing. It can affect a participant's sense of control and increase self-consciousness about how his or her performance is being disseminated and interpreted.

In certain cases, feedback could provoke fear and apprehension. It was not always generated from watching television coverage of the trial itself. One witness, for instance, reported viewing other telecasts that reminded her of the lurid nature of the case. One show singled out was "Inside Edition," a television "tabloid" that had aired a program about the case as the trial was in progress. One segment highlighted photographs of Lisa at play, juxtaposed against photos of the young girl lying comatose after being brought to St. Vincent's Hospital. Dr. Mary Elizabeth Lell, a pediatric neurologist and an expert defense witness, said: "I found it very repulsive where they would show pictures of Lisa on a swing, and then pictures of her bruised body. I just found it disgusting."[8]

The sensational treatment of the Steinberg case heightened her anxiety about her role in the case. Lell feared that this type of coverage might trigger other unstable persons to commit violent acts similar to Steinberg's. "There's a lot of craziness in the world and a lot of craziness in New York," she said. "This was such a sensational case, and television did really extend the viewing audience throughout the country. From that point of view, there's more of a potential that it's going to trigger something in somebody and it might be aberrant behavior." Lell could not state with certainty whether these fears about television coverage carried over into her testimony during the trial, "but at some level there was some concern about that."

JUDGE HAROLD ROTHWAX

Although jurors were excluded from watching television coverage of the trial, other court participants regularly tuned in to the evening news to follow the proceedings. Judge Rothwax watched clips of testimony on the evening news and had his wife tape portions of Nussbaum's testimony. He also asked his sister to record his lengthy charge to the jury, a videotape he was anxious to view. Rothwax "saw himself in little glimpses throughout the trial," but in terms of the camera, he noted, "The only time I became a major player was at the time when I gave my charge to the jury. But apart from that, basically I'm saying 'sustained' or 'overruled.' "[9]

From the brief segments of television news clips, Judge Rothwax said that he was "amazed" by his television image. "My image of myself is always different from the way I see myself on the screen," he said. "Somehow I don't think I sound that way or look that way, but apparently I do. There's a quality of strangeness about it."

Judge Rothwax, like millions of other viewers, was intrigued by Nussbaum's testimony and watched segments of it on videotape. He said that watching the testimony on television was a different experience from observing it in the courtroom. As the presiding judge, he was more concerned with maintaining courtroom procedures and with ensuring that questions to witnesses were clear and relevant and that evidence was being presented to the jury in a coherent manner. But as a television viewer, Rothwax admitted that he operated in "a different mode." He explained: "When I'm a member of the television audience, I sit back and listen and let other things come through, what kind of person she seems to be, and so on. In the courtroom I'm not focused on that, whether she's convincing or not, but on the process moving along."

Judge Rothwax acknowledged that he allowed himself to make judgments on Nussbaum's veracity as a member of the television audience. "As an observer of a television clip, I'm able to sit back and read it the way anybody else does and say, well, she's telling the truth, or she isn't, or it's a bizarre story, or what have you."

When asked how he "read" crucial testimony by Nussbaum as it aired on television, Judge Rothwax declined to answer, stating that "obviously I react the way other human beings do, but I don't feel it's good for me to comment on that while the case is pending." It is an admission that may point to a possible conflict of interest facing judges who preside in a televised trial. Viewing testimony via a highly influential medium like television, can judges separate the "human" judgments formed watching coverage of a trial from their responsibility as a neutral arbiter of the law? Rothwax suggested that it is virtually impossible for judges to disregard personal opinion about a case, whether or not television is present. But he still believes that it is crucial for judges to project an impartial image before the court that is devoid of subjective beliefs and behavior that may be detrimental to objective deliberations of law.

There are two styles of judges. There are judges who say, the judge is not supposed to have an opinion or communicate an opinion to the jury. He's supposed to be a neutral judge, and the jury is not supposed to know how he feels about the case during the trial. Some judges go the whole way and say, since I'm not supposed to have an opinion, I don't have an opinion. I've never been able to reach that level of saintliness, but there are some judges who may maintain it. I maintain that they are out of touch with their feelings if they have no opinion when testimony is vivid. Other judges like myself have opinions. I'm listening in one way, but obviously I'm forming an opinion about those things. But I'm very conscious throughout the whole trial that I must not show it, that there's nothing in my manner, there's nothing in my appearance, my tone of voice, or the way I phrase things, that should indicate I have an opinion. At the end of the trial I don't want to affect their judgments on the facts, and nothing I've said should affect their judgments on the facts. So I have to be very conscious that I am a neutral figure in that courtroom, and I must be perceived that way. So I'm very careful about my tonal quality, my body language, and all the rest of that. It doesn't suggest either approval or disapproval, it's just straight, neutral.

Judge Rothwax contended that he was able to divorce himself in the courtroom from any personal feelings regarding Nussbaum, even after viewing her testimony at home on television. But in a separate incident, televised coverage of other participants angered him and led to a direct confrontation in court. Rothwax had watched Ira London and Adrian DiLuzio conduct mini–press conferences, first in the corridors outside his courtroom and again at home on television. He believed that their behavior not only violated the integrity of the court, but also may have threatened the fair administration of justice. Incensed by the defense lawyers' persistent use of the media to "spin" court proceedings and essentially try their case in the press, he issued a gag order forbidding them to talk to the media. His ruling was subsequently overturned by an appeals court, a decision that Rothwax found upsetting. London and DiLuzio, meanwhile, continued to maintain a high media profile during the remainder of the trial.

Judge Rothwax's anger toward the defense lawyers, which he had managed to temper in the last weeks of the trial, unexpectedly erupted on the final day. After the jury was dismissed for the upcoming weekend, London made a court application to sequester them before deliberations began. It was a legal maneuver that infuriated Rothwax. Still furious at the gag order that had been overturned three months earlier, as well as the defense attorneys' continued play to the media, Rothwax confronted them and accused the lawyers of insensitivity and even grandstanding. The confrontation was recorded in the court transcript:

Rothwax: Now you want to sequester the jury so you can be free to talk to [the media]. . . . It's perfectly okay to interfere with the jury and lock them up for extra days unnecessarily so your rights won't be infringed upon in the smallest degree. For a person who is so concerned with press coverage, it would seem to me you would be well advised to pass a camera once and say, "No comment."

London: I deserve to say. . . .

Rothwax: Don't interrupt me!

DiLuzio: Excuse me, do I have a right to talk?

Rothwax: No.

DiLuzio: If I don't have a right to talk, I'll sit down.

Rothwax: Then sit down.

DiLuzio: You want to scream, I'll sit down.

Rothwax: Then sit *down*!

DiLuzio: You're screaming, I'm sitting down, thank you.

Rothwax: As far as I'm concerned, I've expressed myself with vigor.[10]

Judge Rothwax's attempt to characterize his emotional state for the trial record did not belie the fact that he could no longer contain his anger toward the defense attorneys. For the past four months, he had witnessed constant television coverage of their out-of-court conferences. London and DiLuzio's request that the jury be sequestered now, for fear that they would be subjected to adverse media accounts that they themselves had helped to propagate, seemed to Rothwax absurd and unconscionable. Coming at the very last moment in the trial, the application, if granted, would have burdened jury members. Rothwax said, "They would not have had any overnight clothes, toothbrushes, warnings to their loved ones, and suddenly they wouldn't be home." As he sat in his chambers one week later, his recollection of London's behavior still made him bristle with anger.

So it was observed that it was a grandstand play, it was a thoughtless application at a belated moment in time. And it was not his finest hour. And for him to lock these people up so he can have the freedom to talk to the cameras in the hallway. If I have to balance his freedom to have a hallway press conference or the freedom of 17 people to be free for the weekend, I'd come down on their side and not on his side. Say "No comment" if you're so concerned about press coverage.

Judge Rothwax admitted being annoyed with himself for being unable to control his temper, but added that the defense attorneys' motion to sequester the jury was characteristic of the way in which they had conducted themselves throughout most of the case. He said: "It seemed to be symbolic of so much that was thoughtless that had happened in the trial, so unprepared, so unthought-out."

THE JURORS

One of the most serious concerns about allowing media coverage of trials is that jurors might be encouraged to disobey court instructions and follow television accounts of the case. In other instances, they may inadvertently see glimpses of the coverage while viewing other programming. In the Steinberg trial, several jurors admitted this was, in fact, the case; others said they were diligent in avoiding all news accounts. Some jurors, so compelled to watch the television coverage, circumvented the rules by having friends record accounts of key testimony for future viewing. Given the sensitivity of this issue, some jurors were reluctant to openly discuss their viewing habits during the trial and whether such exposure may have influenced them.

The majority of the court participants, however, believed that most jurors would be unable to avoid the overwhelming media attention devoted to the case and would be exposed to it whether consciously or inadvertently. Tony Guida, a news reporter covering the trial for WNBC-TV, commented that it would be extremely difficult for jurors to ignore the temptation to follow media accounts of a case with such notoriety. "It strikes me unlikely that the jurors were able to avoid television, radio or newspaper," he said.[11]

Judge Rothwax, when asked if he believed that jury members diligently obeyed his instructions to shun news accounts of the case, simply shrugged and replied, "Who knows? I mean nobody knows." But he characterized the Steinberg jury as being "very conscientious." He thought it was "amazing" that the court was able to assemble as good a jury as it did, given all the pretrial publicity in the case. Given the sensationalism surrounding the trial, however, it would not have surprised him if jurors watched at least some trial coverage. "Certainly it would be natural and understandable that a juror would be interested in seeing what happened," he said. "They saw it in court, what's the harm done if they turn on the TV, or what's the harm if all they are doing is reporting what they have seen anyway?" That could be a rationale; the court "might never know about it."

The print press also played a role in creating potential problems for the court. Several weeks into the trial, the *New York Post* ran a banner headline citing a remark made by Mayor Edward I. Koch: the full-page blaring headline that declared Steinberg was "a monster" and should be "dipped in oil." The story reported that Koch, on a television news show, had angrily condemned Steinberg. "I'm so outraged by this monster, it's hard to discuss him rationally," he said. "I'd like to dip him in oil many, many times. This is my personal opinion—the jury must decide his guilt in the death of Lisa Steinberg, but from a moral point of view, he should be dipped in oil several times."[12] Two jurors admitted seeing the headline as they rode the subway to the Criminal Court Building, but insisted that the statement would be disregarded and that they would be able to function normally within the courtroom. Said Judge Rothwax: "They weren't consciously trying to do that, but there it is, they can't deny it."

Most jurors in the case said that they made a conscious effort to obey court instructions to avoid all media coverage. Several added that they went so far as to ask friends to tape television news accounts of the trial and save newspaper clippings to be reviewed later. Allen Jared, a regular viewer of television news, said he was determined to avoid trial coverage, often waiting until the lead stories on the evening news were completed before tuning into the remainder of the program. Fearing he would be influenced by media reports of the case, Jared said that he would have avoided news accounts even if the court had failed to warn him. "I would have feared that the television coverage would have some sort of impact even though, had it happened, I would have tried to disregard it," he said.[13]

Major court participants agreed that the jury appeared diligent in avoiding media accounts. But from the trial's beginnings, the issue continued to be of paramount concern to the prosecuting attorneys and Judge Rothwax. Television news accounts selectively showing sensational segments of the trial outside the broader context of testimony could have a detrimental effect. Peter Casolaro said that he was so disturbed that these newscasts might be reaching jury members that he stopped watching television news altogether. According to Casolaro: "I was concerned about jurors going home and watching the television and getting the wrong impression. That was one of the main reasons I stopped watching because I wasn't about to start worrying about whether or not the jurors are seeing this and start trying to adapt the case to that."[14]

Prosecutor John McCusker also believed that jurors were aware of the enormous media attention and the tremendous public pressure to convict Steinberg. He recalled seeing one juror on television after the verdict and feeling that the jury had suffered from a "backlash effect" due to the media coverage. "They felt they had to be extremely careful not to convict him based on media opinions or based on what the public thought about that," he said.[15]

Court participants were also forced to contend with the ongoing media strategy of the defense attorneys, which included giving regularly scheduled interviews to the press during and after each day's proceedings. "Spinning" became a commonplace occurrence as London and DiLuzio would selectively refine and interpret court testimony. They claimed that their dialogue with the press was intended merely to counter the massive amount of negative publicity that already existed about their client.

DiLuzio angrily dismissed the prosecution's charges that the defense attorneys were trying their case through the media. He maintained that comments to the press were designed to offset the damaging leaks by the prosecution and the massive pretrial publicity that portrayed Steinberg as "a monster" in the public's mind. Denying they were using the medium to, in effect, "reach" the jury, he admitted being aware of the possibility that jurors might watch television coverage of the case. DiLuzio stated that "although we know the jury doesn't read the newspapers, we know they form no opinions, it seems to me that this jury has. I think it would be foolish to think that they hadn't. . . . We really felt that this jury was not going to be reached. I think what was important, if they were going to be reached it was important to balance their commentary."[16]

Other participants charged that the defense attorneys deliberately planned from the beginning to escalate the level of trial publicity based on the likelihood that jurors would watch television news accounts of the trial. Barry Scheck concluded:

To a large degree, no matter what jurors tell you, there is an assumption that the jurors, particularly with respect to television, are going to watch television. And the reason I think is unique to the medium. It's one thing to say I won't read the newspapers because there's more of a conscious act involved in actually reading an article in the paper. You can catch a headline or two, but you can push that aside and consciously avoid reading the article and still read the paper. I think it's much different to avoid television news completely. You never know at what point they are going to put the story on. You have to hide, get out of the room. It's a far more intrusive medium and certainly one's viewing habits involve more passivity and less conscious choice about whether to watch something or not than does the way we experience the print media. So I think there's certainly an assumption that television is a much stronger way to reach the jurors.[17]

As Hedda Nussbaum's attorney, Scheck conceded that he used television to create a more favorable public opinion for his client. Described by court observers as "the third prosecutor" in the trial, Scheck was a highly visible figure as the case progressed and astute about how the press operated. "He was responsible for a lot of publicity that was generated," said John Mc-Cusker. "There's not too many times where a witness's lawyer is in that sort of position."

In using the media as part of his defense strategy, London may have reached too far in a controversial incident that occurred in the middle of the trial. In an interview with *Newsday* columnist Denis Hamill, he remarked that Steinberg was, in fact, probably guilty of criminally negligent homicide. "I know Joel won't like that because he wants nothing short of acquittal, but I don't think he's realistic. He'll probably do jail time."[18] His remarks were widely criticized by legal analysts, and it was reported that Steinberg was outraged and appalled. Even co-counsel Adrian DiLuzio was angry, assuring reporters, "We haven't given up yet."

But according to Perry Reich, the attorney who later replaced London, the comment may have been made as part of a shrewd legal strategy. Assuming that jury members were watching television, London would attempt to persuade them to convict on a lesser charge in a case that was already hopelessly floundering. "I think his theory was, look, I'm dead already on this case and the point is probably some of the jurors are watching television," said Reich. "Let me say, hey, we really don't hope to give this guy a walk, convict him of the lowest thing possible."[19]

The lawyer's perceptions that jurors do, in fact, follow news accounts of the trial, whether deliberately or not, were partially accurate during the Steinberg trial. Two of the more outspoken jurors candidly revealed that television coverage of the trial had infiltrated their lives.

Foreman Jeremiah Cole acknowledged that he was curious about television coverage of the trial and occasionally would watch news accounts with the sound turned off "just to see what [the courtroom] looked like from the camera's vantage point." Said Cole: "If they had gone to a piece of evidence, I would have been off that channel in an instant. But I just wanted to see whether it looked in the television world as it looked to the jurors. In fact, it did pretty much."[20]

Cole would later admit watching the six o'clock news "a couple of times" and leaving just the picture on during London's questioning. "It was satisfying my curiosity," said Cole. He added that he was "fascinated" by London's courtroom performance and asked rhetorically, "Did it look the same on television as it does in real life? To me, it had the same feel as the courtroom did."

Helena Barthell, like other jurors, said she took precautions to avoid media coverage. She recounted that she would deliberately stay in her bedroom while the evening news was being broadcast, waiting for her husband to tell her that the Steinberg portion was over. "On days he wasn't home, I would have the news on and the minute they would say something about the Steinberg trial I'd hit the VCR to record and I'd turn the volume down and then just come back in a minute to see if it was over."[21] Sometimes she would inadvertently catch a glimpse of a witness testifying. On another occasion she saw printed statements from the trial that were broadcast. Barthell admitted to seeing a small segment of Nussbaum's testimony as she was trying to record it on her VCR. She turned off the sound and continued to record until Nussbaum was finished. Comparing Nussbaum's television and court images, Barthell recounted:

She looked better on television. She looked worse in person. She looked more deformed in person, more fragile. She had very little hands, a very slow manner of moving, very slow, methodical, deliberate movements. From what I saw on TV, it just shows her sitting, talking. It doesn't show the movements of her walking in, walking out, fumbling to get her glasses out of her purse, and just being very precise, with her tiny, tiny fingers.

Barthell said that she was aware London was talking to the press about the trial. "My husband told me, he's counting on the jury watching so that he can get to the jury," she said. "So I made doubly sure that I was not paying attention to that."

Angry with London's media tactics, Barthell believed that the defense attorney's statements were, in fact, reaching other members of the jury. She explained: "I was really insulted that he thought the jury could be manipulated. And I guess I was mad because I felt he was probably right, that some of the jurors, I strongly suspected, were watching the news, were watching programs about the trial and were listening to London. And I just thought that was very unethical."

Barthell, who admitted to having a stormy relationship with several jurors, recounted one episode toward the end of deliberations, where she became intensely curious about seeing Steinberg's physical stature and hearing the tonal quality of his voice. When the jury would file into the courtroom each day, Steinberg was already seated at the defense table and left his seat only after the jurors had been dismissed. "We came in last and left first," she said. "I said, I'm dying, I don't know why, I have this very strong desire to hear him speak. He can read from a telephone book, I'm dying to know what his voice sounds like." Barthell recalled several jurors telling her that they had already heard Steinberg's voice. "I just looked at them and they said, 'Oh, forget I said that' because they weren't supposed to know what his voice sounded like," she said. "Obviously they saw something on television where he was speaking, and they knew what his voice sounded like."

Television viewing became the focus in a second jury incident: Barthell was confronted by a jury member who had accused her of watching coverage of the trial. The confrontation developed after she complained about chronic tardiness among jurors that delayed the trial as much as 40 minutes. During the Nussbaum testimony, which was being aired live throughout the day, Barthell had programmed her VCR to record the day's proceedings, but was concerned that she would run out of tape if the trial was delayed. "I looked at my watch. It was one day when it was about 10:40 A.M. and one of the alternates still wasn't there," she said. "And I said, well, I knew that we'd start late, but my VCR is kicked in now so I don't have much room on this tape. I'm wasting space. I'm not going to get it all." At that moment, another juror chastised her for watching television coverage of the trial, even though Barthell told her she had planned to view the tape after the trial's conclusion. Barthell recalled: "She said, 'I don't think that that should be allowed'—and she had a 'I'm-gonna-tell' type attitude. And my attitude was, go jump in a lake. I felt I was one of the most diligent jurors around. I never read a single article, and I tried very hard not to watch television. I suspect others were not as diligent."

THE LAWYERS

The principal lawyers in the Steinberg trial watched at least limited coverage of the case on television, but their reasons for doing so and their reactions to what they viewed varied to a great extent. Peter Casolaro became so disenchanted with news coverage that he was determined "not to watch television as much as possible because I didn't want to see the way [the trial] was reported." Most of the time, he would turn to the news only to watch sports and weather.

In the early stages of the trial, Casolaro acknowledged watching one or two newscasts of witnesses testifying and remembers feeling resigned and unhappy about the coverage. News stations often selected testimony that was sensational and "sold better," but had lesser significance within the legal context. As an example, he cited the coverage given to Dr. Patrick Kilhenny, a resident physician who examined Lisa Steinberg when she first entered the hospital. Virtually all news accounts highlighted a similar segment of testimony. When informed that his daughter had suffered permanent brain damage, Kilhenny recalled that Steinberg had callously remarked that "Lisa's not going to be an Olympic athlete, but she'll survive." The testimony drew a visible reaction among participants and spectators. But according to Casolaro, the real essence of the doctor's testimony was a conversation he had had with Steinberg who denied that his daughter had been beaten, but had instead choked on her own vomit. Recalling his reaction to television news reports, Casolaro stated, "That's just the way journalism is. That's what they do, that's how they sell their newscasts."

The prosecutor said that he was more concerned that jurors at home were watching television and "getting the wrong impression." Apprehensive that television coverage of trial proceedings might eventually affect his own performance in court, Casolaro remarked, "I didn't want to see myself on television. I didn't want to see the witnesses generally on television. I wanted not to let that affect how we tried the case."

John McCusker did not pay that close attention to newscasts either after the initial stages of the trial. At first, he thought that television news accounts could act as a "barometer" to evaluate public opinion and what the jury might be thinking. "I learned after a while that wasn't the case," he said. "From my standpoint there was very little correlation between what was reported on television news that night and what had actually transpired in the courtroom that day."

Like Casolaro, McCusker was anxious that jurors were being exposed to television coverage, particularly reports of sensitive material that had been "leaked" to the media. From the viewpoint of many participants, the Steinberg case was unusual for the number of leaks of confidential information to the media and "evidence" that was often ruled inadmissible in court. McCusker remembers feeling worried when a local station made public portions of Hedda Nussbaum's psychiatric records and a personal letter she had written to Steinberg. These were records that "obviously had come from the defense," materials "that should not have been released, but were released almost every day," he charged. "I was concerned at that point whether the jury had been exposed to a lot of these things. A lot of it was material that I didn't think they would be exposed to in the course of a trial, and I was afraid that they would consider these types of things when they began deliberating the case."

McCusker recalled the prosecution broaching the subject in court and requesting that the judge reinstate a gag order forbidding attorneys to discuss the case with the press. An earlier gag order had been reversed by the court of appeals on the grounds that the court could not prove the origins of the leaks to the press. McCusker said, "We ended up not pursuing it because the bottom line was we would never be able to prove where the leaks were coming from."

While unrestrained television coverage made prosecuting attorneys agitated and apprehensive, the defense attorneys viewed the medium as a tool that could be effectively utilized. Both defense attorneys acknowledged that they would monitor the evening news to gauge public sentiment to discover possible clues as to how well their legal strategy was working and how their case was being received by the jury. Each day, London explained, both he and DiLuzio would watch the six o'clock news in his office. "They're like film dailies, you know, the day's rushes, and we'd get a sense on the six major channels as to how they were responding, and it gave us a clue how we were coming across."[22] In one instance, they were encouraged by news reports criticizing Hedda Nussbaum's testimony, the central component of the prosecution's case against Steinberg. "When the shift began to change that Hedda was no longer perceived as a victim, we knew we were communicating to the jury what we wanted—that Hedda was not a victim," said London.

Encouraged by media reports, London said that he had no specific plan during his cross-examination of Nussbaum other than to allow her to "reveal" herself. He expressed concern about public perceptions of his legal strategy. London was relieved, however, when midway through his cross-examination public opinion "did a total turnabout." He explained: "Before she took the stand, she was the darling of the feminist movement, people felt sorry for her. There isn't any doubt that when she sat down and when she left the witness stand, people saw her as a mother who sold her child's life out."

DiLuzio explained that it was important for the defense to watch television in order to evaluate public reaction to the case because if it leaned one way, "you might infer that the jurors are of a similar mind." "So it was important for us to get that feedback to get a sense of how people were perceiving Joel Steinberg, how they were perceiving the defense team, and how they were perceiving the theories that we were advancing." At one point in the trial, when the defense began to systematically attack Nussbaum's credibility, DiLuzio was gratified to see that television coverage and public sentiment about her were changing. "It suggested to us," he said, "that the jury's mind might also be changing."

Mediated Feedback: The Participant and the Public

Critics of camera experiments fear that the Television Trial magnifies public opinion and intensifies public reactions that may seep back into the courtroom. Even strict adherence to rules forbidding participants to engage in outside discussions often proves futile when a highly engaged public is immersed in a televised trial. Either consciously or unwittingly, participants might find themselves subjected to opinion and comment by family members, friends, and associates who have become knowledgeable about the trial through television reports. This relationship—called *mediated feedback*—threatens the impartiality of a case, should individuals outside the courtroom offer interpretations and subjective opinions not only about the parenthetical issues attached to a case, but also about the specific testimony and personalities involved in the trial. It is a situation exacerbated when television broadcasts extensive coverage of a particular case, as it did during the Steinberg trial.

The dangers of mediated feedback have been articulated by legal and academic scholars. Media theorist George Gerbner warns that by injecting public opinion into the courtroom, the relationship between the media and the courts may be altered. He writes: "A trial must proceed as independently as possible from conventional moral pressures and the popular clamor of the moment. Televising trials may erode the independence of judges to do justice. . . . We may be on the verge of drifting into a major institutional transformation while assuming that we are only making a few public-spirited adjustments."[1]

While most media observers agree that the Steinberg case would have received close public scrutiny regardless of whether it was aired on television, the sensational nature of a televised trial involving child and spouse abuse, with its emotionally charged testimony and graphic images, riveted a huge television audience and provoked enormous public commentary. The degree to which court participants were confronted by public reactions and whether such reactions influenced their performance are central to the camera issue.

JUDGE HAROLD ROTHWAX

Described as a meticulous man and brilliant in the law, Judge Rothwax prided himself on presiding over a well-disciplined courtroom. The Steinberg trial was an example of a "professional trial," he said, in which there "wasn't a great deal of personal acrimony."[2] But according to many court observers Rothwax himself was often infuriated with the conduct of defense attorneys in the early stages of the trial. Punctuating the first six weeks of the case were his dramatic outbursts against the defense attorneys, who had failed to follow court instructions and conduct proper questioning of witnesses. "He was visibly annoyed, frustrated," said reporter Tony Guida. "He made comments in court about the failure [of defense attorneys] to follow what he felt were reasonable instructions."[3]

One example of the tense relationship between Judge Rothwax and the defense team came during the testimony of Dr. John Plunkett. Rothwax sarcastically commented that the lawyers, "as is customary," had failed to take notes.

London bristled at the judge's remark, stating in court, "What I take exception to is your joke at our expense."

Judge Rothwax heatedly responded: "It's not a joke! Frankly, I take it very seriously, Mr. London. I'm not joking at all."[4]

Responding to the judge's remarks, London commented later: "There came a point where I said to him, 'Judge, we feel like we are under attack. We feel like you're angry at us.' And he said, 'No, I'm not. I'm trying to give you a fair trial.' I said, 'Well, it's evident to us if you watch the videotape of yourself, you'll see you're angry at us. You don't handle our objections and arguments the same way you do the prosecution.' "[5]

Prosecutor Peter Casolaro disagreed that Judge Rothwax was "anti-defense" and described him as a judge who "gets annoyed with lawyers when he feels they are not doing what they should be doing."[6]

But virtually all participants noticed a dramatic change in Judge Rothwax's courtroom demeanor about six weeks into the trial. His stern, often confrontational style appeared to mellow, and the sharp verbal exchanges with defense counsel seemed to be curtailed. His argumentative manner appeared to dissolve, replaced by a more conciliatory and temperate attitude. Casolaro speculated that the bicycle accident in which Rothwax suffered two broken wrists may have tempered his volatile interactions with the lawyers. "Whatever difference I noticed in him was after he got hit by the car," he said.

But Casolaro's perceptions proved to be inaccurate. It was not an accident that changed Judge Rothwax's demeanor, but rather a television news account characterizing him as unable to control his emotions. Rothwax's wife had seen the report and warned her husband that he was in danger of losing control of his courtroom by remaining angry and confrontational. Tony Guida recalled: "I did a story about it one day using some of the outbursts that I had collected over a period of weeks and just raised the issue—is the judge running the risk of conveying an image that he is working for the prosecution, or is he just angry over violations of his rules, and is this a good thing to be doing in court?" Shortly after the story appeared, Rothwax noticeably toned down his outbursts.

When asked if Guida's story had influenced him, Judge Rothwax replied, "I don't know if the story made me aware, but my wife made me aware. She said, 'You're too angry.'" Claiming that the news story about him really had little effect, Rothwax rhetorically asked: "But even if it did, what was wrong with that?"

If as a result of [cameras in the courtroom], the lawyers and judge, seeing that they are behaving badly, they are being perceived in a bad light, that they don't like the way they appear, and they change their behavior for the better, it seems to me that's OK. That's not really what happened if I must say. What did happen was that I felt that the anger was counterproductive and that there was a more effective way to deal with it. From time to time we are all going to feel angry, but the idea is to get that anger under control, and basically what I felt, not so much for the public perception, but for my own good, I knew this was going to be a long trial. It's not going to be a good trial for me or for anybody if I'm getting angry. I've got to find a way to deal with this in a way that does not show loss of courtroom control.

In the aftermath of the trial, participants found themselves together again as television talk-show guests, and the Rothwax anecdote was widely circulated. Juror Shirley Unger said that she was asked by London if she felt that the judge favored the prosecution during the trial. She told him that she believed that London had given the judge more cause for reaction and noted that all jurors noticed the change in Rothwax's behavior. "His wife told him he didn't come across so good," she said. "I could really appreciate that. I didn't see him on television, but I did see him in the flesh. He really seemed like he was going to [explode]. But I thought what he was doing was setting the tone and letting people know that he was going to run a tight ship, which he did."[7] Man Fung Tse also recalled that jurors often discussed the perceptible change in Rothwax's demeanor: "We often joked around the jury room about it, 'I think this is Judge Rothwax's twin brother,' because we noticed the difference," he said. "[As compared to the] beginning of the trial, we noticed he wasn't the same person. It was a tremendous difference."[8]

But one major trial participant, who declined to be identified, strongly criticized the judge for allowing his wife to temper his personality and shape his image to conform to television's expectation of him. "[Should] Rothwax have his wife analyzing his behavior and conform his behavior to her psychological, therapeutic suggestions, to temper it for the camera? Whether she's suggesting he should moderate it for living and be a little more open-minded, he's tempering it for his image."[9]

ADRIAN DiLUZIO

Throughout the trial, Adrian DiLuzio and Ira London remained sensitive to public reaction about their client and the case. The lawyers emphasized that when the trial began, they were "off in a hole." The press had portrayed Steinberg as "the most reviled man in America," and the defense team accused the prosecution of leaking information prior to the trial that aroused public anger against their client. The attorneys were determined to direct their legal strategy toward changing those "wrongful" perceptions. Television news reports helped them gauge public sentiment, acting as a barometer to measure how well their case was being received by the public.

Because of their high visibility, the lawyers were besieged by the New York community, and their faces became recognizable even to strangers on the street. DiLuzio believed that the majority of the public were capable of distinguishing his role in the case from the cause he represented. "Most people who were negative to Joel would say things like 'I hate your client and hope he's convicted, but you seem like a nice guy,' or 'it must be an interesting job, it must be tough,'" he said.[10]

DiLuzio contended that the television camera fosters healthy public comment, but he recognized pitfalls as media attention given to trials is expanded. Lawyers could be tempted to use television as a vehicle to enhance public sympathy and understanding with regard to their case. Still he insisted that even this is not necessarily detrimental to the fair administration of justice as long as the public—and even an attending jury member—receives a "balanced" accounting of events. DiLuzio maintained that his daily press interviews during the trial were designed to offset the massive negative publicity against his client. "Once you let the wolves out so to speak, then I think in that situation it's perfectly appropriate to make public comments," he said.

Not only was DiLuzio focused on public attitudes about Steinberg, but also he persisted in developing a sophisticated public relations strategy throughout the trial. By elevating the level of discourse, he hoped that opinions and commentary favorable to Steinberg would ultimately reach the jury. According to DiLuzio, jurors who had followed accounts of the case had entered it with preconceived opinions about Steinberg. It would be naive to think that jurors would not continue to follow media reports, he said, and discuss the trial outside the courtroom in spite of rules prohibiting them from doing so.

I don't think you can insulate the jury completely. People talk to them, they hear comments. Even if they don't read the newspapers, somebody's going to walk up at work and say [something]. Can you really imagine jurors being that disciplined that they say, "No, no, no, you can't talk to me about this case at all"? At some point they'll begin to feel uncomfortable and say, "We shouldn't talk about it anymore." But I think that generally they're going to talk about it.

THE JURORS

Jurors appeared to be most vulnerable to mediated feedback. Unlike other participants in the trial, they were forbidden to discuss the case with friends and associates in order that their verdict be free of extraneous pressures. Still jurors found the separation difficult. Many friends and family members were following the trial via television coverage and were themselves emotionally involved in the issues surrounding the case.

According to Barry Scheck, mediated feedback is a dangerous influence on the jurors' decision-making process. Members of the public audience who have followed coverage of the trial on television may be convinced, said Scheck, that they now have had genuine access to court proceedings and that their opinions and observations are as valid as that of jury members. But, according to Scheck, this is a misguided notion. Brief, fleeting images and fragmented reports cannot possibly present a trial in all its complexities. He warned that such observations in the form of public feedback can place added pressure on jurors. Furthermore, he stated that jurors must realize that once their verdict is reached, "it can be second-guessed much more fiercely by those who claim, 'Well, I saw the trial and you're wrong. How could you have possibly reached that verdict?' They've just got to be aware that the opportunity for second-guessing, an instant replay of the verdict, is much greater when the trial is televised."[11]

Juror Helena Barthell said that comments filtered through to her, sometimes inadvertently by friends and relatives, even though they admitted being cognizant of the court rule forbidding jurors to discuss the case. Barthell recalled one incident in the early stages of the trial where she was given information that was expressly forbidden by the court. Initially selected as an alternate juror, she had replaced a regular jury member who was dismissed after it was learned that she was a victim of domestic violence. Several friends confronted Barthell after watching a television news report that incorrectly identified her. "The news—more than one person said this to me—got our backgrounds mixed up," she recalled. "They had me single with two children and the person who left married and an engineer."[12] Seeking to clear up the misidentification, she was sub-sequently told by a relative that the woman she replaced had been battered by a boyfriend and forced to leave the jury. "I had no idea why she had been excused, and we were told not to contact her and to speculate as to why she had been excused," said Barthell. "I didn't know that, but the damage was done."

Barthell denied that the information seriously affected her judgment during the trial, even if such matters pertaining to family violence were an underlying theme in the case. But clearly the incident pointed to the inherent dangers of having a high-profile, publicized trial. Oftentimes, such outside intrusions were less consequential. But occasionally public feedback was unavoidable, and jurors found that they had to alter patterns of normal social behavior. In some instances, this adjustment even caused personal dilemmas and confrontations with friends and family members.

Barthell said that her husband was quick to discourage anyone from even mentioning the case to her, fearing that more serious matters might surface. On off-days, she would continue working at her job, but she made it clear "right from day one" that she was serious about not discussing the case. "It got so when I showed up for work on Wednesdays, people would look at me and turn away," she said. "I think they were just busting to say something."

In another incident, however, Barthell's unwillingness to discuss the case may have caused a rift between her and a close friend. "I have one close friend [who said], 'I know you can't talk about it, but what do you think of this,' and 'I saw this on TV,' " she said. "And I would say, 'Don't talk to me about it. I mean it.' And she was kind of miffed."

Man Fung Tse also contended that friends and family felt compelled to discuss observations that they had made watching television news accounts. Sometimes those observations would contain ordinary information. In one incident, a relative asked Tse whether he had noticed Steinberg limping into the courtroom after suffering a sprained ankle in a football game at Rikers Island jail. Since jurors enter the courtroom after the defendant is already seated, Tse was unaware of Steinberg's injury. He found such inquiries annoying and found it increasingly difficult to remain private about the trial. He explained: "It's hard to get away from people when they're so involved with the news. When you're involved with the case, you don't want to hear anything about it."

Other jurors noticed the concerted efforts taken by those close to them to prevent inadvertent remarks. Interpersonal relationships soon became a balanc-ing act. Shirley Unger said that her associates made a conscious effort to avoid discussing the trial. "They would say things like, 'I've been watching the trial, but I know I can't talk to you about it. But, boy, when you're through, are we going to talk.' " At times this sensitivity could be jarring. Unger recalled, "When I'd come into a room where there were several people, there'd be a sudden silence." Katherine Anderson's family and friends were equally protective. Her husband would buy the newspaper and cut out articles pertaining to the trial so that Anderson could read news accounts when the trial was over. Her neighbors were also careful and once refused to allow her to enter their apartment until they could turn off the television set.[13]

TELEVISION AND THE RISE OF THE COURTROOM CELEBRITY

With their images broadcast to a national television audience, major participants found it difficult to retain their anonymity and were forced to contend with increasing notoriety and a sudden change in status. As "celebrities," each had to find a way to cope with the rising tide of public recognition. Participants suddenly found themselves thrust into the limelight, besieged with phone calls and mail, much of it congratulatory, some of it condemning them for their role in the trial.

This overwhelming reaction was met with a mixed response. Some comfortably relished their place in the public spotlight. For others, it would be an inconvenient and unwelcome loss of privacy, and they were either indifferent to or shunned public notoriety. The volume of public feedback spilled over into social circles, and invitations were extended to join the "Great Conversation" surrounding the case. Some participants were propelled into instant stardom as guests on the television talk-show circuit. But for others, the feedback took the darker form of threats and intimidation.

Judge Rothwax, too, could not escape the clamor of public demand and resigned himself to accepting the special attention shown him until the interest and furor had a chance to fade. "My phone has been ringing off the hook with family and friends," he said. "They keep on telling me how wonderful I am, that's basically what it is." Rothwax did not relish his newly acquired role as "celebrity judge" and said that his return to anonymity would come as a welcome relief. But he felt compelled to discuss the outcome of the case in interviews for public television and *Vanity Fair* magazine. Realizing how quickly this celebrity status could dissolve, Rothwax said:

I'm very aware that in our society this week's murder is replaced by next week's murder, today's celebrity judge will be replaced by tomorrow's celebrity judge. So it's a very transient thing and I'm very mindful of it. Most people are quite respectful and they don't intrude, they leave me alone. My colleagues, with whom I've worked for many years, treat me the same way they've always treated me, just as I have treated them when they were in the spotlight. By March, hopefully, it will be all over, and it will be forgotten, and I won't be a celebrity any more. I mean, who remembers the judge in the [Bernhard] Goetz case any more? That was a huge case [in which a white subway rider shot three black youths]. You don't even remember his name; he has dropped from sight in that regard. He resurfaced recently when he imposed a sentence on Goetz, but it's Andy Warhol's fifteen minutes of celebrity.

According to Judge Rothwax, had the television camera not been present in the courtroom, his public status and persona would still have remained the same. He argued that even without his media-built image, a news file photo would have effectively thrust him into the public eye. "I don't think that the camera alters that very much," he said. "The camera is reflective of the public interest; it is not the producer of the public interest."

Other participants, however, did not share Judge Rothwax's perception that television merely acted as a mirror that reflected existing public interest. They viewed television as a medium that helped create and arouse public opinion. Peter Casolaro argued that "the camera did have an impact" in generating public response that was often impossible to ignore.

Although the prosecutor insisted on maintaining a low profile during the trial, refusing all opportunities to be interviewed by the media, he still could not avoid being thrust into the spotlight. He was deluged with all kinds of mail, ranging "from very personal letters, to letters about legal strategy, to hate mail, to letters asking us legal questions why this is happening—just the whole range of possible inquiries from the public." Even in the trial's aftermath, Casolaro's office was still receiving correspondence. Many of the letters reflected the narrow and sometimes incorrect perceptions of individuals who had watched the televised coverage of the trial.

I think they were largely based on television coverage because people would write me letters saying "I saw this on television. What does it mean?" This letter I received today was about the posttrial interviews that one woman from Manhattan saw with the defense attorneys and one of the jurors, and she wanted to know if this was right. Why aren't you guys on television? Why don't you present your point of view? That sort of thing.

Despite such public pressure, Casolaro refused to merge his role as prosecutor with that of a public spokesperson responsible for countering the far-ranging comments from critics. He did, however, feel a professional responsibility to answer individual letters directed to his office. By and large, Casolaro found these queries devoid of a true understanding of the judicial system and the defendant's right of due process. "In effect, some of the letters I've received from the public say things like, 'Gee, I saw this on TV. Why did it happen? It seemed so unfair. It doesn't seem right.' And I'd have to write this person a short letter saying 'Well, the rules are these.'"

Casolaro concluded that television was not a very useful educational tool. He took the position that the medium is more effectively used as a source of entertainment, rather than a documentation of courtroom reality. The public, he said ruefully, might be better served "taking a civics course" to learn about the workings of the criminal court system, rather than relying on the in-court camera.

Of all those involved in the case, Ira London was one of the most visible. His meetings with the press became routine, and the television camera focused not only on his courtroom performance, but on his mini–press conferences as well. After a life of relative anonymity, London had quickly become a "celebrity," and he seemed surprised and pleased by the instant recognition.

Adrian and I cannot go anyplace anymore without being recognized. Wherever we go, especially together, people are doing this. So we get a kick out of it and it's also a bit scary. We've learned how celebrities feel when a stranger comes over. You never know if the guy is going to say something nice or look to punch you in the mouth. What is odd, is that the public response to us has been without exception positive. Wherever we go, people say the nicest things to us. People come up to us and say, "You guys are doing a great job. We're really proud of you." We went for a shoeshine yesterday, and the owner came over and he says, "Your money is no good here; this one is on the house. You guys are doing a beautiful job."

London claimed that he received numerous compliments from neighborhood friends in Brooklyn, where he resides, and from "brother lawyers." He recalled only one negative comment that he received from a police officer at the Criminal Court Building "who should have known better."

But London's most recent recollection fails to mention several disconcerting confrontations with the public. During the trial, London confided to some reporters that public reaction to his role as defense attorney was often hostile and threatening. He received considerable hate mail, and at the peak of the trial, nearly a dozen abusive telephone calls per week were recorded by his office. London was particularly hurt when one caller told him: "I want you to know that we don't want you to walk into another Jewish temple in this city again." There were other indications from the public that his case was not being well received. The New York Times reported that at a breakfast meeting at a Brooklyn synagogue, London polled 40 people, asking them if they had "strong feelings" about Steinberg's guilt. All but four raised their hands.

While most jurors were glad to have the trial over and regain a semblance of normalcy in their lives, several opted to join the media spotlight. Moments after the verdict was pronounced, a group of jurors immediately engaged reporters in what has become a growing phenomenon—the postverdict interview. Before the recent trend, jurors in controversial cases would leave the postverdict interviews to attorneys; jury deliberations were usually a private matter that was not publicly announced. At the Steinberg trial, however, at least five jurors appeared eager to discuss the process by which they reached a verdict. They seemed willing to embrace the media recognition, which until then they had tried to avoid. For four months, jury members had remained sheltered from the camera lens, but at the conclusion of the trial, they seemed eager to discard their court-offered anonymity to enter into the media limelight. Under klieg lights in the hallway corridors, jury foreman Jeremiah Cole eagerly reported that the jurors "were almost hopelessly divided," only to persevere and come up with a "compromise" verdict.[14]

Helena Barthell recalled that following the judge's pronouncement of the verdict, a court clerk informed them that their deliberations were confidential and that they could avoid the media by exiting a side door to an awaiting bus which would take them home. Cole was the first juror to agree to talk to the press, and he was soon joined by four others, including Barthell. "I was so tired I just wanted to leave," she said. "Then I got to thinking—why not? My father would like to see me on TV. And so I said, 'I'll talk to the media.' And one or two others said they'll talk to the media. And then there were five of us."

However, Barthell said that she had no inkling that following a rather tumultuous courthouse interview, she would become an instant celebrity, invited to join the rounds of television talk shows. Leaving the court building, Barthell recalled being besieged by media representatives. "They were shoving business cards and little notes in my hand, saying 'We want you to do *Good Morning America*' and 'Oh, you have to do CBS News, we saw you first.'"

But the willingness and enthusiasm of jurors to enter into the media spotlight point to the serious problem raised by postverdict interviews. With the rise of the Television Trial, the media have shown a greater interest in a jury's reasons for reaching a particular verdict. Critics have long held that such interviews abrogate the privacy of the deliberative process. It is a process that allows jurors to voice their conscience about the sensitive issues of a case, candidly revealing their personal concerns—an obvious crucial component of the deliberations. Knowing that their opinions would inevitably be made public, were jurors in the Steinberg trial influenced by that fact? In the corridors outside the Steinberg courtroom, these matters, in fact, became public.

It is worth noting that the postverdict interview may, in fact, severely erode an essential pact between the court and the jury members. The obligation of the court is to protect the verdict from attack, and the law permits a judge to enjoin trial participants from ever questioning jury members about their deliberations or their reasons for their verdict. It is less clear, however, whether that judicial power extends over into the public sphere and therefore the press. Still, as this trend continues and becomes a routine part of the Television Trial ritual, crucial questions are raised as it pertains to a juror's right of privacy and the possible intimidating effect that such accepted practices might have on prospective jurors.

Witnesses had varying reactions to their recent celebrity that resulted from their television exposure during the trial. For most, the fame was momentary and self-contained. The degree of celebrity for some was encapsulated in congratulatory telephone calls from their former college friends or colleagues. Dr. Aglae Charlot said that calls from friends who had seen her on television were reassuring. "I had a lot of people who phoned me from all over the United States. People back in Wisconsin at my alma mater called me and told me I came across well," she said. "So I had a lot of positives as far as my testimony."[15] Dr. Patrick Kilhenny also was overwhelmed by friends seeking to talk to him about the case. "Everyone since grammar school called me, every professional associate," he said. "My phone was ringing non-stop for a week."[16]

For another witness, the rewards of his notoriety were more material. Hedda Nussbaum was reported to have received $100,000 from the CBS network for the rights to her story. Asked why they believed Nussbaum's story was of commercial value, a reticent assistant producer remarked, "That should seem perfectly obvious."[17]

Another witness was also courted by television—even before he had completed his trial testimony. Dr. Azariah Eshkenazi reported that he received a telephone call from the Geraldo Rivera talk show just before his second day of testimony. They requested that he come immediately from the court to the studio "because they were going to interview me and do the whole show [on my testimony]. Eshkenazi said that the query upset him. "I said, 'How could I do that? I'm on the stand, and I'll be testifying tomorrow. And you want me to give you testimony tonight?' It made no sense."[18]

Despite his encounter with the staff member from the Rivera show, Eshkenazi noted that his television appearance seemed to magnify the importance of his role in the minds of his colleagues and friends. "I see the reaction of people around me," he said. "You're a big-time guy now, you know? I've testified twice a week for the last 15 years. Now I've become a big-time guy because I was on TV."

For other witnesses, however, the price of fame took a darker turn. Patricia McAdams reported that she was threatened prior to testifying. Shaken, but unwilling to disclose details, McAdams said that she reported the incident to authorities. Though reluctant to blame television, she speculated that the trial's high visibility could have provoked the threat.[19]

The most outspoken critic of television exposure was Marilyn Walton, who decried the public notoriety she received, claiming that it may have damaged her personally and professionally and could have potentially jeopardized her life.[20] Claiming she had no initial awareness that the trial would be broadcast to her home in Texas, Walton said that when she discovered she "had been all over the national news," she was infuriated. "Being involved in the case in any way, shape, or manner is a negative thing from my standpoint. It just so happens I believe in the guilt of Hedda Nussbaum and in the culpability of Joel Steinberg. Because of these beliefs, I elected to testify, but I did not ever intend, desire, or mean for my testimony or myself to become a focal point."

Walton contended that her exposure on national television may have also jeopardized a business venture in China. "Corporations are very ticklish about their images and the people who represent them," she said. But the most serious problem was of a personal nature. When she arrived home, she was confronted by her mother and boyfriend.

My mother and I had a blood-curdling fight when I got back home. My boyfriend, who is an attorney, is extremely angry. They said, "How could you get involved in this sleazy mess?" They said my reputation was utterly ruined. I was a debutante here in Dallas with some social standing for most of my life. My mother said, "Your father is turning over in his grave." My aunt isn't speaking to me. She was afraid she was going to lose her job. All of this because [the trial] was on television and they saw it. And people sent them copies of the tape. I mean people whom I haven't spoken with in years suddenly were coming out of the woodwork. So, yeah, I'm real mad. I am real mad.

The Steinberg Interview

The most serious risk associated with televised trials is the possibility that they may place a defendant's due process rights in jeopardy. Yet few studies on courtroom cameras have made any meaningful reference to the effect of camera coverage on defendants. This lack of convincing empirical research on the psychological effects of in-court cameras on defendants was acknowledged by the U.S. Supreme Court in the 1981 *Chandler* v. *Florida* decision. Concerned that defendants might be subject to mental harassment during a televised trial, the Court stressed that "particular attention should be paid to this area as the study of televised trials continues."[1] More than a decade after that decision, there are still few references to that concern articulated by the high court.

The delicate task of keeping a jury untainted by prejudicial media coverage can be difficult, but it is crucial for the defendant who may be facing a lengthy prison sentence or even the death penalty. Public defenders have complained that the effects of television on the processes of justice are often detrimental, highlighting sensational elements of the trial on the nightly news while manipulating and inciting public opinion against a defendant. Television coverage is often unavoidable, and jurors are particularly susceptible to information that is widely and quickly disseminated.

Even footage of pretrial hearings can influence prospective jurors and damage a court's ability to empanel an impartial jury. Jonathan Gradess, the executive director of the New York State Defenders Association, testified before the state's senate and assembly Judiciary Committees on Cameras in the Courtroom, and cited the coverage of Steinberg's bail hearing as an example of the inherent dangers of televised proceedings. Although Judge Rothwax's on-air court statements were within legal boundaries, they could potentially be harmful to the defendant. Rothwax stated that Steinberg was "probably guilty" and will "probably be found guilty of second-degree murder" and be sentenced to life imprisonment. The broadcast of those statements "obviously has a severe potential for prejudice" for prospective jurors, said Gradess.[2]

Other jurists also fear that a defendant's right to privacy may be violated in a televised trial. In-court cameras have the potential to hold the defendant up to public ridicule, embarrassing or stigmatizing him before he is proven guilty. A joint *amicus* brief filed by the public defenders in *Chandler* recognized that "a person charged with a crime loses by necessity some of his privacy," but that "the problem arises when a person is displayed to the community for reasons *not necessary* for the court process. The only rights the accused should lose are those *necessary* for the orderly conduct of the court proceedings."[3] The brief likened television exposure to a form of punishment administered to a defendant prior to the proof of his guilt or innocence. It had the potential to scar a person's character permanently and cast him as a pariah even after his release from prison.[4]

Other academic and legal experts examining the camera-in-the-courtroom debate warn that televised trials could further harm a defendant's due process rights. When television presents a case using images that are highly charged and often controversial, the public could be tempted to view the trial as a form of fictional entertainment. George Gerbner writes that the "opaque reality of the courtroom is less illuminating of the judicial process than is translucent fiction." Because courtroom proceedings are complex, the superficial and noncontextual methods used by television are "more likely to conceal than to reveal how the judicial system operates."[5]

In the *Chandler* appeal before the Supreme Court, attorney Joel Hirschhorn charged that broadcasters are interested only in increased ratings and revenues. Trials are not televised for educational purposes, but in an attempt "to feed the American public's almost insatiable desire for the salacious, the sexy, the despair and sorrow of mankind."[6] In her well-documented study on cameras in the court, Susanna Barber opines more than a decade after the *Chandler* decision that Hirschhorn may have been proven correct. She concludes: "Given the nature of most trials televised to date, it would appear that such coverage indeed provides greater appeal to voyeuristic instincts, or to a curiosity to witness the shortcomings and punishments of others, than it does any educational purpose."[7]

BACKGROUND

The Clinton Correctional Facility lies more than 300 miles north of New York City in the small village of Dannemora. About 2,500 inmates are incarcerated there, including criminals who have been the central figures in some of the most notorious cases in the state. David Berkowitz, convicted of the "Son of Sam" murders, spent six years at the prison before being transferred. Jack Abbott, whose book *In the Belly of the Beast* won him a small measure of critical acclaim and social celebrity, was released from prison only to murder again. He is now serving a life sentence at Dannemora.

Since his transfer to Clinton in March 1989, Joel Steinberg has been held in block housing with about 300 inmates. Prison life has been harsh: Steinberg has lost weight, and he appears more haggard than at the time of his arrest in November 1987. There is a grayish pallor to his skin, evidence of someone who has not seen sunlight, and deep lines are etched in his face. His curly brown hair, often disheveled during the trial, is now closely cropped, and he has grown a full beard which is graying. Though once a wealthy lawyer in Greenwich Village, New York, Steinberg seems to have made the adjustment to prison life. There are times, however, when he appears stunned by his current predicament.

At the Dannemora prison, I interviewed Steinberg for thirteen hours over the course of two separate days. Extensive follow-up interviews were also conducted four years later at the Southport Correctional facility outside of Elmira, New York. Steinberg was transferred to this maximum security prison in 1991 and spends his daily hours as a prison librarian. Our initial meeting took place in a cramped room ordinarily used for lawyer-client conferences. Though he did not take the witness stand in his own defense, our discussion offers Steinberg the chance to retry his case, supplying documents that offer a different legal slant to the circumstances surrounding the death of his daughter.

Numerous documents, in fact, dispute prevalent assumptions about his character and actions as reported by the media. Contrary to one media-generated perception that Steinberg was a heavy drug user, police and laboratory reports disclose that the substances found in his apartment after the arrest were not "mountains of cocaine," as had been widely reported, but legal substances.[8] A battery of drug tests performed on Steinberg also proved negative, lending credence to his contention that he was not a drug user, at least not for some time prior to the night in question.[9] Drug charges were in fact dismissed at trial even as the media continued to propagate the perception that the so-called "house of horrors" was a drug den.

More to the heart of his legal defense is the issue of Steinberg's relationship with his daughter Lisa. He repeatedly prods me to just "look at the facts" as documented in the materials—"Don't listen to me," he says. "I have no credibility."[10] Beyond the actual trial material, he is intent on proving that he is an emotionally responsive, sensitive, and caring father, one who would never hurt his child. "This is not a kid living in a house of horrors," he says. "I didn't have one moment where I'd raise a hand to her."

Legal documents, marked as confidential by the district attorney's office, are used to buttress his point. Although the prosecutor put on the stand a witness who testified to seeing marks on Lisa's face prior to the tragic events which occurred at the Steinberg household on November 1, 1987, a Board of Education report undermines the state's contention that Steinberg was an abusive father in the days leading up to her death. The document cites a half dozen teachers and school authorities who were interviewed about Lisa Steinberg and testified to her outward physical condition and psychological state of mind before her death.[11] Elliot Korman, the school's principal, stated that the girl was "extremely articulate and verbal," a "beautiful kid to look at," and that there were "no signs whatsoever" that the girl had been abused. Korman added that in the previous few weeks, Lisa "looked a little more disheveled but not to the degree that would cause an alarm." Elizabeth Kasowitz, Lisa's former kindergarten teacher, also told investigators that the six-year-old "was bright, never cried, popular, participated in activities and showed no signs of depression." Further, she stated that she continued to have a close relationship with Lisa after she left kindergarten for the first grade and "never saw any marks, bruises or any signs of battering" on the girl. To emphasize this crucial contention, Steinberg cites a page from the prosecutors' brief, which refers to a pre-sentencing report stating that "allegations of child abuse had been determined to be unfounded" by the court.[12]

We also reviewed medical records that called into question the charge that Lisa had died from a subdural hematoma, a brain injury caused by a blow to the head. This issue is, in fact, at the crux of his case. During the trial, witnesses giving medical testimony took varying viewpoints as to the type of injury sustained by the girl. Dr. Douglas Miller, a New York City neuropathologist testifying for the prosecution, believed that Lisa Steinberg had been hit by three powerful blows to her jaw, the back of her head, and her right temple, with a force comparable to the impact of an automobile collision or a fall from a third-floor window. The girl had died of a subdural hematoma caused by the blow to her right temple, Miller stated.

But other witnesses contended that such a conclusion was inconsistent with hospital medical findings. For Dr. John Plunkett, a defense witness and a forensic pathologist from Minneapolis, the reports suggested that Lisa had been shaken and "propelled into a solid surface"—a rapid "acceleration-deceleration" movement to the head causing a "shearing" of the interior part of the brain known as the subarachnoid region. The result was a fatal swelling of the brain.

Another analysis by the University of Pennsylvania, a report never disclosed in court, supported Plunkett's determination that the injuries were "ischemic" in nature—caused by a gradual swelling obstructing the flow of blood to the brain—and were not caused by a traumatic blow to the head.[13] Citing the absence of epidural hemorrhaging or fractures to the exterior of the skull—clear signs that Lisa had been beaten—the report casts doubt as to whether the six-foot-tall, 180-pound Steinberg fatally injured his daughter. While prosecution and defense attorneys both acknowledged that Lisa's death was a homicide, Plunkett stated that the six-year-old girl's injuries could have been caused by an adult of any size, raising the possibility of Nussbaum's culpability in the incident.

While media reports continued to press Steinberg's criminality in the case, in the end, the evidence moved jury members against a second-degree murder charge (murder showing depraved indifference and recklessness). Steinberg was convicted for first-degree manslaughter (a charge defined by the court as the intent to inflict serious physical injury and the causing of Lisa Steinberg's death by failing to expeditiously seek medical care). The verdict, coming after eight days of deliberations, was perceived as a compromise reached by jury members divided between a verdict of murder and outright acquittal.

Beyond the specific legal and medical contentions surrounding his daughter's death is an overriding public picture portraying Steinberg as a domineering and abusive companion to Hedda Nussbaum. Maligned during the trial for his relationship with Nussbaum, Steinberg says that press reports depicting him as her "guru" are false. He did not control her life, nor did he isolate her from her family and continually beat her. To illustrate the point is a personal letter from Nussbaum dated November 15, 1987, written just ten days after Lisa was pronounced dead. Nussbaum wrote the letter from the hospital where she was being treated for various injuries. We reviewed the letter as proof of her independence and assertiveness. "Is this a woman I control?" he asks. "She controls, I never tell her what to do."

The three-page letter is written coherently and, at times, poignant. "Note: I eat every bit of food I'm given except for one meal of baked fishy fish. Did you hear Joan Bonano [a neighbor] say on "20/20" that I went from being a beautiful woman and have become an old hag? I looked in the mirror. She's right. I will change that. I will be beautiful again." One passage, in particular, elicits a tender response from Steinberg. Nussbaum writes, "And yes, I do." It is the private code between them, meaning "I love you." For the first time, Steinberg's face flushes and his voice cracks with emotion.

He is still fascinated by Nussbaum and pulls from his file a photograph of Nussbaum taken in the early 1980s. They are seated together in a restaurant with two other people. They both look remarkably young. Steinberg, holding his ever-present cigarette, displays a boyish grin. Nussbaum is beautiful, with dark hair and expressive eyes. He suggests that I closely examine her eyes. Look how clear and intelligent those eyes are, he says. They are not the eyes of a woman who has been described as being abused and beaten.

Steinberg denies that Nussbaum was a battered woman, and emphasizes that he was never charged for such a crime: Nussbaum's history of mental illness combined with a sadomasochistic lifestyle led to the deterioration that was so visible on the television screen. Testimony during the trial, however, pointed to an existence that had grown increasingly fractured, with Nussbaum herself testifying over the course of six days about a life of abuse and degradation. At times, it was smaller incidents that proved most revealing. During her testimony, she accused Steinberg of forcing her to sleep on the floor without a cover and with the windows open. When faced with the accusations, Steinberg hunches his shoulders and gestures with his hands as if to say, "What choice did I have?" Nussbaum was a drug user, a bad example for the children. When Lisa crawled into their bed, Steinberg explained, he told Nussbaum, then under the influence of drugs, to leave the room. She insisted on staying, however, making the floor her bed. Steinberg said that he had no other choice but to remove the cover and open the window to prompt her to leave.

Following Lisa Steinberg's death, whatever ties connected Steinberg and Nussbaum—who shared a lifestyle endlessly critiqued by a zealous media— were soon enmeshed in the workings of the law. To avoid prosecution, Nussbaum spent hundreds of hours with the district attorney's office to help prepare the case against her long-time companion. Four years after the trial, her civil suit against Steinberg is still pending.

THE MEDIA AND THE PUBLIC

Throughout our lengthy discussions, it becomes evident that Joel Steinberg is an astute observer of the media. His comments indicate the dangers to a defendant inherent in a sensational case, dangers compounded by the court camera. He insists that the public is largely ignorant of the facts surrounding his case and that the media, aided by the in-court television camera, are largely to blame for these misconceptions. While endorsing the press's right to inform the public, he critically questions how the public can understand and draw conclusions about the case from media coverage that he describes as biased and sensational.

"The election of what they cover is critical," he says, "and there's too much latitude. I mean, they can create an image any way they want to. The public's right to know is an issue that's been covered, but I don't know that that knowledge is necessarily encompassed in two things; in one, having cameras in the courtroom; and, two, that the press really informs the public."

During the trial, Steinberg closely followed coverage of the case in news-papers and on television. He was able to watch limited segments of the trial at Riker's Island "if you could turn off the cartoons or the rock music. You know, there's not a lot of electiveness there." He remains critical of the medium that he feels selectively chose images and information to deliberately present a biased and slanted view of his case, rather than giving the public a balanced representation. Emotionally charged visuals, constantly repeated, only rein-forced the notion that he was guilty, even in the light of what he states to be overwhelming evidence to the contrary. Prompted by leaks from the district attorneys' office in the year prior to his trial, media created a climate of guilt that made it all but impossible for a fair evaluation in court. Medical and police reports were misrepresented to a press eager to label him as a "monster."

Comparing the media to the criminal justice system, Steinberg observes that a fair trial is dependent on the adversarial interplay between the defense and the prosecutor in order to reach a fair assessment of a defendant's guilt or innocence. Similarly, the press also presents its evidence and renders a verdict, but their facts and representations are usually distorted and unrestricted. "When the press is the only controller of the dissemination and they select a theme," he says, "then they can be devastating to either side and they can push an issue any way they want to."

During the trial, he states that he was as much a prisoner of the media as he was of the legal system. Choosing images that were one-sided and biased, the media created an avalanche of public opinion calling for his conviction.

Because of their enormous repetition, you have to correct an image by reality. When you don't recall reality because you haven't heard it repeated, it's like still believing Beech Nut foods are the best for babies even though you vaguely recall that they were prosecuted for tainting and adulterating their infant foods. And yet, you hear their music box theme song and buy Beech Nut and you're just thinking these lovely things about baby and that's the great American pie image. It's bull. . . . The recollection of fact is going to dissipate itself by the repetition of nonsense.

He blames the press for not vigorously pursuing information that went beyond a prepared "script" orchestrated by the prosecution. The press was selective and it was "viciously self-serving." When asked if his situation can be likened to the protagonist in Tom Wolfe's novel *Bonfire of the Vanities*, Steinberg immediately brightens with recognition. He himself has made the comparison to Sherman McCoy, the central character who finds himself inextricably sinking into a morass of media sensationalism after being falsely accused of murder. Like the fictionalized character, Steinberg believes part of his legal battle lies in countering a massive and highly negative media campaign that has irrevocably distorted reality and branded him.

The only people I see who feel [outraged] are people close enough to the courthouse to know what's going on and they get ticked, and inmates who have enough perceptivity to know [because] they've been through it. What Shakespeare said, "He scoffs at pain and [never] suffered a scar." You've got to feel it happen to someone close to you before you really want to do something about it.

Steinberg contends that television, in particular, creates stereotypical themes in order to form a strong narrative line. Images and information that do not conform are either disregarded or de-emphasized. The outcome is a one-sided and highly biased picture of the case put forth to the public. As an example, he cites an incident in which he "hopped into court" after suffering an ankle injury playing football at Riker's Island. "Michelle Launders [Lisa's natural mother] was laughing. It was a friendly laugh." Steinberg claims that television failed to capture the interaction. Instead, it repeatedly suggested how the audience should react to conform to a preconceived media image. This was effectively accomplished by seating Launders behind him in the courtroom so that the image of "the victim" was purposely juxtaposed with that of the defendant. "You don't let a purported victim or someone who has an interest sit behind the defendant so that there's a constant imaging of the defendant in relation to her reactions," he says.

Steinberg also illustrates that the nasal surgery performed on Nussbaum was designed to further dramatize her image as a battered woman for the public and for television. After her arrest, Nussbaum was taken to Bellevue Hospital where a doctor's preliminary report cited an old nose injury and an ulcerated leg. But the post-arrest photos of Nussbaum show a much fuller bridge on her nose. Only after facial reconstructive surgery did her nose seem flattened, seemingly caved in.

CAMERAS IN THE COURT

Steinberg singles out the in-court camera as being particularly damaging to his case. Analyzing the way that television news stations operate, he contends that the use of short clips of testimony on the nightly news only serves to sensationalize the trial and to present information and images out of context. As a highly competitive industry, television is not interested in balanced reporting, but in focusing on sensational elements of the trial to boost ratings. "The only balance was the coverage of Hedda because it was complete, and even that, there was no precursor to it, it was all set up with an image." Even with gavel-to-gavel coverage of Nussbaum's testimony, the television audience is still manipulated by the camera because of its limited capacity to portray "the totality of the person."

Perceiving himself as merely an object of the camera lens, Steinberg believes that television helped foster an image of insensitivity by the use of close-ups and camera angles and by the choice of particular shots. "I saw very little coverage that fairly expressed my sentiments, my natural manner," he says. "It was almost selective to reactions. I found it unfavorable and unflattering." The purpose of such coverage "is to bolster a negative image, and the reason for that was the more sensationalism, the more [public] interest."

Other participants also reported a different reaction to Steinberg's television image as compared to the persona he manifested in court. But for the most part, they agreed that on television Steinberg appeared noticeably less nervous and agitated than he had been at moments during the trial. According to assistant district attorney Peter Casolaro, Steinberg looked more "stoic" on television, an image contradicted by what he had seen of him in court.[14]

Helena Barthell, a juror, also agreed that the television audience viewed only short snippets of Steinberg reacting to court proceedings. Because that image was ephemeral, and not part of a broader context, it allowed the audience members to retain their hostile attitude toward him, without being challenged by other, more sustained and perhaps contradictory images. She explained:

A lot of people had in their minds already convicted him, thought of him as a monster, and they would look at him for five seconds [on television] and say, "There's that slime." When you're sitting all day [in court], and he's behaving perfectly respectable, he's in a nice suit, he's in a shirt and tie. He's obedient, he's not making noise, he's not being disruptive, he's not doing anything violent, you sit and see this man looking very studious and taking notes continuously, and I think you can't quite look at him and think "monster, monster, monster!" It's like the human brain doesn't let you keep that intense emotion for such a long period of time.[15]

TELEVISION, PRIVACY, AND SELF-CONSCIOUSNESS

Steinberg believes that the only valid purpose of cameras in the courtroom is to give a balanced public presentation "which is almost a sociological, in-depth study, the type of thing you'd see on the public news media." But he contends that the public is not fully prepared to watch a trial in its entirety and dispassionately deal with the complexities that arise during court proceedings. They turn on the television to view the sensational, the brief explosive moments that are occasionally interspersed within the extended, often dry recapitulation of testimony. Televising a trial is based on the same considerations made when televising any other type of entertainment. "How do you sell a soap opera?" he asks rhetorically. "You give a little flick of skin, a little flick of violence, a little flick of suggestiveness, of something exciting, and people want to watch."

Television can use a trial "to create its own milieu," one that is based on entertainment values, even if it means insensitively invading the privacy rightfully afforded courtroom participants. He compares media coverage of the contemporaneous Robert Chambers murder trial and the Tawana Brawley case to that of his own trial. In the Brawley case, involving a young black woman who charged that a group of white men had sexually assaulted her, the media initially showed explicit pictures of the woman's alleged injuries. Responding to complaints by Brawley's lawyer, the media backed off from such sensational photographic coverage. In the Chambers case as well, he notes, the press had access to photographs of the naked, brutally slain body of Jennifer Levin, but was careful to handle such material discreetly, unlike at his own trial where the press was much more willing to make sensitive and graphic photographs of Hedda Nussbaum public. The images depicted a woman who had been without sleep for three days, whose physical state had deteriorated, and who suffered from multiple bruises and a leg that was severely infected. "Hedda," he says, "was treated with such disregard and disrespect. [Television] wouldn't have lost anything by not sensationalizing, showing photographs and visualizations of areas of her body. It's an invasion. It's a by-product of her counsel Barry Scheck's self-aggrandizement, who unlike Brawley and Levin's lawyers failed to protect her dignity and integrity."

Media coverage also exacerbated his relationship with his own chief defense counsel. He is reluctant to criticize leading participants in the trial for fear it might jeopardize him on appeal, but during his sentencing and in open court, Steinberg accused Ira London of pandering to the press. He reiterated the complaint in our interview, stressing that his former counsel was more intent on building a media image to advance his career than on properly presenting a cogent defense. He maintains that London was far less aggressive than he would have been had the cameras not been present. London, he says, did not want to look "cumbersome" in the courtroom by presenting information that would not be well received by the judge. "It's very difficult when you're a lawyer to try to bring the information the judge is giving you resistance on, that might be impeached, that you have to spend a long time looking cumbersome to present, when you want to look good."

Steinberg says the camera further stymied his defense. He found the cameras to be inhibiting and a serious consideration in his refusal to take the stand. Adding that legal ramifications prevented him from testifying, Steinberg concedes that he "certainly didn't want to go before the cameras."

Look, if you were pulled in tomorrow and falsely accused of a rape case, would you really want to be photographed by a camera when you were defending yourself on the stand? Would you? Why not? You have the opportunity to show your own composure, your own candor, your own character, and the public could see you. Because what you'd be worrying about is that they would characterize you, right? And the characterization would be defeating to you. It wouldn't show your guilt or innocence, but we're all uncomfortable about having somebody cast stones that you can't respond to. And if you had a year's worth of publicity about how this, and how that, and you didn't do this, and it's false, you can't even deny it. I think that almost any defendant who's charged with something doesn't want the exposure. Nobody wants the exposure to negative aspects. You're subject to being accused of things you can't answer. You're really galled by falseness and you just can't come up and say but [look at this].

Admittedly, Steinberg was self-conscious about the cameras during sentencing. He was hopeful that his statement to the court, refuting allegations that he believed had gone unsubstantiated during the trial, would be picked up by the media. At the same time, he was particularly concerned that he would, again, be misrepresented by the prosecution as being a violent personality. He cites the court-authorized probation report that included several psychiatric evaluations. The documents illustrate further proof that he "had no propensity toward violence." He recognizes, too, that appearing before the camera put him at a distinct disadvantage. For example, at a point during his statement to the court, Steinberg openly questioned Rothwax's gestures. "He's looking at me as if to say, 'What are you trying to pull on me?'" he says. "And the public gets this view that Steinberg takes a challenging attitude and the judge just shuns it aside."

After that particular exchange with Rothwax, Steinberg remained composed and quietly took his seat. But he contends that if circumstances had been different and if television had not been present, he would have reacted more forcefully. "In a proceeding where there weren't cameras, we could have called a few names and said, 'Look, let's cut this nonsense. This is what the prosecutor did. This is what I'm accused of. . . . This is what's going on, judge. Let's cut it out." But in front of the camera, Steinberg says, the usual give-and-take between counsel and judge is stilted, the proceedings predetermined to fit a prescribed television format that will appeal to a vast audience. Rhetorically, he asks, "Don't you think the publicity, and the way it was geared, forces [the judge to respond that way]? Where do you take a man who had no prior offenses and who's lived a remarkably clean life and bang him out for a max?"

Had he shown remorse and taken responsibility for Lisa's death, Steinberg believes he would not have been given the maximum sentence. "I mean, I knew [Rothwax would] give me a substantially reduced sentence," he said. But he says that he was unwilling to make a false statement of contrition in open court and before the public. Refusing to "play the game," he states: "I could have easily said I feel remorse—I do feel enormous loss, I feel great pain—but this is *not* a battered child at all. This is not a child who lacks clothing. She had an enormous wardrobe; every schoolteacher thought she was perfect and delightful. Hedda testified that it was a joyous relationship; Joel was an exceptional, superb father."

During the trial, Steinberg perceived that other participants, especially witnesses, were also self-conscious about appearing before the in-court camera. He warned that television could serve as a charismatic tool for witnesses intent on observing themselves and then putting forth a particular image before the camera lens. "Hedda was self-conscious, at all times," he says, noting the changes in her dress and mannerisms during her testimony. In fact, Nussbaum admitted in open court that she had watched televised coverage of her testimony and had adjusted her presentation as a result.

He also cites Dr. Patrick Kilhenny, a physician who had first attended to Lisa when she was hospitalized, as another example. From Steinberg's perceptions, Kilhenny's manner and statements to the court differed from the doctor he had first encountered at the hospital. According to the records, Kilhenny's original diagnosis stated that Lisa had suffered a neurological deficit, but would survive. But Steinberg noted that Kilhenny was more visibly nervous on the witness stand than he had been at the hospital. "He was also under great pressure from the district attorney, which allowed for the situation to be more staged. He's performing for a camera and confrontationally and critically being viewed by his hospital peers."

Steinberg speculated that jurors, too, were affected by being part of a televised trial. Despite repeated court warnings to avoid media coverage, Steinberg believes it would have been highly unlikely for them to remain untainted. "There is no juror who didn't see during a football game or a show—'trial continues'—a little flash of 30 seconds or one minute," he says. "They can't avoid it. How can any member of the jury say they didn't see media coverage?" He recognizes that one "can't open the floodgates to litigation every time somebody has a little press exposure. But when it is this overwhelming, and it has that potential, it's damaging."

The massive negative publicity, Steinberg contends, has made it virtually impossible for him to ever reenter the social mainstream, even if his conviction is subsequently overturned by the appellate court. Repeatedly, he has been characterized by the media as "a monster," someone who lived "in a house of horrors," a man that Mayor Ed Koch demanded be "dipped in oil." He asks: "Don't you feel that there's no possibility at all of me reentering society, not being able to overcome the labeling, even though an appellate court could find that improper? And don't you suffer as a citizen by what happens to me?"

Reflections: Television and the Steinberg Trial

Echoes of the Steinberg trial continue to resonate. Through the in-court television camera, the trial reached American living rooms on a daily basis. Its images struck deep emotional chords, compelling us to acknowledge and examine the darker side of human existence. As the courtroom scene played on television, a national audience was moved by the visuals that still continue to haunt.

Beneath the stark reminders and controversial issues, another debate ensued, one that was to have far-reaching consequences for both the judicial system and the media. For the first time under New York State's newly enacted camera legislation, television would provide extensive accounts of court proceedings. As television monitored the Steinberg trial, we monitored the medium itself in an attempt to answer a general question that has yet to be resolved in a debate nearly 40 years old: Could television be compatible with the workings of the court without altering or even damaging the foundation on which this critical institution of justice stands?

This study is but one example of how the medium worked within a particular setting. It should be noted that its aim is not to judge whether or not television as a journalism tool performed well during the trial, but rather to identify a new mediated judicial entity that has become the Television Trial—one in which the court participant is tied to an intricate legal and social environment that extends from the courtroom well to the public soapbox. It is an environment in which fragmentary images rule and advance story lines designed to fit the assumptive world of the media. In this universe, both the public and the trial participant are induced to participate, whether or not they are knowingly aware of the mediated pressures and influence surrounding them. At the Steinberg trial, the specter of public opinion was so palpable that one prosecuting attorney was prompted to speculate that the jury verdict may have been the result of undue pressure, a fact that may have worked against the prosecution's case.[1]

Cameras also allowed participants to evaluate their ongoing trial per- formances and then, following the verdict, comment on their role—as judge, witness, lawyer, or juror—as guests on popular talk shows. The "celebrity" status afforded to participants in a televised trial may not bode well for a judicial system concerned with the public's perceptions of justice. This rise of the postverdict interview—a trend instigated by in-court television—may also send an ominous signal, most notably to prospective jurors in other high-profile trials who might expect their once private deliberative process and verdict to be subject to media scrutiny. The increasing visibility and vulnerability of jury members, caused by television coverage, is an area of genuine concern. Such fears were realized in the aftermath of the 1992 Rodney King trial, when jurors returned home frightened and intimidated by public outrage directed toward them following an unpopular verdict.

From the defendant's vantage point, Joel Steinberg spoke of the qualitative shifts in trial coverage fostered by the camera that endangered his ability to receive a fair trial. While recognizing that his self-interests are at stake, Steinberg's critique still represents a voice that has been long neglected in camera research. The constitutionally mandated purpose of a trial hinges on the court's ability to ensure a defendant's rights of due process. But in the year before the case came to court and throughout the four-month trial itself, the media were unrestrained in labeling what they perceived to be the criminal act as well as the criminal himself. Pretrial publicity that characterized Steinberg as a "monster" and his home "a house of horrors" was validated by sound bites and in-court camera visuals chosen for their imagistic intensity. According to Steinberg, mediated public perceptions worked to severely prejudice public opinion and may have changed the way in which key participants performed during the trial. Ultimately, he concluded, the media characterizations and public pressures brought to bear on the case may have influenced the outcome of the trial.

With the rise of the Courtroom Television Network, a national 24-hour-a-day, 7-day-a-week cable network (along with an equally aggressive Cable News Network), we can only anticipate that the media furor created around the Steinberg case will be replicated at dozens of other trials across the country. The early results appear to ratify that conclusion. While the Claus von Bulow and the New Bedford gang rape cases were such examples in the 1980s, they pale in comparison to the William Kennedy Smith trial in 1991 that was telecast to a national and global audience. While the legal issues surrounding the Smith case were hardly outstanding, the trial telecast may ultimately be a defining moment in the history of the American courtroom. With the birth of what can be described as a new media "genre," the Television Trial may represent the next class of popular entertainment for a country approaching the twenty-first century.

CAMERA "EFFECTS"

The Steinberg trial yielded evidence that television could shape attitudes and behavior in subtle, yet definitive, ways—a mediated mindset that was often inescapable. Even proponents, who argue that the in-court camera is a benign technology that mirrors the events taking place before it, concede that underlying and sometimes inexplicable shifts were taking place during the Steinberg trial. Remarks from court participants demonstrate that these changes are often subtle, to the degree that trial members may not even be conscious or aware of them as they occur. For some, the study afforded them their only opportunity to articulate thoughts and feelings that had evolved as a result of their participation in a televised trial.

A common thread seemed to link many of their observations. Television's influence and "effect" on participants appear to be directly correlated with a court member's own perception of the medium itself. That is, each participant held a unique perspective of how television operates and of its role and function within a societal framework. This perspective about the medium often had direct consequences as to the manner in which a participant performed. The camera, with its ability to transmit images to an audience, was not merely "a piece of the furniture," but a viable entity to be taken seriously. Strikingly, many participants appeared to "live up" to the expectations that they believed the medium had of them, and it was that peculiar interaction that played a part in their performance during the trial.

Television, in fact, held no single identity among these participants. It was alternately viewed as a medium for entertainment, propaganda, public opinion, self-promotion, self-analysis, news, information, and commentary. The way in which a participant defined the medium had a marked effect on the interaction taking place within the courtroom. In certain cases, it had a direct bearing on his performance.

The examples are illuminating. For one witness, the camera was representative of a crass and exploitative entertainment medium designed to promote ratings. Dr. Mary Elizabeth Lell perceived that the medium, through its sensational programming, had little regard for the sensitivities involved in the case. She went so far as to express deep concern for children unshielded from television trial coverage and other related programming for fear such "entertainment" would be harmful. This perception that television trivialized issues for commercial exploitation carried into the courtroom. Facing the camera prompted Lell to realize that her testimony could be used as grist for the medium mill. The camera served to remind her "of the reasons for it to be there," and it was that perception that made her more self-conscious and cautious about her role in the trial. According to Lell, the case had received so much "dramatization" that she had no wish "to stir things up" before the camera lens.[2]

Other major participants, as well, were wary that the primary role of the camera was to "boost ratings" for local television stations, rather than educating or informing the public about the issues in the case. Coverage was selected insofar as it represented the conflicts, the visual, or the controversial elements of the trial. So disturbed were the prosecutors by the television reports (and fearful that such coverage might even be seen by jury members) that they avoided watching nightly accounts of the trial altogether.

Still other participants perceived the medium as a vehicle used to gauge and perhaps influence public opinion. Those who could use the medium to their own benefit did so by making concerted efforts to influence public perceptions throughout the trial. The defense attorneys admitted an awareness of television's role in profoundly influencing a vast audience, and they readily incorporated it as part of their legal strategy. Through daily commentary and hallway press conferences, they attempted to create a more favorable public milieu. Surmising that their remarks would seep back to the jurors and perhaps influence the verdict, the lawyers took advantage of a medium they regarded as ideally suited as a communications link to the public's thinking about the case.

During Hedda Nussbaum's testimony, in particular, they watched "dailies" on the six major television channels to evaluate how they were "coming across." The reports encouraged them to believe that Nussbaum was "no longer being perceived as a victim" and that perhaps a turning point had been reached in the public's mind about her culpability. Following her testimony, they changed their legal strategy, admitting for the first time that a homicide had taken place. But it was Nussbaum, and not Steinberg, who had committed the crime.[3]

Nussbaum herself was anxious and concerned about public perceptions of her role in the case. The camera was a vehicle by which she could exonerate herself while concomitantly posing as a symbol for other battered women. Other witnesses also had their own agendas and were sensitive to the way in which television characterized their remarks.

The perspective that television is a medium that could engender public opinion also had a direct bearing at a later juncture in the case. Perry Reich abandoned controversial legal motions during the sentencing for fear that they "would have ripped the country open." Through the lens of the camera, such statements, he believed, could be taken out of the context of the courtroom environment and thrust into the wider realm of public opinion, a move that could eventually damage his client on appeal.[4] From Steinberg's own observations, the presence of the camera had an inhibiting effect on the defense team's efforts to negotiate during sentencing.[5]

Judge Harold Rothwax believed that if the camera had, in fact, coerced participants to behave more properly and "civilized," it is an argument for its continued use. But camera opponents realize that if the camera can provoke changes deemed desirable, in other instances it may not. Rothwax himself was not immune from such telegenic pressures. After learning of a news report showing trial footage of him angry at defense attorneys, he conceded that he modified his behavior, albeit to fit the mold of the proper judge.[6] The conformity to media-generated public pressure is a component of the Television Trial that presents an ominous challenge to the American courtroom.

THE IMPACT ON NEWS COVERAGE

Another participant at the Steinberg trial was the media. While it was not the study's original intention, one could not help but observe a dramatic change in the way news was covered and reported to the public—a change inspired by the camera. With proceedings widely disseminated on videotape, the camera became a new "competitor," altering the way journalists work and report the news. "This was a very, very important story for virtually every news organization, but even more for the broadcasters because, indeed, we did have cameras there," said Paul Smirnoff, executive producer for Fox News.[7]

Beyond changing the nature and scope of the court story, the in-court camera coverage shifted the balance of authority that has existed between the reporter and the news editor. With live courtroom visuals available, editors played a greater role in making news decisions and instructing reporters on news coverage, a circumstance that made some reporters uneasy. During the televising of Hedda Nussbaum's testimony, for instance, reporters found their judgments second-guessed—and their autonomy jeopardized—by editors compelled to express their own opinions. "They would tell me what to do on the basis of what they'd seen," said Mike Pearl, a reporter for the *New York Post*. "It was a very unusual situation. For those six days it did, in effect, put my editors into the courtroom. They had as much input [into the story] as I did."[8]

At the Steinberg trial, the relationship between the electronic and the print press also changed. The availability of visuals of court proceedings gave the trial the highest priority, and television reporters were allotted additional air time for their stories. As television coverage increased, newspapers were induced to join the media bandwagon, and print coverage expanded. Print reporters, like their television counterparts, became much more unrestrained in reporting stories derived from confidential sources. As newspapers allotted more space for the Steinberg trial, reporters could write more commentary and news analysis. The upward spiral of media coverage continued throughout the trial, fueled by a competitiveness wrought by the courtroom camera.

With greater access to both the print press and television, trial participants became media savvy, some presenting information or opinions that comfortably fit the constraints of the television news story. The trial also gave rise to the sound bite, and participants became knowledgeable about the lexicon and the processes of the media. The defense attorneys, in particular, perfected their techniques of "spinning" the day's testimony in hallway press conferences. And, in a curious scenario, competing interests within the confines of the courtroom spilled over into the corridors as different groups vied for the attention of the media. Lawyers, doctors, women's rights activists, and others saw the media as a vehicle to present their opinions. Other participants, once shielded in relative anonymity, felt pressured to present their viewpoints. While such a situation has existed in other high-profile cases, the link between the courtroom camera and the cameras in the corridors magnified television's role in promoting its own creation: the media-trial event.

Timothy Clifford, a *New York Newsday* reporter, contended that television and newspapers "fed each other," creating a wider circle of publicity that was lacking in other sensational nontelevised trials.[9] More sustained television coverage prompted newspaper editors "to give better play and more space to newspaper coverage," he said. Clifford compared the Steinberg case to the Robert Chambers murder trial, another sensational case in New York that contained similar emotional overtones, but that was not televised. He concluded that the Steinberg case was given considerably more front-page coverage in all major daily newspapers and was more often a prominent lead story on local stations.

According to Clifford, the shift in news coverage was most blatant in the *New York Times*. The newspaper ran a story each day that court was in session, unlike the Chambers trial where coverage was sporadic. He noted that the Steinberg case also received greater "play," frequently appearing on the front page of the metropolitan section of the *Times*, whereas the Chambers trial was relegated to a more obscure back page. Referring to his own reporting, Clifford said that it stretched as long as 40 consecutive days when stories about the trial were featured in *Newsday*. His reporting also became more aggressive.

Clifford believed that it was essential that members of the print press expand their reports and explore other areas of the case once considered less interesting or off-limits. Using a sports analogy to make his point, he noted that after watching television the public already knew "the score" before picking up the newspaper the following day. With visuals provided by a courtroom camera, the print press was under pressure to find new and different "angles" other than just recounting the day's key testimony. "Because of television and radio," said Clifford, "we lost what was a monopoly for print reporters . . . it's no longer enough to say [just] what happened."

An offshoot of this competition was that print journalists became more concerned with events not only as they happened within the courtroom, but also as they existed beyond the parameters of the camera lens. Under the rules, the camera was forbidden to photograph the spectators and the jury. Clifford found himself focusing on the reactions of those participants that could not be photographed. The result was a report that might emphasize the emotional responses of the jury or of prominent spectators such as Michelle Launders, Lisa's natural mother. In these instances, television reports were at their weakest, since they were unable to show these off-camera reactions.

Michael Callaghan, the managing editor for WNBC-TV news, said that it was inevitable that print reporters would shift the focus of their stories, since they could not compete with television's ability to present live testimony. "If I were an editor of a newspaper and one or more of the local stations were broadcasting coverage of the trial gavel-to-gavel, I would probably be pushing my people to come up with more sidebar material because the testimony was already available probably the day before and people had already seen and heard it."[10]

Fox News executive Paul Smirnoff noted that whenever television is allowed to broadcast any social or political event, print reporters invariably "have to work a little harder." At the Steinberg trial, he found this supposition to be true. "They became more analytical," he said. "And that happens every time cameras have been allowed anywhere. If [television] covers a live event from an inaugural, an election night, even sports, what does that leave the print reporter?"

During the Steinberg trial, an interesting turnabout occurred. Television could now concentrate on covering live testimony once considered the exclusive "domain" of the print press. The visual images greatly enhanced its effectiveness in conveying testimony. Ironically, according to reporters, this stimulated the print press to concentrate more on the "theatrics" and personalities of the trial, once material on the periphery of their coverage.

LEAKS

To counter the extensive television coverage, reporters admittedly became more aggressive in writing stories that did not necessarily emanate from court proceedings alone. Clifford acknowledged that many of his stories were, in fact, built around sources and "leaks" to the press. Leaks were particularly relevant to stories having to do with Hedda Nussbaum and her relationship with Joel Steinberg. "Because of the high level of interest, it gave more range to the print reporters to use these kinds of stories," he said. "Editors were interested in it and would give space to it."

The expanding attention given to the trial created a new and profound way in which editors, reporters, and sources interacted. Since editors were encouraging reporters to provide more in-depth coverage of the case, reporters were becoming more aggressive in cultivating sources. And as the case attracted more media coverage, sources became more relaxed in providing information to reporters. According to Clifford, in a nontelevised trial there was "no urgency" to speak with the source. But with television's expanded role and with fierce competition among the media, Clifford was more aggressive with his sources, pushing them "to give us some information that's not going to be on television." He noted that his sources were amenable to such requests, believing that their input had become critical. "Not only has it pushed us to try to get more off-the-record information, somehow it has made it easier [for the source] to give it to us," he said.

According to some observers, the Steinberg trial was notable for the overwhelming number of leaks and out-of-court statements made by key participants. Several participants attribute this situation to the presence of the courtroom camera. With testimony and other proceedings now broadcast on television, those participants with special interests felt increasingly obligated to present to the public what was once considered to be confidential information.

Leaks became increasingly routine, and attorneys utilized the medium to reach the public through their "spins." Barry Scheck commented that cameras tended to increase the pressure on lawyers to "spin" the media.[11] He, too, was active in responding to the press, but noted that other lawyers in recent nontelevised trials had also utilized the press. Jack Litman and Barry Slotnick, defense attorneys who represented, respectively, Robert Chambers and Bernhard Goetz, were cited as two examples who "did that very effectively." Scheck maintained that such high-profile cases mandate that the press be used to sway public opinion and create a more favorable climate for the defendant. But even the Chambers and Goetz cases paled in contrast to the "unbelievable number of leaks" that occurred during the televised Steinberg trial.

According to Scheck: "I submit that the extraordinary leaks that occurred happened here because you have cameras in the courtroom in the fashion that they were. There is a tremendous competition that begins to evolve between the television reporters and the print reporters for something new and different on the story."

Mike Pearl also noted that television reporters, under the strain of producing several news stories per day, became "greedy," often "speeding up" reports that perhaps needed more verification. "The pressure on television was something that I had never seen before in my 22 years [as a reporter]," he said. "When there wasn't anything going on in the courtroom, or it was dull, then they felt compelled to give their viewers something as startling as they thought the rest of the trial was. I don't know if it made them more aggressive, but they became more impatient."

Attorneys took advantage of this "impatience" by the media, using the wide access given to them by reporters. The lawyers even joked about their interactions with the media. When Ira London criticized Scheck for statements praising Hedda Nussbaum, characterizing the remarks as "brilliant fraudulent packaging," Scheck wryly responded: "My only complaint is that he should have mentioned my name more."

Postscript: Gray Endings

Gray areas, shadowy questions that have no satisfactory answers, still surround the Steinberg case. For Joel Steinberg, the verdict has been rendered. He will serve up to 25 years in prison. His appeal for a retrial, citing among other points that the media unfairly prejudiced the trial, was turned down in June 1992.

Through the lens of the camera, a personal tragedy was turned into a public drama. But for some, a residue of doubt still lingers as to what happened November 1, 1987, at Steinberg's Greenwich Village apartment on West 10th Street. Writer Maury Terry states, "The only eyewitnesses were two children at the mercy of two perverse adults, and one of them is dead."[1]

Certainly the social issues raised by the Steinberg trial continue to exist. The case compelled us to confront the issues of wife battering, child abuse, and homicide. They serve to remind that such violence is prevalent within the mainstream of American culture. Statistics reveal that the Joel Steinberg case was not an aberration. The same year he was arrested, more than 3 children died each day in America, victims of domestic violence, while nearly 2 million women were beaten by their spouses. Says writer Anne Summers, "We are not talking about a small problem or one confined to a single social class or region. This violence is pervasive [reaching into] a future almost too horrible to fathom."[2]

In the shattered remnants of the trial's aftermath, Hedda Nussbaum has begun to start her life over. At one point she was attending a New York area college for paralegal studies. Her tenuous connection to Steinberg, the man she once professed to worship, now exists only in the courtroom. Following the trial, she filed a multimillion-dollar lawsuit against him.

Against this backdrop of personal tragedy and devastation, the camera-in-the-courtroom experiment gave the public a voyeuristic glimpse into the events surrounding the death of a six-year-old girl named Lisa Steinberg. The personalities and issues involved in the case were held up to public scrutiny, as was television itself. Reservations about television's role in the courtroom led lawmakers in New York to eventually allow the camera experiment to end before grudgingly reinstating it with further restrictions.

Surely this legislative wavering continues to confound journalists and others who narrowly perceive the debate as a First Amendment issue. Moves to ban television from the courtroom are viewed as an infringement on the press's right to report the news and the public's "right to know." They are perplexed as to why the medium, so accepted in other arenas of American social and political life, is still being viewed with so much suspicion by a segment of the legal establishment. Ellen Fleysher, an experienced television journalist at WNBC-TV in New York City, maintains that given the chance, television can compatibly mesh with the workings of the court system.

There are a lot of question marks about cameras in the courtroom. There are a lot of question marks unresolved. I do not know the answer. And I do not think anybody does. All I can say is that I believe with all my heart that the more open and accessible any branch of government is, the better it's going to be. I do believe that. And therefore I believe the courtroom should be open to the examination of a camera as an extension of the pens and pencils of our brothers and sisters in the print press. Do I think it should be limitless, without reservation? No, no. Because I am aware of the power of what we do. But do I believe the answer lies in arbitrarily shutting them down? No. I think that's just as foolish. And I think that very reasonable people have to sit down and say how can this best serve the public interest, and then go ahead and do it.[3]

Yet other concerns remain that alarm social and media critics as they attempt to elevate the camera debate to a more theoretical plain. It is there that they issue a warning about American obeisance to their technology. "Nothing comes free, especially technology," states Neil Postman. "Culture always pays a price for technology."[4]

The Steinberg case was actually a rare example where we questioned how a powerful technology like television works, what it can create within the courtroom—and what its "cost" is to the nation's justice system. Our conclusions are not necessarily reassuring for a culture ensconced in a technological era where perceptions of and beliefs about American sociopolitical life are strongly linked to the images packaged by the media. These visuals are a symbolic reference point that connotes that the "system" is working, a comforting notion to us at a time when we increasingly are enveloped by television's pictures, and their meaning, of the world.

In such an environment, the Television Trial may be a welcomed cousin, a family relative with stories to tell about the American courtroom. Unquestionably, these tales are fascinating and alluring—and therein lies our challenge, should we choose to recognize it. Indeed, it is the medium's acute familiarity— its "mythic" quality, as Roland Barthes reminds us—that has obscured our vision and has deflected our justifiable concerns and fears.

In loving a medium that seduces our senses, perhaps we have too easily become enchanted by its power, and, in doing so, not only has television become a part of culture, but also we have become a part of it. By extension, in the age of the Television Trial, the threat is not that the medium will somehow fail to adjust to the sensitive intricacies of the courtroom, but that the American courtroom itself will become a manifestation of the medium. In a vast media experiment that is no longer new and rarely questioned, this is the peril that lies in the long shadows cast by the fusion of the trial and the technology.

Appendix

The following sources were interviewed by the author between January 1988 and June 1993.

PART ONE—THE AGE OF THE TELEVISION TRIAL

Roy Black, attorney, William Kennedy Smith trial, W. Palm Beach

Steven Brill, president and editor in chief, Courtroom Television Network, *The American Lawyer* magazine

Merrill Brown, senior vice president of corporate and program development, Courtroom Television Network

Pamela Ferrero, assistant district attorney, McMartin trial, Los Angeles

Ellen Fleysher, assistant news director, NBC-TV

Walter Goodman, critic, *New York Times*

Jack Litman, attorney, Robert Chambers trial, New York

Marty Rosenbaum, director of judicial and legislative services, New York State Defenders Association

Paul Smirnoff, executive producer, Fox News

PART TWO—THE STEINBERG TRIAL: A CASE STUDY

Harold Rothwax, presiding judge

Ira London, lead defense counsel

Adrian DiLuzio, defense counsel

Perry Reich, defense counsel
Peter Casolaro, assistant district attorney, Manhattan
John McCusker, assistant district attorney, Manhattan
Barry Scheck, lawyer representing Hedda Nussbaum

Witnesses:

Dr. Aglae Charlot
Dr. Azariah Eshkenazi
Dr. Patrick Kilhenny
Dr. Mary Elizabeth Lell
Patricia McAdams
Dr. Douglas Miller
Hedda Nussbaum
Dr. John Plunkett
Marilyn Walton

Jurors:

Katherine Anderson
Sharon Bailey
Helena Barthell
Jeremiah Cole
Allen Jared
Anne King
Gillian Llinas
John Sullivan
Man Fung Tse
Shirley Unger

Defendant:

Joel Steinberg

Journalists and Media Executives:

David Bookstaver, administrator, New York Broadcasters Courtroom Pool
Susan Brownmiller, author of *Waverly Place*
Michael Callaghan, managing editor, WNBC News
Pat Clark, reporter, *New York Daily News*

Timothy Clifford, reporter, *New York Newsday*

Roger Colloff, vice president and general manager, WCBS News

Tony Guida, news reporter, WNBC-TV

Peter Hamill, columnist, *New York Post*

Colleen Hunt, news reporter, WPIX-TV

Mary Murphy, news reporter, WCBS-TV

Steve Paulus, assistant news editor, WCBS-TV

Mike Pearl, reporter, *New York Post*

Paul Smirnoff, executive producer, Fox News

Notes

INTRODUCTION

1. "Televised Trial, World's Attention Attracted to 1955," *Waco Tribune Herald*, July 23, 1978, p. C1. The article's attention to the Washburn trial was in part a reaction to the push by many states to endorse the use of courtroom cameras. Florida in particular brought attention to the issue after a year-long study in 1977, which concluded that television did not hinder the workings of the court.

2. Neil Postman, Betsy Kaufman Memorial Speech, Second International Conference on Early Childhood Education, Tel Aviv, Israel, June 1987. Postman is also to be credited with coining the "Faustian Bargain" as a metaphor for the conflicting elements that are inherent within a technological society.

3. It should be noted that camera legislation varies across the country. In the majority of states, cameras are permitted for criminal and civil trials as well as for the appellate courts. Some states, however, allow courtroom cameras under more restricted provisions.

4. Both Paul Newman and William Hurt were defendants in televised civil cases: Newman was embroiled in a Connecticut dispute over the legal rights of his brand food line; Hurt was the defendant in a palimony suit in New York. Zsa Zsa Gabor was charged in a criminal action for slapping a Los Angeles police officer.

5. Interview with Pamela Ferrero, January 1991.

6. In Maryland, during a court-supervised 18-month experiment in 1980–81, television cameras were allowed access to criminal trials. In 1981, the state legislature banned such coverage, and that remains Maryland law as of June 1993.

7. Anna Quindlen, "The Glass Eye," *New York Times*, December 18, 1991, p. A29.

8. Ibid.

CHAPTER 1

1. Neil Postman, *Amusing Ourselves to Death* (New York: Viking, 1985) is an intriguing analysis of television and the decline of public discourse and social institutions.

2. George Gerbner, "Trial by Television: Are We at the Point of No Return?" *Judicature* 63(79), 1980: 426.

3. Ibid.

4. Ibid., p. 420.

5. Michael Hoyt, "Steven Brill Builds an Empire," *Columbia Journalism Review*, September-October 1990, p. 46.

6. Ibid.

7. "Murder in Beverly Hills," "Prime Time Live," ABC-TV, May 17, 1990.

8. Robert Entner, "Encoding the Image of the American Judiciary Institution: A Semiotic Analysis of Broadcast Trials to Ascertain Its Definition of the Court System" (Ph.D. diss., New York University, 1993), p. 15.

9. Barry Brummett, "Mediating the Law: Popular Trials and Mass Media," in *Popular Trials: Rhetoric, Mass Media and the Law*, ed. Robert Hariman (Tuscaloosa, AL: University of Alabama Press, 1990), p. 183.

10. Entner, p. 11

11. David Altheide, "TV News and the Social Construction of Justice," in *Justice and the Media*, ed. Ray Surette (Springfield, MA: Charles C. Thomas, 1984), pp. 299–301.

12. Ibid.

13. Ibid.

14. Entner, p. 162. The author credits the idea of television's "associative grammar" and the decline of public reasoning to Kathleen Jamieson, *Elegance in the Electronic Age: The Transformation of Political Speechmaking* (New York: Oxford University Press, 1988).

15. Entner, p. 9. The author also cites the work of Stuart Hall as important in understanding the structuring systems of the media. See Hall's essay, "Determinations of News Photographs," *The Manufacture of News*, ed. S. Cohen and J. Young (Beverly Hills, CA: Sage, 1973), pp. 176–190.

16. Entner, pp. 73–75.

17. Edward J. Epstein, *News from Nowhere* (New York: Vintage Books, 1973).

18. Entner, p. 158. The television audience is not the only entity influenced by television's imagistic portrait. Of particular concern is whether trial participants are "reading" TV messages—and then reconstructuring their own performance to conform to the agenda of the medium. The effect of televising trial participants is explored later in Chapter 1 and is an integral component of the Steinberg case study in Part Two.

19. Ibid.

20. Kiku Adatto, *Sound Bite Democracy: Network Evening News Presidential Campaign Coverage, 1968–1988* (Cambridge: Joan Shorenstein Barone Press Politics Center, John F. Kennedy School of Government, Harvard University, June 1990), p. 4.

21. Richard L. Berke, "Sound Bites Grow at CBS, Then Vanish," *New York Times*, July 11, 1992, p. A7. See also a related article, "Campaign Sound Bites Become Smaller Mouthfuls," *New York Times*, January 23, 1992, pp. A1, A18.

22. Postman, *Amusing Ourselves to Death*, p. 130.

23. For more on the modern-day televised political scene, see Postman's essay, "Reach Out and Touch Someone," in *Amusing Ourselves to Death*, pp. 125–141.

24. Adatto, p. 5.

25. Ibid., p. 4.

26. Susan Brownmiller, quoted in Sidney Schanberg, "The Rape Trial," *New York Times*, March 27, 1984, p. A31.

27. See Katha Pollitt's thought-provoking essay "Media Goes Wilding in Palm Beach," *Nation*, June 24, 1991, pp. 833, 847–52. For perspectives by Pollitt and Alan Dershowitz regarding the media's role in high-profile rape and sexual assault cases, see "Exchange," *Nation*, September 9, 1991, pp. 250, 280.

28. Ruth Jones, quoted in James Barron, "Experts on Rape Back Smith's Acquittal," *New York Times*, December 12, 1991, p. B20.

29. Public Defense Backup Center, *The Intrusion of Cameras in New York's Criminal Courts: A Report by the Public Defense Backup Center* (Albany: New York State Defenders Association, May 12, 1989), pp. 9–10.

30. Ibid., p. 9.

31. Cited by Jonathan E. Gradess, executive director, New York State Defenders Association, in testimony before the New York State Senate and Assembly Judiciary Committees on Cameras in the Courtroom, April 23, 1991.

32. Cited by Marty Rosenbaum, director of judicial and legislative services, New York State Defenders Association, in testimony before the New York State Senate and Assembly Judiciary Committees on Cameras in the Courtroom, March 13, 1989.

33. Interview with Joel Steinberg, June 1989.

34. Interview with Jack Litman, January 1989.

35. Ibid.

36. The Criminal Justice Section of the New York State Bar Association also argued the issue in a position paper on legislation authorizing audiovisual coverage in the civil and criminal courts. See Section Six, "The Study of the Experiment Released by the Office of Court Administration Is Fatally Flawed, and Completely Inadequate," pp. 3–5.

37. *Report of the Chief Administrative Judge to the New York State Legislature, the Governor and the Chief Judge on the Effect of Audio-Visual Coverage on the Conduct of Judicial Proceedings*, March 1989.

38. See Public Defense Backup Center, p. 11.

39. *People* v. *Hazelwood*, no. 8297 (Supreme Court, Suffolk County, New York, 1989).

40. Ibid.

41. Interview with Jack Litman, January 1989. Also, the New York State Defenders Association joined in the criticism, stating that "there was little doubt that Justice Rohl's decision to set such excessive bail was influenced . . . by the national television coverage the proceedings received." Public Defense Backup Center, p. 11.

CHAPTER 2

1. Cited in Jack B. Weinstein and Diane L. Zimmerman, "Let the People Observe Their Courts," *Judicature* 61(4), October 1977: 157. The authors dispute this point, contending that rather than "preserving the sanctity of the judiciary," the courts have become more a "mysterious private rite than an exercise in public governance."

2. *People* v. *Munday*, 280 Ill. 32, 67, 117 N.E. 286, (1917).

3. Still and newsreel cameras still were present at several sensational trials of the 1920s, most notably the Leopold-Loeb and Scopes trials. See an excellent study by Richard Kielbowicz, "The Story Behind the Adoption of the Ban of Courtroom Cameras," *Judicature* 63(1), 1979: 17.

4. Kielbowicz cites Raymond Schuneman, "The Photograph in Print" (Ph.D. diss., University of Minnesota, 1966), p. 289.

5. Kielbowicz, p. 15.

6. Ibid.

7. Susanna Barber, *News Cameras in the Courtroom: A Fair Trial–Free Press Debate* (Norwood, NJ: Ablex, 1987), p. 2.

8. Ibid.

9. Ibid.

10. Ibid.

11. Kielbowicz, p. 16.

12. Barber, p. 2

13. Ibid.

14. Quoted in Kielbowicz, p. 17.

15. For summaries of the events surrounding the Hauptmann trial, see the following sources: Barber, pp. 3–10; Kielbowicz, pp. 14–23; Oscar Hallam, "Some Object Lessons on Publicity in Criminal Trials," *Minnesota Law Review* 24(4), 1940: 454–508; David Reed, *Canon 35: Flemington Revisited 1*, Freedom of Information Center Report No. 177 (Columbia, MD, 1967).

16. Kielbowicz, p. 17. The author emphasizes that news reports of the Hauptmann trial took on somewhat mythic overtones even decades after the event. He states that 33 years after the trial an editor of the *Portland Oregonian*, still enamored of the drama of the event, stated that the trial "was a Roman holiday." He described photographers who "clambered on counsel's table and shoved their flash-bulbs into the faces of witnesses. The judge lost control of his courtroom and the press photographers lost control of their senses." Kielbowicz noted that Malcolm Bauer, the associate editor, later conceded that he had been confused over the media events surrounding the trial.

17. Ibid. Still these observations fail to connect the actions of photographers to their role outside the courtroom. Intense photo coverage was given immediately after Lindbergh reported the disappearance of his 18-month son on March 1, 1932, and then when the body of Charles, Jr., was discovered in a shallow grave near the Lindbergh home. During the next two years, as police investigated the murder, Lindbergh and his wife were continually harassed by the photo-press. When Hauptmann, a German immigrant, was arrested on September 18, 1934, newsreel companies descended on the New York City police station where the suspect was being interrogated.

18. Ibid.

19. Quoted in Hallam, p. 486.

20. Ibid., pp. 478–481.

21. "Both Guilty," *New Republic*, February 27, 1935, p. 62.

22. Richard Knight, "Trial by Fury," *Forum*, January 1936, pp. 8–10. See also Barber, p. 5.

23. Barber, p. 7.

24. Hallam, p. 454.

25. Ibid.

26. Ward Stone and Shiel G. Edlin, "TV or Not TV: Televised and Photographic Coverage of Trials," *Mercer Law Review* 29(4), 1978: 1120. Canon 35 has been a "lively public issue" for a number of scholars and jurists. See Robert Underwood, "Observations Regarding Canon 35," *Illinois Bar Journal* 55(3), 1966: 194–203; Albert E. Blashfield, "The Case of the Controversial Canon," *American Bar Association Journal* 48(4), 1962: 429–435.

27. Kielbowicz, p. 23.

28. Barber, p. 11.

29. Ibid.

30. "Televised Trial, World's Attention Attracted to 1955," *Waco Tribune Herald*, July 23, 1978, p. C1.

31. Abner V. McCall, "Courtroom Television," *Texas Bar Journal* 19(2), February 1956; 73–74, 106–110. See also Gilbert Geis, "A Lively Public Issue: Canon 35 in the Light of Recent Events," *American Bar Association Journal*, May 1957, pp. 420–421.

32. Quoted in Blashfield, p. 432.

33. Frank White, "Cameras in the Courtroom: A U.S. Survey," *Journalism Monograph* 60, 1979: p. 3. White credits Colorado as the first state to enact legislation allowing television access to the courts in 1956. Prior to the 1965 *Estes* decision, only Texas and Oklahoma had joined Colorado. Texas had not adopted Canon 35, and Oklahoma had adopted the canon, but had not enforced it. By late 1978, 19 states were allowing courtroom cameras under various provisions.

34. Barber, pp. 12–13.

35. Geis, pp. 421–422.

36. White, p. 3.

37. *Estes* v. *Texas*, 381 U.S. 532 (1965). See also Barber, pp. 47–49; John Broholm, "Electronic Media in the Courtroom," *Case and Comment* 85(3), 1978: 3–4.

38. Stone and Edlin, pp. 1121–1122.

39. Cited in Joseph A. Boyd, Jr., "Cameras in Court—*Estes* v. *Texas* and Florida's One-Year Pilot Program, *University of Miami Law Review* 32, 1978: 819.

40. *Estes* v. *Texas*, 381 U.S. 532 (1965).

41. Ibid. See also Broholm, p. 4. The author notes that the *Estes* decision, even as it closed courtroom doors, left those same doors open for television to come back at a later time. Still, while the ruling did not represent a collective will, it set out succinctly the Court's philosophical concerns about maintaining a "dignified" courtroom setting, free from the possible tainting effects of an in-court camera.

42. *Estes* v. *Texas*, 381 U.S. 532 (1965). See also Broholm, pp. 4–5; Stone and Edlin, pp. 1122–1123.

43. *Estes* v. *Texas*, 381 U.S. 532 (1965). See also Charlotte Carter, "Television in the Courts," *State Court Journal* 5(1), 1981: 12; Broholm, pp. 4–8.

44. *Estes* v. *Texas*, 381 U.S. 532 (1965). See Stone and Edlin, p. 1123. See also Stephen Wasby, "Laying Estes to Rest: A Case Note," *Justice System* 5(1), 1979: 59–60.

45. Barber, pp. 20–21.

46. Ibid.

47. Elder Witt, "Television in the Courtroom," *Editorial Research Reports*, 1(2), 1981: 25. The author notes that the state's legal brief also addressed another recent Florida trial involving five Dade County policemen charged with the beating death of a black Miami insurance salesman, Arthur McDuffie. The state declared that if the media bore any responsibility for subsequent riots in Miami, it was due to initial inflammatory news reports and not the televising of the trial. The brief concluded that had the entire trial been broadcast and had the public seen the administration of justice, the explosion of public fury may not have occurred. It is an argument that loses strength in light of an analogous situation in Los Angeles in 1992. A trial involving several police officers accused of viciously beating a black man, Rodney King, ended in acquittal, and the city exploded in a full-blown riot. In this episode, televised gavel-to-gavel coverage over Court TV may apparently have served to fuel community unrest.

48. S. R. Craig, "Cameras in the Courtroom in Florida," *Journalism Quarterly* 56, 1979: 703–710. See also Boyd, p. 835.

49. *United States* v. *Chandler*, 449, U.S. 560 (1981).

50. Witt, p. 25.

51. Barber, pp. 17–20.

CHAPTER 3

1. Susanna Barber, *News Cameras in the Courtroom: A Fair Trial–Free Press Debate* (Norwood, NJ: Ablex, 1987), p. 113.

2. Cited in Barber, p. 113.

3. R. W. Power, "Television in the Courtroom: Von Bulow and *The Jazz Singer*," *St. Louis University Law Journal*, 25, 1982: 813–820.

4. David Berreby, "Von Bulow: Examining the Tactics," *National Law Journal*, March 29, 1982, pp. 1, 11–13.

5. Ruth Hochberger, "Von Bulow Lawyer No Fan of Cameras in Courtroom," *New York Law Journal*, March 18, 1982, pp. 1–2.

6. Herald Price Fahringer, "Cameras in the Courtroom," *Trial*, January 1981, pp. 6, 18–20.

7. Hochberger, p. 2. See also Barber, p. 113.

8. Susan Drucker and Janice Platt Hunold, in *Popular Trials: Rhetoric, Mass Media and the Law*, ed. Robert Hariman, (University of Alabama Press, 1990), p. 138. This essay examines televised trials as a clash between societal agendas and the rights of trial participants.

9. Barber, p. 114.

10. Power quoted by Barber, p. 114.

11. Barber, p. 100.

12. B. De Silva, "The Gang-Rape Story," *Columbia Journalism Review*, May-June 1984, pp. 42–44.

13. Ibid., p. 43.

14. Ibid., p. 42.

15. "Pool Table Sex Assault Charged to Boy, Twelve," *New York Times*, April 18, 1984, p. A14.

16. Barber, p. 115.

17. Sidney Schanberg, "The Rape Trial," *New York Times*, March 27, 1984, p. A31.

18. Joe Queenan, "What's in a Middle Name?," *Time*, December 16, 1992, p. 32.

19. Robert Goldberg, "Mr. Smith in the Dock and on the Tube," *Wall Street Journal*, December 9, 1991, p. A12.

20. Jeff Greenfield, "Nightline," ABC-TV, December 10, 1991.

21. Richard Lacayo, "Trial by Television," *Time*, December 16, 1991, p. 31.

22. Ibid.

23. Susan Estrich, quoted in James Barron, "Experts on Rape Back Smith's Acquittal," cited by *New York Times*, December 12, 1991, p. B20.

24. George Bush, quoted in Walter Goodman, "When Broadcast Matter Is Considered Offensive," *New York Times*, December 21, 1991, p. 47.

25. Walter Goodman, "Sex? Viewers Are Shocked. Shocked!" *New York Times*, December 22, 1991, II, *Arts and Leisure*, p. 1.

26. "That Night on the Beach and on the Lawn," *New York Post*, December 11, 1991, p. 5.

27. Murray Weiss, "Defendant Now a Solid Bet to Win Acquittal," *New York Post*, December 11, 1991, p. 4.

28. Steven Brill, "Nightline," ABC-TV, December 10, 1991.

29. Queenan, p. 32.

30. Ibid.

31. Mim Udovitch, "Fear and Loathing in Palm Beach," *Village Voice*, December 25, 1991, pp. 41–42.

32. Jeff Greenfield, "Nightline," ABC-TV, December 10, 1991.

33. Ibid.

34. Fox Butterfield and Mary R. W. Tabor, "Woman in Florida Rape Inquiry Fought Adversity and Sought Acceptance," *New York Times*, April 17, 1991, p. A17.

35. Ibid.

36. William Glaberson, "Times Article Naming Rape Accusor Ignites Debate on Journalistic Values," *New York Times*, April 26, 1991, p. A14.

37. Cited in Glaberson, p. A14.

38. Interview with Walter Goodman, July 1992.

39. Ibid.

40. Murray Weiss, "Ted Tried to Bribe Son's Rehab Buddy," *New York Post*, December 10, 1991, pp. 4–5.

41. Timothy McDarrah, "Jackie O Fears She's Susceptible to Alzheimer's," *New York Post*, December 10, 1991, p. 4.

42. Amy Pagnozzi, "Time Stops for No Woman in Ticking Judge's Courtroom," *New York Post*, December 10, 1991, p. 5.

43. Joe Nicholson, "Judge Boots Reporter for Smiling," *New York Post*, December 10, 1991, p. 5.

44. Joe Nicholson, "'It's a Hanging Jury,' say Legal Experts," *New York Post*, December 19, 1991, p. 4.

45. Ibid.

46. Orbach's comment during *voir dire* was aired repeatedly by CNN and other major networks in November 1991.

47. David Bianculli, "Shame on You, CNN," *New York Post*, December 11, 1992, p. 60.

48. Charles Jaco, cited in Walter Goodman, "From Jury Box and TV, Rape Trial Is Seen on Very Different Channels," *New York Times*, December 10, 1991.

49. Anna Quindlen, "The Glass Eye," *New York Times*, December 18, 1991, p. A29.

50. Don Pember, *Mass Media Law* (Dubuque, Iowa: W. C. Brown, 1987), p. 404.

51. George Critchlow, "Rodney King: Justice Denied?," *Cultural and Comparative Studies, Bulletin of the American, British, French and German Centers in Sibiu*, No. 1, 1993, pp. 1–3.

52. Ibid.

CHAPTER 4

1. The anecdote about the origins of Court TV came from an interview with Merrill Brown, February 1992, and also from press reports. See Marlys Harris, "Making Crime Pay: Steve Brill's Court TV Shows America the Law, Torts and All," *People*, April 20, 1992, p. 93.

2. Warren Berger, "Cable in the Court!" *New York*, August 12, 1991, p. 46.

3. Michael Hoyt, "Steven Brill Builds an Empire." *Columbia Journalism Review*, September-October 1990, pp. 41–42.

4. Steven Brill, "Headnotes: Watching the Drama of Justice," *American Lawyer*, July-August 1990, pp. 1–4.

5. Ibid.

6. Sam Howe Verhovek, "News Cameras in Courts? New York Law Disputed," *New York Times*, May 28, 1991, p. B1.

7. Sam Howe Verhovek, "Permission Expires for Cameras in Court," *New York Times*, June 1, 1991, p. 25. See Chapter 5, "The Forty-Fifth State," for a fuller analysis of the New York experiment.

8. Walter Goodman, "The Wheels of Justice Live on Cable," *New York Times*, July 3, 1991, p. C17.

9. Harry Waters, "Courting Courtroom Junkies," *Newsweek*, July 1, 1991, p. 58.

10. Interview with Steven Brill, February 1992.

11. Ibid.

12. Steven Brill, "How the Willie Smith Show Changed America," *American Lawyer*, January-February 1992, pp. 3, 98–102.

13. "Smith Trial Puts Court TV in the News," *Court TV in Session* (newsletter of the Courtroom Television Network), February 1992, p. 4.

14. Ibid., p. 1.

15. Brill, "How the Willie Smith Show Changed America," p. 3.

16. Ibid.

17. Roy Black, quoted in Brill, "How the Willie Smith Show Changed America," p. 100.

18. Ibid., p. 98.

19. Alan M. Dershowitz, "How Not to Televise Trials," in *Contrary to Popular Opinion* (New York: Pharos Books, 1992), pp. 312–314.

20. Ibid.

21. Interview with Merrill Brown, July 1993.

22. By late 1992, Court TV operations consolidated and were centered at 600 Third Avenue in Manhattan.

23. Interview with Merrill Brown, February 1992.

24. Ibid.

25. Ibid.

26. *Profiles: The People Behind the Network* (Courtroom Television Network, 1992).

27. Ibid.

28. Berger, p. 41.

29. Charles Claffery, "Interview with Steven Brill," *Boston Globe*, Living section, July 31, 1991, p. 25.

30. Berger, p. 42.

31. F. Lee Bailey, quoted in Berger, p. 42.

32. Alan Dershowitz, quoted in Berger, p. 41.

33. Dershowitz, pp. 312–314.

34. Ibid.

35. Ibid.

36. Dottie Enrico, "Will Court TV Appeal? The Verdict's Not in Yet," *Newsday*, December 16, 1991, p. 35.

37. Interview with Steven Brill, February 1992.

38. Enrico, p. 35.

39. Susan Drucker, "Cameras in the Court Revisited," *New York State Bar Journal*, July-August 1992, p. 47.

40. Ibid.

41. Quoted in Robert Goldberg, "Mr. Smith in the Dock and on the Tube," *Wall Street Journal*, December 9, 1991, p. A12.

42. Harris, p. 93.

43. Letter from Judge Steve Russell to Steve Brill, June 18, 1992.

44. Ibid.

45. James Wolcott, "On Television—Prime Time Justice," *New Yorker*, November 30, 1992, pp. 158–159.

46. Ibid.

47. Ibid.

48. *Court TV Trials Aired to Date* (as of February 6, 1992) (Courtroom Television Network, 1992).

49. Drucker, pp. 47–48.

50. Brill, "Headnotes," p. 3.

51. Ibid.

52. Cited in Berger, p. 46.

53. Ibid.

54. Interview with Barry Scheck, December 1992.

55. Berger, p. 46.

56. Brill, "Headnotes," pp. 1–3.

57. Interview with Steven Brill, February 1992.

58. Interview with Barry Scheck, December 1992.

59. Ibid.

60. Interview with Steven Brill, February 1992.

61. Brill, "Headnotes," p. 3.

62. Brill, "How the Willie Smith Show Changed America," p. 101.

63. Ibid., p. 100.

64. David Kaplan and Bob Cohn, "Palm Beach Lessons," *Newsweek*, August 5, 1991, pp. 30–31.

65. Brill, "How the Willie Smith Show Changed America," p. 101.

66. *Court TV Trials Aired to Date* (as of June 22, 1993) (Courtroom Television Network, 1993).

67. Interview with Marty Rosenbaum, September 1992.

68. Ibid.

69. George Gerbner, quoted in Claffery, p. 25.

70. Susan Drucker, "Television Comes to the Courtroom" (scholarly paper for Hoftra University, 1992), p. 12.

71. Howard Kurtz, "Media Notes: Courting the Coup Plotters," *Washington Post*, April 9, 1992, The *Post* describes the agreement with Russia as "a sort of electronic cultural exchange." In return for Russian satellite feeds of trials, Ostankino will be allowed to use Court TV footage and will have the right to broadcast American trials to audiences in the CIS, Europe, and Asia.

72. Interview with Steven Brill, February 1992.

CHAPTER 5

1. List compiled by the Information Service, National Center for State Courts (Williamsburg, VA: September 1992).

2. Ibid. Following New York, South Carolina began its experiment in a single courtroom in January 1992, but that limited plan was soon replaced by a more ambitious one. Even before the six-month experiment had expired, a new blueprint was enacted to include the televising of criminal and civil courts in various counties. Jurists were so enamored with television that by October 1992 a judicial oversight committee had already devised plans to allow the broadcast of state and appellate courts. South Carolina has also taken the unique step—and, one might argue, a precarious one—of permitting camera coverage of family courts (raising a host of problems pertaining to the confidentiality of minors involved in such proceedings).

3. Anthony Genovesi, Deliberations on Bill A77-B, New York State Senate, June 2, 1987.

4. Robert King, ibid.

5. New York State Assembly, Bill A77-B, 1987.

6. Ibid.

7. Thomas A. Demakos and Saul Weprin, quoted in Sam Roberts, "TV in the Court: Titillation or Education?" *New York Times*, November 26, 1987, p. B1.

8. Ibid.

9. Ibid.

10. Ibid.

11. Ibid.

12. Statistics compiled by the Office of Court Administration in New York City, June 1989.

13. Richard Heffner, "Cameras in the Courtroom: A Bad Idea Whose Time Has Come," *New York Law Journal*, April 17, 1989, pp. 1–3.

14. Matthew Crosson, as part of an extensive opinion regarding the New York experiment in the *New York Law Journal*, May 1, 1991, p. 40.

15. Public Defense Backup Center, *The Intrusion of Cameras in New York's Criminal Courts: A Report by the Public Defense Backup Center* (Albany: New York State Defenders Association, May 12, 1989), p. 24. The report maintained that "the research conducted by OCA [Office of Court Administration] is merely a continuation of the 'unsophisticated and unreliable' research that has been conducted elsewhere. OCA chose not to engage in a controlled experiment. Instead, it sought to determine the impact of cameras on trial participants solely through survey research. [Such results] cannot provide information on the *actual* psychological effects. . . . "

16. Cited in an interview with Ellen Fleysher, January 1989.

17. Public Defense Backup Center, pp. 21–22.

18. Ibid.

19. Cited by Jonathan E. Gradess, executive director, New York State Defenders Association, in testimony before the New York State Senate and Assembly Judiciary Committees on Cameras in the Courtroom, April 23, 1991.

20. Ibid.

21. Sam Howe Verhovek, "Permission Expires for Cameras in Court," *New York Times*, June 1, 1991, pp. 22, 27.

22. Sam Howe Verhovek, "News Cameras in Courts? New York Law Disputed," *New York Times*, May 28, 1991, p. B1.

23. As previously noted, the Maryland legislature curtailed an experiment in 1981 that was implemented through judicial initiatives.

24. Dale Volker, quoted in Gary Spencer, "Embattled Cameras-in-Courts Bill May Face Close Vote in Senate," *New York Law Journal*, June 8, 1992, p. 1.

25. College of Criminal Justice, Northeastern University, Massachusetts, *Cameras in the Courtroom Make New Yorkers Reluctant to Testify* (Boston: Northeastern University).

26. National Victim Center, *Rape in America* (National Victim Center, April 23, 1992).

27. News release by the Executive Chamber of the state of New York, June 23, 1992.

28. William Petkanas, "Cameras on Trial: An Assessment of the Educational Effects of News Cameras in Trial Courts" (Ph.D. diss., New York University, 1990), p. 112.

29. C. R. Nesson and A. D. Koblenz, "The Image of Justice: *Chandler* v. *Florida*," *Harvard Civil Rights–Civil Liberties Law Review* 16, Fall 1981: 400–413.

30. Jack B. Weinstein and Diane L. Zimmerman, "Let the People Observe Their Courts," *Judicature* 61(4), October 1977: 156–165.

31. Anthony Genovesi, Deliberations on Bill A77-B, New York State Senate, June 2, 1987.

32. Richard Heffner, pp. 1–3.

33. Interview with Paul Smirnoff, January 1989.

34. Interview with Ellen Fleysher, January 1989.

35. David Altheide, "TV News and the Social Construction of Justice," in *Justice and the Media*, ed. Ray Surette (Springfield, MA: Charles C. Thomas, 1984), pp. 300–301.

36. Robert D. McFadden, "Custody Fight Intensifies as Girl Tells of Her Ordeal," *New York Times*, January 16, 1993, p. 26.

37. George Gerbner, "Trial by Television: Are We at the Point of No Return?" *Judicature* 63(79), 1980: 416–426.

38. "Amy Fisher: My Story" aired on NBC-TV, December 28, 1992; "Casualties of Love" on CBS-TV, January 3, 1993; and "The Amy Fisher Story," on ABC-TV, January 3, 1993.

39. John J. O'Connor, "The Line Between Dramas and Lies," *New York Times*, December 31, 1992, pp. C11, C25.

40. Prime time ratings compiled by A. C. Nielson Co. for December 29, 1992, through January 3, 1993. Reported in the Ft. Lauderdale *Sun Sentinel*, January 7, 1993, p. 4E.

41. Jose Pretlow, quoted by Jon Lafayette, "Courting Viewers: TV Plays for Ratings with High-Profile Trials," *Electronic Media*, February 8, 1993.

42. Steve Bornfeld, "Tele-Courts Open to Mockery," *Times Union* (Albany, NY), February 17, 1993, p. C–6.

43. "The Trial That Had to Happen: The People versus Amy Fisher," "A Current Affair," Fox Network, February 1–4, 1993.

44. "HBO Jury Finds James Earl Ray Not Guilty in King Assassination," *Journal Gazette*, April 5, 1993.

45. Ibid.

46. Gerbner, p. 421.

47. Philip Hager, "Bid to Televise Execution Becomes Broad Court Test," *Los Angeles Times*, June 6, 1991, p. A1.

48. Ibid. See also Philip Hager, "U.S. Judge Upholds Ban on TV Cameras at Executions," *Los Angeles Times*, June 8, 1991, p. A1.

49. *Bridges* v. *California*, 314 U.S. 252 (1941).

50. *U.S.* v. *Dickinson, 465 F.2d 496, 499* (1972), quoted in Susanna Barber, *News Cameras in the Courtroom: A Fair Trial–Free Press Debate* (Norwood, NJ: Ablex, 1987), p. 31.

51. Barber, pp. 31–32.

52. Jack G. Day, "The Case Against Cameras in the Courtroom," *Judges Journal* 20(1), 1981: 19.

53. Weinstein and Zimmerman, pp. 156–157.

54. Barber, p. 33.

55. *Sheppard* v. *Maxwell*, 384 U.S. 333 (1966).

56. Matthew T. Crosson, "Cameras in Court Do Not Adversely Affect Conduct of Court Proceedings," *New York Law Journal*, May 1, 1991, p. 40. Crosson's opinion closely echoes the judicial stance taken by the Westchester County Court of Appeals in *Westchester Rockland Newspapers* v. *Leggett*, 48 N.Y. 2d 430 (1979).

57. Tarky Lombardi, Deliberations on Bill A77-B, New York State Senate, June 1, 1987.

58. Charlotte Carter, "Television in the Courts," *State Court Journal* 5(1), 1981: 6–12, 24–28. See also Shelly B. Kulwin, "Televised Trials—Constitutional Constraints, Practical Implications, and State Experimentation," *Loyola University Law Journal* 9(4), 1978: 910–934.

59. *Cox Broadcasting Corporation* v. *Cohn*, 420 U.S. 469 (1975).

60. Ray Surette, *Media, Crime and Criminal Justice: Images and Reality* (Pacific Grove, CA: Brooks/Cole, 1992), p. 197.

61. Werner Heisenberg, *The Physicist's Conception of Nature* (San Diego: Harcourt Brace, 1958).

62. Marshall McLuhan, *Understanding Media: The Extensions of Man* (New York: McGraw-Hill, 1964), p. 177.

63. Susan Sontag, *On Photography* (New York: Farrar, Straus & Giroux, 1977), p. 85.

64. Ibid., p. 88.

65. Halla Beloff, *Camera Culture* (New York: Basil Blackwell, 1985).

66. Roland Barthes, *Camera Lucida: Reflections on Photography* (New York: Hill & Wang, 1981), pp. 10–11.

67. Abigail McCarthy, "The American Family and the Family of Man," *Atlantic Monthly*, July 1973, pp. 72–76.

68. Ibid., pp. 72–76.

69. *Estes* v. *Texas*, 381 U.S. 352 (1965).

70. "Justice in New York, Observed." *New York Times*, May 24, 1989, p. A30.

CHAPTER 6

1. The study includes extensive background information pertaining to the death of Lisa Steinberg taken from archival records such as judicial, police, hospital, and legal documents as well as media reports. Among the better books that discuss the early morning events at the Steinberg apartment on November 2, 1987, is Joyce Johnson's *What Lisa Knew: The Truth and Lies of the Steinberg Case* (New York: G. P. Putnam's Sons, 1990).

2. Interview with Pete Hamill, January 1989.

3. Interview with Susan Brownmiller, January 1989.

4. Interview with Harold Rothwax, January 1989.

5. Erika Munk, "Crocodile Tears," *Village Voice*, April 4, 1989, pp. 11, 51.

6. My prefatory remarks include a general description of the study's methodology. Specifically, I used three distinct "tools" to gather information: unobtrusive observation, the in-depth interview, and the follow-up interview. This form of triangulation helped to present an insightful and less biased analysis of the perceived effects of the courtroom camera on trial participants.

As an organizing framework, I analyzed four common problems associated with the televised courtroom: the distraction factor (the extent to which cameras are conspicuous and intrusive on court proceedings), the self-consciousness factor (the extent to which participants are psychologically affected by the presence of television), the direct feedback effect (the degree to which trial members become aware of their own performance after watching themselves on television and the extent to which that televised perception changes their behavior and judgments within the courts), and the mediated feedback effect (the degree to which participants are affected by persons who saw them on television).

CHAPTER 7

1. Interview with Pete Hamill, January 1989. Throughout this chapter all quotes from Hamill are from that January 1989 interview with the author.
2. Interview with Harold Rothwax, January 1989. Throughout this chapter all quotes from Rothwax are from that January 1989 interview with the author.
3. Interview with Ira London, January 1989. Throughout this chapter all quotes from London are from that January 1989 interview with the author.
4. Interview with Adrian DiLuzio, January 1989. Throughout this chapter all quotes from DiLuzio are from that January 1989 interview with the author.
5. Interview with Peter Casolaro, January 1989. Throughout this chapter all quotes from Casolaro are from that January 1989 interview with the author.
6. Interview with Tony Guida, January 1989.
7. Interview with David Bookstaver, January 1989.
8. Interview with Helena Barthell, January 1989. Throughout this chapter all quotes from Barthell are from that January 1989 interview with the author.
9. Interview with Allen Jared, January 1989. Throughout this chapter all quotes from Jared are from that January 1989 interview with the author.
10. *Estes* v. *Texas*, 381 U.S. 532 (1965).

CHAPTER 8

1. *Estes* v. *Texas*, 381 U.S. 532 (1965).
2. The broader context of this case study takes into account courtroom variables that are operating whether or not cameras are present. The courtroom cannot be considered a sterile environment free from societal influence. Studies have noted that even before a camera is introduced into a courtroom environment, pretrial publicity may have already worked to influence the mindset of the jurors. Even the fact that a defendant has been arrested and accused of a crime may be prejudicial and create juror bias. Jurors are also a reflection of their environment and may not be able to rid themselves of such cultural biases during a trial.
3. Interview with Ira London, January 1989. Throughout this chapter all quotes from London are from that January 1989 interview with the author.
4. Interview with Peter Casolaro, January 1989. Throughout this chapter all quotes from Casolaro are from that January 1989 interview with the author.
5. Interview with Adrian DiLuzio, January 1989. Throughout this chapter all quotes from DiLuzio are from that January 1989 interview with the author.
6. Interview with Harold Rothwax, January 1989. Throughout this chapter all quotes from Rothwax are from that January 1989 interview with the author.

7. Interview with Barry Scheck, January 1989. Throughout this chapter all quotes from Scheck are from that January 1989 interview with the author.

8. Interview with Azariah Eshkenazi, January 1989. Throughout this chapter all quotes from Eshkenazi are from that January 1989 interview with the author.

9. Interview with Douglas Miller, January 1989. Throughout this chapter all quotes from Miller are from that January 1989 interview with the author.

10. Interview with Marilyn Walton, January 1989. Throughout this chapter all quotes from Walton are from that January 1989 interview with the author.

11. Live broadcast of Joel Steinberg sentencing, WCBS-TV, March 1990.

12. Ibid.

13. Ibid.

14. Ibid.

15. Interview with Perry Reich, June 1989. Throughout this chapter all quotes from Reich are from that June 1989 interview with the author.

16. Interview with John McCusker, January 1989. Throughout this chapter all quotes from McCusker are from that January 1989 inteview with the author.

17. Interview with Mary Elizabeth Lell, January 1989. Throughout this chapter all quotes from Lell are from that January 1989 interview with the author.

18. Interview with Patrick Kilhenny, January 1989. Throughout this chapter all quotes from Kilhenny are from that January 1989 interview with the author.

19. Interview with Allen Jared, January 1989. Throughout this chapter all quotes from Jared are from that January 1989 interview with the author.

20. Interview with Helena Barthell, January 1989. Throughout this chapter all quotes from Barthell are from that January 1989 interview with the author.

21. Jeremiah Cole, WCBS-TV, March 1990.

CHAPTER 9

1. Sam Ehrlich, *Lisa, Hedda and Joel: The Steinberg Murder Case* (New York: St. Martin's Press, 1989).

2. Interview with Roger Colloff, January 1989. Throughout this chapter all quotes from Colloff are from that January 1989 interview with the author.

3. Interview with Susan Brownmiller, January 1989. Throughout this chapter all quotes from Brownmiller are from that January 1989 interview with the author.

4. Interview with Harold Rothwax, January 1989.

5. Interview with Pete Hamill, January 1989. Throughout this chapter all quotes from Hamill are from that January 1989 interview with the author.

6. Hedda Nussbaum testimony, December 1–12, 1988.

7. Interview with Ira London, January 1989.

8. Interview with Adrian DiLuzio, January 1989.

9. Interview with Barry Scheck, January 1989. Throughout this chapter all quotes from Scheck are from that January 1989 interview with the author.

10. Interview with Helena Barthell, January 1989.

11. Interview with Shirley Unger, January 1989.

12. Interview with John McCusker, January 1989.

13. Interview with Peter Casolaro, January 1989.

14. Interview with Harold Rothwax, January 1989.

15. Interview with Michael Callaghan, January 1989.

16. Interview with Paul Smirnoff, January 1989.

17. Interview with Steve Paulus, January 1989. Throughout this chapter all quotes from Paulus are from that January 1989 interview with the author.

CHAPTER 10

1. Erving Goffman, *The Presentation of Self in Everyday Life* (Garden City, NY: Doubleday Anchor Books, 1959), pp. 7–16.

2. Ibid.

3. Interview with Azariah Eshkenazi, January 1989.

4. Interview with Aglae Charlot, January 1989. Throughout this chapter all quotes from Charlot are from that January 1989 interview with the author.

5. Interview with Douglas Miller, January 1989. Throughout this chapter all quotes from Miller are from that January 1989 interview with the author.

6. Interview with Patrick Kilhenny, January 1989. Throughout this chapter all quotes from Kilhenny are from that January 1989 interview with the author.

7. Interview with Marilyn Walton, January 1989. Throughout this chapter all quotes from Walton are from that January 1989 interview with the author.

8. Interview with Mary Elizabeth Lell, January 1989. Throughout this chapter all quotes from Lell are from that January 1989 interview with the author.

9. Interview with Harold Rothwax, January 1989. Throughout this chapter all quotes from Rothwax are from that January 1989 interview with the author.

10. From court transcripts of the Steinberg trial.

11. Interview with Tony Guida, January 1989.

12. Edward I. Koch, quoted in "Dipped in Oil," *New York Post*, November 1988, p. 1.

13. Interview with Allen Jared, January 1989.

14. Interview with Peter Casolaro, January 1989. Throughout this chapter all quotes from Casolaro are from that January 1989 interview with the author.

15. Interview with John McCusker, January 1989. Throughout this chapter all quotes from McCusker are from that January 1989 interview with the author.

16. Interview with Adrian DiLuzio, January 1989. Throughout this chapter all quotes from DiLuzio are from that January 1989 interview with the author.

17. Interview with Barry Scheck, January 1989.

18. Ira London, quoted in Denis Hamill, "Dull End to Lisa's Tragic Tale," *New York Newsday*, January 20, 1989, p. 5.

19. Interview with Perry Reich, June 1989.

20. Interview with Jeremiah Cole, January 1989. Throughout this chapter all quotes from Cole are from that January 1989 interview with the author.

21. Interview with Helena Barthell, January 1989. Throughout this chapter all quotes from Barthell are from that January 1989 interview with the author.

22. Interview with Ira London, January 1989. Throughout this chapter all quotes from London are from that January 1989 interview with the author.

CHAPTER 11

1. George Gerbner, "Trial by Television: Are We at the Point of No Return?" *Judicature* 63(79), 1980, pp. 417–418.

2. Interview with Harold Rothwax, January 1989. Throughout this chapter all quotes from Rothwax are from that January 1989 interview with the author.

3. Interview with Tony Guida, January 1989. Throughout this chapter all quotes from Guida are from that January 1989 interview with the author.

4. From court transcript of the Steinberg trial, October 1988.

5. Interview with Ira London, January 1989. Throughout this chapter all quotes from London are from that January 1989 interview with the author.

6. Interview with Peter Casolaro, January 1989. Throughout this chapter all quotes from Casolaro are from that January 1989 interview with the author.

7. Interview with Shirley Unger, January 1989. Throughout this chapter all quotes from Unger are from that January 1989 interview with the author.

8. Interview with Man Fung Tse, January 1989. Throughout this chapter all quotes from Tse are from that January 1989 interview with the author.

9. Interview with source (quote not for direct attribution), January 1989.

10. Interview with Adrian DiLuzio, January 1989. Throughout this chapter all quotes from DiLuzio are from that January 1989 interview with the author.

11. Interview with Barry Scheck, January 1989. Throughout this chapter all quotes from Scheck are from that January 1989 interview with the author.

12. Interview with Helena Barthell, January 1989. Throughout this chapter all quotes from Barthell are from that January 1989 interview with the author.

13. Interview with Katherine Anderson, January 1989.

14. Interview with Jeremiah Cole, January 1989.

15. Interview with Aglae Charlot, January 1989.

16. Interview with Patrick Kilhenny, January 1989.

17. Interview with source (quote not for direct attribution), June 1989.

18. Interview with Azariah Eshkenazi, January 1989. Throughout this chapter all quotes from Eshkenazi are from that January 1989 interview with the author.

19. Interview with Patricia McAdams, January 1989.

20. Interview with Marilyn Walton, January 1989. Throughout this chapter all quotes from Walton are from that January 1989 interview with the author.

CHAPTER 12

1. *Chandler* v. *Florida*, 449 U.S. 560 (1981).

2. Jonathan E. Gradess, executive director, New York State Defenders Association, in testimony before the New York State Senate and Assembly Judiciary Committees on Cameras in the Courtroom, 1989.

3. *Amicus Curiae* Brief for the California State Public Defenders Association et al., 1979, p. 3.

4. Ibid.

5. George Gerbner, "Trial by Television: Are We at the Point of No Return?" *Judicature* 63(79), 1980, p. 420.

6. Joel Hirschhorn, *Amicus Curiae* Brief in opposition to petition of Post-Newsweek Stations, Florida, Inc. for change of code of judicial conduct, submitted to the Florida Supreme Court, 1979, p. 4.

7. Susanna Barber, *News Cameras in the Courtroom: A Fair Trial–Free Press Debate* (Norwood, NJ: Ablex, 1987), p. 113.

8. Police Department Forensic Laboratory Report, November 2, 1987.

9. Reports from the Bellevue-NYU Medical Center, Eye, Ear, Nose, Throat Division.

10. Interview with Joel Steinberg, June 1989. Steinberg was transferred afterward to Southport Correctional Facility in Pine City, New York, and remains incarcerated there as of October 1993. Throughout this chapter all quotes from Steinberg are from that interview with the author, as well as follow-up interviews which occurred during the period October 1992–August 1993 at the Southport Correctional Facility.

11. Board of Education Report, July 29, 1988. Redacted portions presented to defense counsel Ira London from assistant district attorney Peter Casolaro, marked Confidential IG 482 87/88.

12. Brief for Respondent—Vol. 11. The brief cites the following: "Defendant's third objection was that the [pre-sentencing] report improperly mentioned allegations of child abuse which had been shown to be unfounded" (PSM14; PSR11). But the judge pointed out that the report itself stated that these allegations had been determined to be unfounded (S37-38), and played no role in defendant's sentencing.

13. Report issued by the Hospital of the University of Pennsylvania, Neuroradiology Section, March 3, 1988. Dr. Robert A. Zimmerman reviewed copies of radiographic studies performed by New York City's Medical Examiner's Office and St. Vincent's Hospital.

14. Interview with Peter Casolaro, January 1989.

15. Interview with Helena Barthell, January 1989.

CHAPTER 13

1. Interview with John McCusker, January 1989.

2. Interview with Mary Elizabeth Lell, January 1989.

3. Interview with Ira London, January 1989.

4. Interview with Perry Reich, June 1989.

5. Interview with Joel Steinberg, June 1989.

6. Interview with Harold Rothwax, January 1989.

7. Interview with Paul Smirnoff, January 1989. Throughout this chapter all quotes from Smirnoff are from that January 1989 interview with the author.

8. Interview with Mike Pearl, January 1989. Throughout this chapter all quotes from Pearl are from that January 1989 interview with the author.

9. Interview with Timothy Clifford, January 1989. Throughout this chapter all quotes from Clifford are from that January 1989 interview with the author.

10. Interview with Michael Callaghan, January 1989.

11. Interview with Barry Scheck, January 1989. Throughout this chapter all quotes from Scheck are from that January 1989 interview with the author.

POSTSCRIPT

1. Maury Terry, "Joel Steinberg's Version," *Vanity Fair*, May 1988, p. 184.

2. Anne Summers, "The Hedda Cunundrum," *Ms.*, April 1989, p. 54.

3. Interview with Ellen Fleysher, January 1989.

4. Neil Postman, Betsy Kaufman Memorial Speech, Second International Conference on Early Childhood Education, Tel Aviv, Israel, June 1987.

Selected Bibliography

ABA Adopts New Cameras Rule. *Judicature* 66(6), December-January 1983.

ABA Makes It Perfectly Clear on Cameras in the Courtroom—It Wants Them Out. *Broadcasting*, February 1979, p. 58.

Adler, R. A., ed. *Understanding Television: Essays on Television as a Social and Cultural Force.* New York: Praeger, 1981.

Altheide, David. TV News and the Social Construction of Justice. In *Justice and the Media*, ed. Ray Surette. Springfield, MA: Charles C. Thomas, 1984.

Altheide, David. *Creating Reality: How Television News Distorts Events.* Beverly Hills, CA: Sage, 1988.

Barber, Susanna. News Cameras in the Courtroom: A Review of the Empirical Literature. *Progress in Communication Sciences*, 1986: 177–212.

Barber, Susanna. *News Cameras in the Courtroom: A Fair Trial–Free Press Debate.* Norwood, NJ: Ablex, 1987.

Barthes, Roland. *Camera Lucida: Reflections on Photography.* New York: Hill & Wang, 1981.

Beloff, Halla. *Camera Culture.* New York: Basil Blackwell, 1985.

Berger, Warren. Cable in the Court. *New York*, August 12, 1991.

Blashfield, Albert E. The Case of the Controversial Canon. *American Bar Association Journal* 48(4), 1962: 429–435.

Boyd, Joseph A., Jr. Cameras in Court—*Estes* v. *Texas* and Florida's One-Year Pilot Program. *University of Miami Law Review* 32, 1978: 815–838.

Brill, Steven. Headnotes: Watching the Drama of Justice. *American Lawyer*, July-August 1990.

Brill, Steven. How the Willie Smith Show Changed America. *American Lawyer*, January-February 1992: 3, 98–102.

Broholm, John. Electronic Media in the Courtroom. *Case and Comment* 85(3), 1974: 3–4, 8–10.

Brownmiller, Susan. Madly in Love. *Ms.*, April 1989, pp. 56–59.

California State Public Defenders Association et al. *Amicus Curiae* Brief Filed with the U.S. Supreme Court in *Chandler* v. *Florida*, October 1979.

Carter, Charlotte. Television in the Courts. *State Court Journal* 5(1), 1981: 6–12, 24–28.

Chandler v. *Florida*, 499 U.S. 560 (1981).

College of Criminal Justice, Northeastern University. *Cameras in the Courtroom Make New Yorkers Reluctant to Testify.* Boston: Northeastern University, 1991.

Cox Broadcasting Corp. v. *Cohn*, 420 U.S. 469 (1975).

Craig, S. R. Cameras in the Courtroom in Florida. *Journalism Quarterly* 56, 1979: 703–710.

Crosson, Matthew T. Courtroom Proceedings Not Adversely Affected by Media Coverage. *Buffalo Law Journal*, May 18, 1989.

Cuomo Faults Changes in Cameras-in-Court Bill. *Syracuse Post Standard*, May 26, 1989, p. B–13.

Davis, Norman. Television in Our Courts—The Proven Advantages, the Unproven Dangers. *Judicature* 64(2), 1980: 85–92.

Day, Jack G. The Case Against Cameras in the Courtroom. *Judges Journal* 20(1), 1981: 18–21, 51.

Drucker, Susan. The Televised Mediated Trial: Formal and Substantive Characteristics. *Communication Quarterly* 37(4), Fall 1989: 305–318.

Drucker, Susan. Cameras in the Court Revisited. *New York State Bar Journal*, July-August 1992, pp. 44–48.

Drucker, Susan, and Hunold, Janice Platt. The Claus von Bulow Retrial: Lights, Camera, Genre? In *Popular Trials: Rhetoric, Mass Media and the Law*, ed. Robert Hariman, pp. 133–147. Tuscaloosa, AL: University of Alabama Press, 1990.

Ehrlich, Sam. *Lisa, Hedda and Joel: The Steinberg Murder Case.* New York: St. Martin's Press, 1989.

Entner, Roberta. "Encoding the Image of the American Judiciary Institution: A Semiotic Analysis of Broadcast Trials to Ascertain Its Definition of the Court System." Ph.D. diss., New York University, 1993.

Epstein, Edward J. *News from Nowhere.* New York: Vintage Books, 1973.

Estes v. *Texas*, 381 U.S. 352 (1965).

Floren, Leola. *Cameras Come to Court.* Report No. 396. University of Missouri School of Journalism Freedom of Information Center, Columbia, MO, October 1978.

Frankel, Marvin. The Search for Truth: An Umpireal View. *University of Pennsylvania Law Review* 123(5), 1975: 1031–1059.

Freedman, W. *Press and Media Access to the Criminal Courtroom.* New York: Quorum Books, 1988.

Geis, Gilbert. A Lively Public Issue: Canon 35 in the Light of Recent Events. *American Bar Association Journal*, May 1957, pp. 419–422.

Gerbner, George. Trial by Television: Are We at the Point of No Return? *Judicature* 63(79), April 1980: 416–426.

Graber, D. *Crime News and the Public*. New York: Praeger, 1980.

Hall, Stuart. Determinations of News Photographs. In *The Manufacture of News*, ed. S. Cohen and J. Young, pp. 176–290. Beverly Hills, CA: Sage, 1973.

Hallam, Oscar. Some Object Lessons on Publicity in Criminal Trials. *Minnesota Law Review* 24(4), 1940: 454–508.

Hawaii State Bar Association Committee on Cameras in the Courtroom. *Final Report*. 1982.

Heffner, Richard. Cameras in the Courtroom: A Bad Idea Whose Time Has Come. *New York Law Journal*, April 17, 1989, pp. 1–3.

Heisenberg, Werner. *The Physicist's Conception of Nature*. San Diego: Harcourt Brace, 1958.

Hirschhorn, Joel. Does Television Make a Fair Trial Impossible?—A Debate. *Judicature* 64(3), September 1980: 145–146.

Hoyt, James. Cameras in the Courtroom: Another Chance. *Public Telecommunications Review* 6(3), May-June 1978: 28–34.

Hoyt, James. Courtroom Coverage: The Effects of Being Televised. *Journal of Broadcasting* 12(4), 1978: 487–495.

Hoyt, Michael. Steven Brill Builds an Empire. *Columbia Journalism Review*, September-October 1990, pp. 41–46.

Johnson, Joyce. *What Lisa Knew: The Truth and Lies of the Steinberg Case*. New York: G. P. Putnam's Sons, 1990.

Justices Limit TV in Courtroom. *New York Times*, June 8, 1965, p. A1.

Kielbowicz, Richard. The Story Behind the Adoption of the Ban of Courtroom Cameras. *Judicature* 63(1), 1979: 14–23.

Kulwin, Shelly. Televised Trials—Constitutional Constraints, Practical Implications, and State Experimentation. *Loyola University Law Journal* 9(4), 1978: 910–934.

McCall, Abner V. Courtroom Television. *Texas Bar Journal* 19(2), February 1956: 73–74, 106–110.

McCarthy, Abigail. The American Family and the Family of Man. *Atlantic Monthly*, July 1973, pp. 72–76.

McLuhan, Marshall. *Understanding Media: The Extensions of Man*. New York: McGraw-Hill, 1964.

MacNeilly, M. D. The Electronic Courthouse. *Judicature* 60(4), 1976: 188–192.

Miller, G. R., and Fontes, N. E. *Videotape on Trial: A View from the Jury Box*. Beverly Hills, CA: Sage, 1979.

National Victim Center. *Rape in America*. National Victim Center, April 23, 1992.

Nesson, C. R., and Koblenz, A. D. The Image of Justice: *Chandler* v. *Florida*. *Harvard Civil Rights–Civil Liberties Law Review* 16, Fall 1981: 400–413.

New York State Assembly. Deliberations on Bill A77-B, May 1987.

New York State Defenders Association. Testimony Before the New York State Senate Judiciary Committee and the New York State Assembly Judiciary Committee on Cameras in the Courtroom, 1989.

New York State Senate. Deliberations on Bill A77-B, June 2, 1987.

Petkanas, William. Cameras on Trial: An Assessment of the Educational Effects of News Cameras in Trial Courts. Ph.D. diss., New York University, 1990.

Postman, Neil. *Amusing Ourselves to Death*. New York: Viking, 1985.

Postman, Neil. *Conscientious Objections: Stirring Up Trouble About Language, Technology, and Education*. New York: Alfred A. Knopf, 1988.

Postman, Neil, and Powers, Steve. *How to Watch TV News*. New York: Penguin, 1992.

Public Defense Backup Center. *The Intrusion of Cameras in New York's Criminal Courts: A Report by the Public Defense Backup Center*. Albany: New York State Defenders Association, May 12, 1989.

Radio and Television News Directors Association et al. Joint Brief for *Amici Curiae* Filed with the U.S. Supreme Court in *Chandler* v. *Florida*, October 1979.

Reed, David. *Canon 35: Flemington Revisited*. Freedom of Information Center Report No. 177. 1967, pp. 1–5.

Report of the Chief Administrative Judge to the New York State Legislature, the Governor and the Chief Judge on the Effect of Audio-Visual Coverage on the Conduct of Judicial Proceedings, 1989.

Research and Information Service, National Center for State Courts. *Summary of TV Cameras in the State Courts*. Williamsburg, VA, 1987.

Roberts, Sam. TV in the Court: Titillation or Education? *New York Times*, November 26, 1987, p. B1.

Sharp, Allen. Postverdict Interviews with Jurors. *Case and Comment*, September–October 1983, pp. 3–15.

Sheppard v. *Maxwell*, 384 U.S. 333 (1966).

Silverstein, Duane. TV Comes to the Courts. *State Court Journal*, Spring 1978, pp. 14–19, 49–55.

Slater, Dan, and Hans, Valerie. Methodological Issues in the Evaluation of Experiments with Cameras in the Courts. *Communications Quarterly* 39, 1982: 376–380.

Sontag, Susan. *On Photography*. New York: Farrar, Straus & Giroux, 1977.

Stone, Ward, and Edlin, Shiel G. TV or Not TV: Televised and Photographic Coverage of Trials. *Mercer Law Review* 29(4), 1978: 1119–1135.

Storozynski, Alex. Judicial Attraction. *Empire State Report*, May 1991, pp. 38–45.

Summers, Anne. The Hedda Cunundrum. *Ms.*, April 1989, p. 54.

Surette, Ray. *Media, Crime and Criminal Justice: Images and Reality*. Pacific Grove, CA: Brooks/Cole, 1992.

Tans, M., and Chaffee, S. Pretrial Publicity and Juror Prejudice. *Journalism Quarterly* 43, 1966: 647–654.

Televised Trial, World's Attention Attracted to 1955. *Waco Tribune Herald*, July 23, 1978, p. C1.

Terry, Maury. Joel Steinberg's Version. *Vanity Fair*, May 1988, pp. 120–123, 184.

Underwood, Robert. Observations Regarding Canon 35. *Illinois Bar Journal* 55(3), 1966: 194–203.

Wasby, Stephen. Laying Estes to Rest: A Case Note. *Justice System* 5(1), 1979: 58–69.

Weinstein, Jack B., and Zimmerman, Diane L. Let the People Observe Their Courts. *Judicature* 61(4), October 1977: 156–165.

Whisenand, J. D. Cameras and Courtrooms: Fair Trial–Free Press Standards. *Florida Bar Journal* 64, 1978: 1860–1864.

White, Frank. Cameras in the Courtroom: A U.S. Survey. *Journalism Monographs* 60, April 1979: 3–41.

Wilson, Jerome. Justice in Living Color: The Case for Courtroom Television. *American Bar Association Journal* 60, 1974: 294–297.

Winick, C., and Winick, M. Courtroom Drama on Television. *Communication* 24(4), 1974: 67–74.

Witt, Elder. Television in the Courtroom. *Editorial Research Reports* 1(2), 1981: 19–29.

Index

About the Author

PAUL THALER is the Director of Journalism and Media at Mercy College in New York, a post he has held since 1982. Dr. Thaler was the Fulbright Senior Lecturer in Journalism at the University of Bucharest in 1993. *The Watchful Eye* is the culmination of six years of research into the media and the criminal justice system.

ISBN 0-275-94215-5

90000>

9 780275 942151

HARDCOVER BAR CODE